Lecture Notes in Computer Science　8900

Commenced Publication in 1973
Founding and Former Series Editors:
Gerhard Goos, Juris Hartmanis, and Jan van Leeuwen

T0212805

Achim D. Brucker   Fabiano Dalpiaz
Paolo Giorgini   Per Håkon Meland
Erkuden Rios (Eds.)

Secure and Trustworthy Service Composition

The Aniketos Approach

 Springer

Volume Editors

Achim D. Brucker
SAP SE, Vincenz-Priessnitz-Str. 1, 76131 Karlsruhe, Germany
E-mail: achim.brucker@sap.com

Fabiano Dalpiaz
Utrecht University, PO Box 80.089, 3508 TB Utrecht, The Netherlands
E-mail: f.dalpiaz@uu.nl

Paolo Giorgini
University of Trento, DISI, Via Sommarive 5, 38123 Povo Trento, Italy
E-mail: paolo.giorgini@unitn.it

Per Håkon Meland
SINTEF ICT, Strindveien 4, 7465 Trondheim, Norway
E-mail: per.h.meland@sintef.no

Erkuden Rios
TECNALIA Research & Innovation
Parque Tecnológico de Bizkaia, Edificio 202, 48170 Zamudio, Spain
E-mail: erkuden.rios@tecnalia.com

Cover illustration: The Aniketos approach to making composite services secure and trustworthy for the service end user.

ISSN 0302-9743   e-ISSN 1611-3349
ISBN 978-3-319-13517-5   e-ISBN 978-3-319-13518-2
DOI 10.1007/978-3-319-13518-2
Springer Cham Heidelberg New York Dordrecht London

Library of Congress Control Number: 2014955202

LNCS Sublibrary: SL 4 – Security and Cryptology

Typesetting: Camera-ready by author, data conversion by Scientific Publishing Services, Chennai, India

Printed on acid-free paper

Springer is part of Springer Science+Business Media (www.springer.com)

Foreword

The Future Internet envisions a move toward widespread use of services as a way of networked interaction. However, while the technologies for developing and deploying services are well established, methods for ensuring trust and security are fewer and less mature. In particular, current service security standards and technologies tend to be focussed on specific areas, such as security at the communication level.

Lack of trust and confidence in composed services and in their constituent parts is reckoned to be one of the significant factors limiting widespread uptake of service-oriented computing. Citizens and businesses alike need to have greater confidence in online services for the digital economy to flourish.

For example, the security claims of a service should be known in advance, and a user should be able to make judgments about the trustworthiness of a service and its likelihood of fulfilling these claims. This should apply to services running in isolation, as well as those comprised of other services from different providers. In order for users to be confident that their legitimate security requirements are being satisfied, advances in tools and methods are required.

This was the common understanding that brought 17 European partners from 10 countries to join forces in the Aniketos project. The motivation was to overcome some of these obstacles.

The results of the project are now available, and this book presents them in condensed form. In addition to the written word, the project has produced software tools wrapped in four packages, each serving a group of typical security needs, ranging from the specification of security and trustworthiness requirements, through improved tools for designing secure composite software systems services, and to support for runtime monitoring and dynamic recomposition of secure behavior.

Enjoy!

August 2014

Richard Torbjørn Sanders
Project Manager of Aniketos

Preface

The Future Internet will provide an environment in which a diverse range of services are offered by multiple suppliers, and users are likely to unknowingly invoke underlying services in a dynamic and ad hoc manner. Moving from today's static services, we will see service consumers that transparently mix and match service components depending on service availability, quality, price, and security attributes. Consequently, the applications that end users see may be composed of multiple services from many different providers, and the end user may have little assurance about the compliance of a particular service supplier with the declared security policies.

Thus, there is the need for services platforms that build the foundation of a Future Internet that is responsive to threats and changes in services. This book presents the Aniketos platform that was developed during the Aniketos project, and that is the central element of the Aniketos approach to secure and trustworthy service composition. This approach can help establish and maintain trustworthiness and secure behavior in a constantly changing service environment. It integrates methods for analyzing, solving, and sharing information on how new threats and vulnerabilities can be mitigated. The Aniketos approach is holistic in the sense that it addresses the following three areas:

1. *Socio-technical perspective*: Dynamically composed services have to handle not only technical issues, but also organizational and business aspects such as responsible parties, business models, different security legislations, as well as end-user usability and assurance.
2. *Design-time composition support*: Services cannot be created the same way as we have been doing so far. Security, as well safe and secure behavior, needs to be described not only from a technical point of view, but also from the organizational and businesses perspective. Moreover, there is a need for methods and tools to analyze and model the variability of services and their composition as a response to the evolution of the environment.
3. *Run-time service adaptation and composition:* At run-time, the trust established from design-time artifacts and activities needs to be maintained, and safe and secure service behavior needs to be continuously verified. Run-time monitoring and automatic adaptation of services are needed due to an evolving environment of threats and operating conditions. Down-time is costly; a composed service must be able to operate even during an attack (with possible limitations or change of behavior), taking risks and adaptation costs into account.

The book is divided into five parts. Part one provides a summary of the state of the art in secure and trustworthy composite services, thereby being the most suitable starting point for readers who want to get a quick overview on why we need secure and trustworthy composite services, the threats that they need to consider as well as a first insight into techniques for building secure and trustworthy such services. Readers that are already familiar with the topic might skip directly to Part two, which provides an overview of the Aniketos platform. This is, so to speak, the "must read" part of the book if one wants to get an overview of the Aniketos approach to trustworthy composite services. Moreover, this part helps decide which of the following chapters one wants to deep-dive into. Part three discusses selected details of the design-time support of the Aniketos platform, i.e., how to gather the requirements for secure and trustworthy services and transfer these requirements into a system design that is eventually implemented. We continue the journey on designing and operating secure and trustworthy composite services in Part four, which discusses selected features of the run-time support of the Aniketos framework. Finally, in Part five, we present two large case studies in which the Aniketos platform was used, as well as a report on challenges in evaluating such a complex and feature-rich platform.

This book is the result of the collective effort of all project participants that contributed to the success of Aniketos, which arises from the many brainstorming and discussion sessions. The project participants also acted as reviewers for the book chapters; each chapter was reviewed by at least two reviewers. We would like to thank them all for their serious effort. In particular, we would like to thank Richard Sanders, the project leader of Aniketos, the EU Project Officer Manual Carvalhosa and Rodrigo Mendes, who supported the project during its lifetime, the reviewers Giampaolo Bella, Dirk Khulman, Martin Koyabe, and Patrick Legand, who provided valuable feedback at the project reviews, and, last but not least, Eleonora Anzini, Valentino Meduri, and Alessandra Tedeschi, who designed the image featured on the title page of this book.

October 2014

Achim D. Brucker
Fabiano Dalpiaz
Paolo Giorgini
Per Håkon Meland
Erkuden Rios

Table of Contents

Run-Time Support Framework

Case Studies and Evaluation

Composite Services with Dynamic Behaviour

Per Håkon Meland

SINTEF ICT, N-7465 Norway
per.h.meland@sintef.no

Abstract. The characteristics of dynamic composite services opens up to new possibilities as well as potential dangers. We need to be aware of both sides of this coin when designing and providing such services, as well as when we are consuming them. This chapter explains the characteristics of composite services, and gives a brief overview of related literature, projects, tools and standards as a backdrop to the Aniketos project.

Keywords: Service-Oriented Computing, Composite Services, Dynamic behaviour, Security, Trustworthiness.

1 Introduction

As the Internet extends into an Internet of Services, composite services [28] are expected to become enablers of a more open and agile business environment. Design-time service composition involves the manual tailoring of a service based on planning, discovery, analysis and composition. The typical work styles of composing a service range from *top down* approaches, where a user specifies an abstract description of a desired composite service, to *bottom-up* approaches where users directly edit and compose existing services [45]. In the event of a change, a manual or (semi-)automatic recomposition is done before the service can be replaced. Currently, many WS-* specifications address security concerns, but most of the focus is on secure message exchange [30], and current orchestration and choreography lack support for the specification and enforcement of process level requirements, such as secure operational styles [57]. These higher order interactions must become a part of composition; otherwise service composition represents a real threat for the security of services and network integrity. Static service composition suffers from an inherent drawback, the absence of information about the dynamic structure of the network. Usually, the variance between a static approximation and the real behaviour of a system is huge. Papazoglou et al. point out that *many of the existing approaches towards service composition largely neglect the context in which the composition takes place* [41]. These considerations outline the importance of dynamic adaptation/composition environments, where a composite service can automatically react and respond to change. Fully automatic service composition is still at a very immature stage [41,47,48] but partial adaptation and/or replacement of service components is possible given that there are adaptation plans or alternative service configurations.

A.D. Brucker et al. (Eds.): Secure Service Composition, LNCS 8900, pp. 1–9, 2014.
© Springer International Publishing Switzerland 2014

New paradigms and new challenges tend to go hand in hand. Just as flexibility is a way of dealing with unforeseen changes and threats, it is also a serious risk to security, trustworthiness, and dependability. Traditional engineering paradigms suggest to check systems against these properties through design-time verification techniques (à la model checking [31]). Unfortunately, these approaches are inapplicable for dynamically composed services given that (i) a service behaves as a black-box, thus a composite service's building blocks are not necessarily inspectable; (ii) at runtime, service components may be replaced by new ones; and (iii) the interaction among different services leads to non-deterministic outcomes [50]. When developing new methods and technologies we need to make sure that we do not introduce new problems that are greater than the ones we had before.

The purpose of this chapter is to explain the characteristics (section 2) of composite services with dynamic behaviour as a backdrop for the rest of this book, and to give a brief overview of related work in this area (section 3). In section 4 we conclude the chapter with some comments on the research challenges we have faced in the Aniketos project.

2   Characteristics

Creating complex systems by combining smaller services as components is one of the fundamental concepts in *Service Oriented Architecture* (SOA). For Web services, composition and integration usually fall under the terms *choreography* and *orchestration* [33]. With a *dynamic* composite service, service components can be replaced during execution time [56], for example if a component fails, or a cheaper, faster, or otherwise better one can be found. This is usually termed runtime *adaptation* or *recomposition*. There are different grades of adaptation, from simply replacing a single service component with another one performing the same task, to a total reconfiguration of roles and a completely new set of service components with different functionalities. Alternative service compositions may have been defined in advance at design-time, or may involve real-time reasoning, planning, discovery and binding.

We know that the threat picture of a service is in constant evolution. This is due to the fact that new methods and motivations for performing an attack emerge, changing operating conditions and that the services themselves are updated at various intervals. Within a composite service, this is even more of a challenge, since each individual service component will have a fluctuating threat picture and the total attack surface of the composite service will be broader as the number of involved service components increases. It is important to understand the characteristics of dynamic composite services in order to understand the threats to them. We can summarize these characteristics as:

- A *composite* service is an aggregation of multiple *sub-services* or *service components*. These more fine-grained services may be atomic services or other compositions themselves.

- A service *consumer* is the one requesting a service, while a service *provider* tries to fulfill the request. A service provider can also be a service consumer (acting as a service *mediator*).
- The service components are delivered by service providers from within or outside the consumer's organization. The consumer may know very little about these providers.
- Composite services have much more *distributed* nature than isolated services, and this is something that makes the detection of attacks much harder than in single systems. The attack surface is also much broader, giving the attacker several more options on where to attack.
- A *dynamic* composite service can replace service components or reconfigure itself during execution time. This kind of adaptation or re-composition at run-time may affect the functionality or efficiency of the remaining services. Crisis situations are prime examples where dynamic behaviour is needed.
- A service component has the nature of a black box, meaning that the external interface is exposed, but it is very difficult to check what the component actually does internally.
- Service components are primarily selected from functional service *descriptors*, secondly from other types of properties such as costs and QoS[1].
- Service descriptors are available in different types of service marketplaces (most common are yellow/green pages for UDDI), making it possible to discover relevant service components for a composition.
- The expected behavior of a service component is often expressed in a type of contract between the service consumer and service provider. Today this is mostly limited to availability, price and performance.

We can illustrate some of the characteristics through a practical service example. Consider a service provider offering a travel assistance service which lets the end user read about various points-of-interest (POI), access local maps, calculate routes and pay for tickets online. Under the hood of such a composite service there will be a range of service components from independent providers, but this is hidden from the service end user.

Consider the case where a ticket purchasing component becomes exposed to a threat (for instance recall the DDOS attacks on VISA, Mastercard and PayPal in 2010 [58]), lowering its assurance level or availability. The composite service should consequently react to this, and for instance replace that service component with something that is available and will not cripple the service as a whole. This could be a service component that allows you to use an electronic invoice, charge your mobile phone bill, or in the worst case - direct you to the nearest ticketing machine where you can pay by cash. Figure 1 illustrates this composition example, where the composition is puzzled together by a set of roles played by a set of generic services. The original payment service is later considered to be too risky at runtime, influencing the total security and availability of the composite service. This leads to a substitution of the service with another one

---

[1] The term QoS does not usually include security, the contractual focus is in most cases related to dependability, measured as service availability.

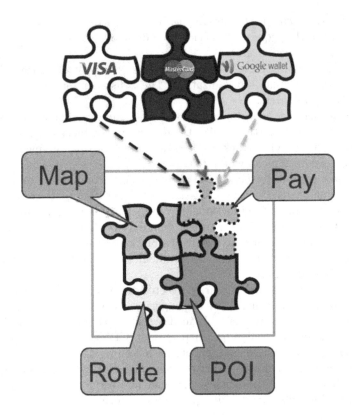

Fig. 1. The travel assistance composite service example

that has an equivalent business functionality, but is considered more secure and trustworthy at that time.

Whether the end users should be notified about such service changes must be determined on a case-by-case basis. An end user will probably not care if the service providing the map changes on a regular basis, but would probably want an explanation if the payment part suddenly does so. *Ignorance is bliss*, but *knowlegde is power*.

3   Related Work

3.1   Literature

Service composition, especially with automatic methods and tools, has been high up on the research agenda for a long time now. The most cited are publications by Milanovic and Malek [40], Hamadi and Benatallah [34], Rao and Su [46], Canfora et al. [26], Casati et al. [29], and Srivastava and Koehler [51]. These were all published before 2005, at a time that seems to be a peak when it comes to publications in this area. After this period, there has been a steady number of publications up until today. For instance, Alrifai et al. [20] have developed an approach for service selection based on QoS parameters, Hwang et al. [35] have taken dynamic service selection further, El Hadad et al. [32] have worked on selection and composition based on transactional properties and QoS characteristics between service components, and Sohrabi and McIlraith [49] have looked at the trade-off between offline and online composition. Richer overviews of existing publications can be found in the many survey works. Strunk [53] published a survey on service composition in 2010, as did Bronsted et al.[25] and Ibrahim et al. [36] the same year, but with a stronger focus on pervasive computing. Maigre [37] also wrote a survey in 2010 on the topic of service composition tools. Later surveys have followed, such as [27,24,54,42,52], but these are currently not as much quoted in the literature.

3.2   Projects

Our Aniketos project started in 2010 with the goal of enabling practical solutions to secure and trustworthy composite services. Alongside with Aniketos, there have been other European research projects tied to our work, such as SecureChange [14], which started in 2009 and targeted to develop new models, methodologies and processes to ensure security, privacy and dependability requirements during software evolution. The AVANTSSAR (Automated Validation of Trust and Security of Service-oriented Architectures) project [2] developed a formal language for specifying trust and security properties of services, their associated policies and their composition into service architectures, as well as automated techniques to reason about services, their dynamic composition, and their associated security policies into secure service architectures. NESSOS [10] has been a *network of excellence* on the security challenges for the future software services. COMPAS [5] implemented a framework to ensure dynamic and on-going compliance of software services. FI-WARE [6] is developing a catalogue of so-called generic enablers that can be included in services to perform specific tasks. SOA4All [16] developed an infrastructure for easier service composition and application mash-ups. COIN [4] worked for self-adaptive service systems, and CHOReOS [3] with large-scale service choreographies.

3.3   Tools and Standards

In Aniketos, we have based our tool technology on open source platform from Activiti [1], which uses BPMN as a service specification and execution language. There are several other open source tools for service composition and execution, for instance Sword [44], ZenFlow [39], JOpera [8], METEOR-S [19] and Flow Editor [43]. These are mostly academically driven. On the commercial tool side, we are aware that e.g. Microsoft Visual Studio [9], Oracle SOA Suite [12], IBM Business Process Manager [7] and SAP NetWeaver [13] are commonly used for service composition/integration. Interoperability between these these tools is very limited, though there exist a plethora of standards for service descriptions, service process specifications and service interaction. For instance SoaML [15], WS-BPEL [11], BPML [55], DAML-S [21], WSCI [22], WSCL [23], WS-CDL [18], OWL-S [38] and WSMO [17]. Having these standards has not lead to a wide uptake and implementation, and most of them are now outdated.

4   Conclusion

The characteristics of dynamic composite services opens new possibilities as well as potential dangers. We need to be aware of both sides of this coin when designing and providing such services, as well as when we are consuming them. Service composition is one of the key principles of service oriented architecture, the research field gained a lot of attention between 2003-2005 and has kept a steady pace ever since. This chapter has explained the common backdrop of the Aniketos project, with a brief overview of the most notable related publications, projects, tools and standards. Still, even after fifteen years of research and development, there are many roads yet to be discovered and very few composite services that are self-managed and trustworthy at the same time. We hope that the Aniketos methods and technology will help bring this field a lot further, both from an academic and industrial point of view.

References

1. Activiti BPM Platform, http://activiti.org/ (cited May 2014)
2. Automated VAlidatioN of Trust and Security of Service-oriented ARchitectures (avantssar), http://www.avantssar.eu/ (cited May 2014)
3. CHOReOS, http://www.choreos.eu/ (cited May 2014)
4. Coin, http://www.coin-ip.eu/ (cited May 2014)
5. COMPAS - Compliance-driven Models, Languages, and Architectures for Services, https://sites.google.com/site/mashtn/eu-projects/compas (cited May 2014)
6. FI-ware, http://www.fi-ware.eu/ (cited May 2014)
7. Ibm business process manager, http://www-03.ibm.com/software/products/en/business-process-manager-family (cited May 2014)
8. JOpera for Eclipse, http://www.jopera.org/ (cited May 2014)
9. Microsoft Visual Studio, http://www.visualstudio.com/ (cited May 2014)
10. Network of Excellence on Engineering Secure Future Internet Software Services and Systems (NESSoS), http://www.nessos-project.eu/ (cited May 2014)
11. OASIS Web Services Business Process Execution Language (WSBPEL), https://www.oasis-open.org/committees/wsbpel/? (cited May 2014)
12. Oracle SOA Suite, http://www.oracle.com/technetwork/middleware/soasuite/ (cited May 2014)
13. SAP NetWeaver Technology Platform, http://scn.sap.com/community/netweaver (cited May 2014)
14. Securechange, http://www.securechange.eu/ (cited May 2014)
15. Service Oriented Architecture Modeling Language (SoaML), http://www.omg.org/spec/SoaML/ (cited May 2014)
16. Service Oriented Architectures for All (SOA4All), http://www.soa4all.eu/ (cited May 2014)

17. Web Service Modeling Ontology (WSMO), `http://www.w3.org/Submission/WSMO/` (cited May 2014)
18. Web Services Choreography Description Language Version 1.0, `http://www.w3.org/TR/ws-cdl-10/` (cited May 2014)
19. Aggarwal, R., Verma, K., Miller, J., Milnor, W.: Constraint driven web service composition in METEOR-S. In: Proceedings of the IEEE International Conference on Services Computing (SCC) 2004, pp. 23–30. IEEE (2004)
20. Alrifai, M., Skoutas, D., Risse, T.: Selecting skyline services for qos-based web service composition. In: Proceedings of the 19th International Conference on World Wide Web, pp. 11–20. ACM (2010)
21. Ankolekar, A., et al.: DAML-S: Web service description for the semantic web. In: Horrocks, I., Hendler, J. (eds.) ISWC 2002. LNCS, vol. 2342, pp. 348–363. Springer, Heidelberg (2002)
22. Arkin, A., Askary, S., Fordin, S., Jekeli, W., Kawaguchi, K., Orchard, D., Pogliani, S., Riemer, K., Struble, S., Takacsi-Nagy, P., et al.: Web service choreography interface (WSCI) 1.0. Standards proposal by BEA Systems, Intalio, SAP, and Sun Microsystems (2002)
23. Banerji, A., Bartolini, C., Beringer, D., Chopella, V., Govindarajan, K., Karp, A., Kuno, H., Lemon, M., Pogossiants, G., Sharma, S., et al.: Web services conversation language (WSCL) 1.0. W3C Note 14 (2002)
24. Bartalos, P., Bieliková, M.: Automatic dynamic web service composition: A survey and problem formalization. Computing & Informatics 30(4) (2011)
25. Bronsted, J., Hansen, K.M., Ingstrup, M.: Service composition issues in pervasive computing. IEEE Pervasive Computing 9(1), 62–70 (2010)
26. Canfora, G., Di Penta, M., Esposito, R., Villani, M.L.: An approach for qos-aware service composition based on genetic algorithms. In: Proceedings of the 2005 Conference on Genetic and Evolutionary Computation, pp. 1069–1075. ACM (2005)
27. Cardinale, Y., El Haddad, J., Manouvrier, M., Rukoz, M.: Transactional-aware web service composition: A survey. IGI Global-Advances in Knowledge Management (AKM) Book Series, pp. 116–141 (2011)
28. Casati, F., Ilnicki, S., Jin, L., Krishnamoorthy, V., Shan, M.-C.: Adaptive and Dynamic Service Composition in eFlow. In: Wangler, B., Bergman, L.D. (eds.) CAiSE 2000. LNCS, vol. 1789, pp. 13–31. Springer, Heidelberg (2000)
29. Casati, F., Ilnicki, S., Jin, L., Krishnamoorthy, V., Shan, M.C.: Adaptive and dynamic service composition in eflow. In: Advanced Information Systems Engineering, pp. 13–31. Springer (2000)
30. Charfi, A., Schmeling, B., Heizenreder, A., Mezini, M.: Reliable, Secure, and Transacted Web Service Compositions with AO4BPEL. In: 4th European Conference on Web Services, ECOWS 2006, pp. 23–34 (December 2006)
31. Clarke, E.M., Emerson, E.A.: Design and Synthesis of Synchronization Skeletons Using Branching-Time Temporal Logic. In: Workshop on Logic of Programs, pp. 52–71. Springer, London (1982)
32. El Hadad, J., Manouvrier, M., Rukoz, M.: Tqos: Transactional and qos-aware selection algorithm for automatic web service composition. IEEE Transactions on Services Computing 3(1), 73–85 (2010)
33. Erl, T.: Service-Oriented Architecture: Concepts, Technology, and Design. Prentice Hall PTR, Upper Saddle River (2005)
34. Hamadi, R., Benatallah, B.: A petri net-based model for web service composition. In: Proceedings of the 14th Australasian Database Conference, vol. 17, pp. 191–200. Australian Computer Society, Inc. (2003)

35. Hwang, S.Y., Lim, E.P., Lee, C.H., Chen, C.H.: Dynamic Web Service Selection for Reliable Web Service Composition. IEEE Transactions on Services Computing 1(2), 104–116 (2008)

36. Ibrahim, N., Le Mouël, F.: A survey on service composition middleware in pervasive environments. International Journal of Computer Science Issues (IJCSI) 7(4) (2010)

37. Maigre, R.: Survey of the tools for automating service composition. In: ICWS, pp. 628–629 (2010)

38. Martin, D., Burstein, M., Hobbs, J., Lassila, O., McDermott, D., McIlraith, S., Narayanan, S., Paolucci, M., Parsia, B., Payne, T., et al.: OWL-S: Semantic markup for web services. W3C member submission 22, 2007–2004 (2004)

39. Martinez, A., Patino-Martinez, M., Jimenez-Peris, R., Perez-Sorrosal, F.: ZenFlow: a visual Web service composition tool for BPEL4WS. In: 2005 IEEE Symposium on Visual Languages and Human-Centric Computing, pp. 181–188. IEEE (2005)

40. Milanovic, N., Malek, M.: Current solutions for web service composition. IEEE Internet Computing 8(6), 51–59 (2004), http://dx.doi.org/10.1109/MIC.2004.58

41. Papazoglou, M.P., Traverso, P., Dustdar, S., Leymann, F.: Service-oriented computing: A research roadmap (2008)

42. Pejman, E., Rastegari, Y., Esfahani, P.M., Salajegheh, A.: Web service composition methods: A survey. In: Proceedings of the International MultiConference of Engineers and Computer Scientists, vol. 1 (2012)

43. Pi, B., Zou, G., Zhong, C., Zhang, J., Yu, H., Matsuo, A.: Flow Editor: Semantic Web Service Composition Tool. In: 2012 IEEE Ninth International Conference on Services Computing (SCC), pp. 666–667. IEEE (2012)

44. Ponnekanti, S.R., Fox, A.: Sword: A developer toolkit for web service composition. In: Proc. of the Eleventh International World Wide Web Conference, Honolulu, HI (2002)

45. Rao, J., Dimitrov, D., Hofmann, P., Sadeh, N.: A Mixed Initiative Approach to Semantic Web Service Discovery and Composition: SAP's Guided Procedures Framework. In: Proceedings of the IEEE International Conference on Web Services, ICWS 2006, pp. 401–410. IEEE Computer Society, Washington, DC (2006), http://dx.doi.org/10.1109/ICWS.2006.149

46. Rao, J., Su, X.: A survey of automated web service composition methods. In: Cardoso, J., Sheth, A.P. (eds.) SWSWPC 2004. LNCS, vol. 3387, pp. 43–54. Springer, Heidelberg (2005)

47. Schaffner, J., Meyer, H.: Mixed initiative use cases for semi-automated service composition: A survey. In: Proceedings of the 2006 International Workshop on Service-oriented Software Engineering, SOSE 2006, ACM, New York (2006), http://doi.acm.org/10.1145/1138486.1138489

48. Sirin, E., Parsia, B., Hendler, J.: Composition-driven filtering and selection of semantic web services. In: AAAI Spring Symposium on Semantic Web Services, pp. 129–138 (2004)

49. Sohrabi, S., McIlraith, S.A.: Preference-based web service composition: A middle ground between execution and search. In: Patel-Schneider, P.F., Pan, Y., Hitzler, P., Mika, P., Zhang, L., Pan, J.Z., Horrocks, I., Glimm, B. (eds.) ISWC 2010, Part I. LNCS, vol. 6496, pp. 713–729. Springer, Heidelberg (2010)

50. Srivastava, B., Koehler, J.: Web Service Composition-Current Solutions and Open Problems. In: ICAPS 2003 Workshop on Planning for Web Services (2003)

51. Srivastava, B., Koehler, J.: Web service composition-current solutions and open problems. In: ICAPS 2003 Workshop on Planning for Web Services, vol. 35, pp. 28–35 (2003)
52. Stavropoulos, T.G., Vrakas, D., Vlahavas, I.: A survey of service composition in ambient intelligence environments. Artificial Intelligence Review 40(3), 247–270 (2013)
53. Strunk, A.: Qos-aware service composition: A survey. In: IEEE 8th European Conference on Web Services (ECOWS), pp. 67–74 (December 2010)
54. Syu, Y., Ma, S.P., Kuo, J.Y., FanJiang, Y.Y.: A survey on automated service composition methods and related techniques. In: IEEE Ninth International Conference on Services Computing (SCC), pp. 290–297. IEEE (2012)
55. Thiagarajan, R.K., Srivastava, A.K., Pujari, A.K., Bulusu, V.K.: Bpml: a process modeling language for dynamic business models. In: Fourth IEEE International Workshop on Advanced Issues of E-Commerce and Web-Based Information Systems, WECWIS 2002, pp. 222–224. IEEE (2002)
56. Tsai, W.T., Chen, Y., Paul, R., Liao, N., Huang, H.: Cooperative and group testing in verification of dynamic composite web services. In: Proceedings of the 28th Annual International Computer Software and Applications Conference - Workshops and Fast Abstracts, COMPSAC 2004, vol. 2, pp. 170–173. IEEE Computer Society, Washington, DC (2004), http://dl.acm.org/citation.cfm?id=1025118.1025616
57. Xu, D.H., Qi, Y., Hou, D., Wang, G.Z., Chen, Y.: An improved calculus for secure dynamic services composition. In: 32nd Annual IEEE International Computer Software and Applications, COMPSAC 2008, pp. 686–691 (July 2008)
58. Zuckerman, E., Roberts, H., McGrady, R., York, J., Palfrey, J.: Distributed Denial of Service Attacks Against Independent Media and Human Rights Sites. Tech. rep., The Berkman Centre for Internet & Society and Harvard University (December 2010), http://cyber.law.harvard.edu/sites/cyber.law.harvard.edu/files/2010_DDoS_Attacks_Human_Rights_and_Media.pdf

Security and Trustworthiness Threats to Composite Services: Taxonomy, Countermeasures, and Research Directions

Per Håkon Meland[1], Muhammad Asim[2], Dhouha Ayed[3], Fabiano Dalpiaz[4],
Edith Félix[3], Paolo Giorgini[5], Susana Gonzáles[6], Brett Lempereur[2],
and John Ronan[7]

[1] SINTEF ICT
per.h.meland@sintef.no
[2] Liverpool John Moores University
{m.asim,b.lempereur}@ljmu.ac.uk
[3] Thales Services
{dhouha.yahed,edith.felix}@thalesgroup.com
[4] Utrecht University
f.dalpiaz@uu.nl
[5] University of Trento
paolo.giorgini@unitn.it
[6] ATOS
susana.gzarzosa@atos.net
[7] Waterford Institute of Technology
jronan@tssg.org

Abstract. This chapter studies not only how traditional threats may affect composite services, but also some of the new challenges that arise from the emerging Future Internet. For instance, while atomic services may, in isolation, comply with privacy requirements, a composition of the same services could lead to violations due to the combined information they manipulate. Furthermore, with volatile services and evolving laws and regulations, a composite service that seemed secure enough at deployment time, may find itself unacceptably compromised some time later. Our main contributions are a taxonomy of threats for composite services in the Future Internet, which organises thirty-two threats within seven categories, and a corresponding taxonomy of thirty-three countermeasures. These results have been devised from analysing service scenarios and their possible abuse with participants from seventeen organisations from industry and academia.

Keywords: Threats, taxonomy, countermeasures, service composition, security, trustworthiness.

1 Introduction

The capability to effectively cope with unexpected changes and threats is desirable for any system. Systems residing on the Internet are no exceptions, as the

A.D. Brucker et al. (Eds.): Secure Service Composition, LNCS 8900, pp. 10–35, 2014.
© Springer International Publishing Switzerland 2014

Internet is a volatile and vulnerable environment that poses difficult challenges for researchers and systems engineers. Representatives from European industry and academia [17] have already stated in their Future Internet vision that *a primary research direction is to make the Internet—and the systems deployed over it—more secure, dependable, reliable, and flexible.*

This chapter investigates both how traditional threats will affect composite services, and some of the new challenges that shall be accounted for in the emerging Future Internet. For instance, while atomic services may in isolation comply with privacy requirements, a composition of the same services could lead to violations due to the use and manipulation of combined information. Furthermore, with volatile services and evolving laws and regulations, a composite service that seemed secure enough at deployment time may become non-compliant.

Our main contribution is a taxonomy of threats—organised within seven categories—and corresponding countermeasures for composite services in the Future Internet. These results have been devised from analysing service scenarios and their possible abuse with participants from seventeen organisations from industry and academia.

This chapter is organised as follows. Section 2 describes the research method that we followed. Section 3 presents our taxonomy of threats and Section 4 suggests possible countermeasures to these threats. Section 5 outlines research directions to tackle the threats as well as the implementation of countermeasures. Section 6 gives and overview of related work and, finally, Section 7 concludes the chapter.

2   Research Method

In order to study the threats related to composite services, we have employed a scenario-driven method to identify the most relevant types of threats based on both the knowledge of the present situation as well as what different stakeholders envision concerning the near future.

As service composition is still an emerging field, one cannot simply look at incidents in the past to determine what will be the greatest challenges. The scenario development process involved the seventeen organisations in the Aniketos project, with their different expertise and domain knowledge related to service technology. Together, these organisations cover private and public service providers, Cloud providers, security companies, researchers (institutes and universities) on secure service engineering and end-users.

The organisations were encouraged to focus on their expertise domains during scenario description. However, in order to have a comprehensive catalog of threats, we also allowed scenarios related to other domains, even beyond the project case studies. The scenario development was done iteratively, starting off with rough sketches of the usage and behaviour of service environments. A chosen moderator gathered the scenario descriptions and performed an initial review of their relevance. This was followed by a refinement process, where each scenario was updated by the scenario creators in collaboration with the moderator. Afterwards, there were several iterations where the group as a whole determined necessary steps to remove ambiguousness and gaps.

The rough scenarios consisted of short text with focus on the normal situations and behaviour. They were then refined into a more structured template consisting of a summary, workflow description, workflow deviations, stakeholders involved, and expected outcome. For each scenario, we tried to identify how the service environment could be exploited for malicious intents through misuse/abuse case scenario descriptions. They were similarly structured with a short description, stakeholders (the attackers), outcome, assets involved, and possible countermeasures/mitigations. Figure 1 illustrates the overall process.

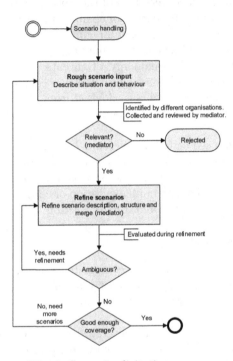

Fig. 1. Scenario elicitation process

The first round of scenario creation resulted in more than fifty scenarios for normal situations, and twenty misuse cases identifying threat events and threat agents. These scenarios have been our main information source for defining threats and countermeasures. A second round of scenario elicitation was performed two years later. Eleven additional scenarios were identified then, and we have been updating the classification itself and the threat description over a period of four years as technology and service uptake have progressed.

We chose to focus on and classify threats that are critical for composite services; thus, the taxonomy should not be regarded as a complete overview for software systems in general. To sort out what is already established threats, we have studied the dictionary of Common Weakness Enumeration (CWE) [2], the dictionary of Common Vulnerabilities and Exposures (CVE), and results from various research project such as Forward [3] (extensive list in section 6).

3   A Taxonomy of Threats for Composite Services

Trustworthiness and security in composite services have the same foundations as in traditional information systems. They are grounded by the security needs which shall roughly be aligned with classical needs as addressed by the information security field, for example confidentiality, availability, integrity, trustworthiness, privacy, access control, non-repudiation as defined in [16].

However, composite services present specific vulnerabilities and threats that do not affect traditional information systems. A threat is defined as a potential for violation of security, which exists when there is a potential for accidentally triggering or intentionally exploiting a specific vulnerability. Vulnerabilities are instead security weaknesses or flaws that make a system susceptible to an attack, whereas attacks consist in the exploitation of such vulnerabilities, being the actual materialization of threats [18,19]. Countermeasures are defensive security mechanisms used for mitigating system vulnerabilities. If a vulnerability is detected within a service, this would typically reduce the trustworthiness of the service until it has been repaired or mitigated.

Taking into account the special characteristics of dynamic composite services, we have defined a set of categories and classes of threats following the method presented in Section 2. Categories are more abstract than classes, and help with organisation. Our categories share similarities with the STRIDE[1] categories [10], which are widely used for modelling threats to traditional software systems, but we have specialized them for our domain. A threat class can belong to more than one category, and represents more specific unwanted events. Note that the threat classes have different levels of abstractions as well, and can in some cases partly overlap/subsume each other. The reason for this is that they have been collected from different industry domains. In our work, we had to make a balance between making the threat classes generic enough for wider use, and preserving them in their original form in terms of name and level of detail. For each threat class we have also indicated a threat impact value within the range of low, medium, high. These values must be considered as an indicative starting point, as they are based on how they would affect the scenarios they originate from. For further reuse, these values may need to be re-assessed based on the system under consideration. Section 3.1 explains our categories, while Section 3.2 lists and explains the threat classes. Table 1 summarizes the relationship between categories and threats, along with their impact value.

3.1   Threat Categories

[TC-1] Incompatibility: Service composition can be a highly complicated task, and such complexity tends to cause security issues concerning incompatibility. Functionality should not be the only criteria while considering composition. Other non-functional constraints such as efficiency, redundancy, resource, and

---

[1] Spoofing, Tampering, Repudiation, Information disclosure, Denial of service and Elevation of privileges.

synchronisation issues may all result in a composition failure. The interface of the component services have to be secure and compatible with each other. A composite service might seem to work correctly from a functional point of view, but there may be violations of security requirements. Even though a composite service only consists of components that are considered to be safe and secure individually, their combination might increase overall vulnerability to threats. The incompatibility category is related to *information disclosure*. If we consider for example, that a travel assistance service provider is committed to ensure customer information privacy, a *point of interest* (POI) service provider that uses data related to user preferences, and sells the data to advertisement companies, should not be selected in the composition.

If one service component is insecure this may compromise the overall security of the composite service. It is unlikely that each component will be fully secure, but the objective is to make them secure enough for their purpose.

[TC-2] Constraints: The services within a composition can be geographically distributed and composed, in turn of other services with different capabilities and constraints, such as security policies, laws or technical and conceptual restrictions. All these new features must be considered in order to avoid the appearance of incompatibilities between the integrated services. Thus, it is necessary to be conscious of the component services to assure a reliable result.

It is possible that each component service has its own security policy. Incompatibility policies may result in a security breach or may lead to different vulnerabilities being exposed. For example, the composite services of the travel assistance service can be deployed in several countries that have incompatible confidentiality laws which can cause an incompatibilities between confidentiality policies of the composition. The constraints category is related to *information disclosure*.

[TC-3] Unaccountability: Unaccountability is related to *repudiation*. It should be possible to hold service providers of composite services and service components accountable on how data is managed, used and transferred. Responsible parties should be defined in contracts, but this can be difficult in a complex and dynamic environment. With composite services, information exchanged between different services is typically maintained in the form of logged data. This logged information can be used for accountability and chain-of-evidence. Also, the logged data may contain sensitive information (such as user's bank account details), and therefore its integrity and confidentiality have to be protected.

[TC-4] Malicious Activity: Composite services are not spared from malicious activities or *tampering*. Attacks are launched with varying motivations. Examples include financial gain, competitive advantage, and damaging reputation. An attacker can, for instance, first gain access to a single service component before it compromises the overall composition. The component service can be either maliciously coded (e.g., by the service developer) or can offer a vulnerability that the attacker can exploit. Malicious activities always have an intention of damaging the composite service or related assets, and can be performed by insiders or external agents.

[**TC-5**] **Overtrust:** By building trust relationships and establishing trustworthiness, service providers and organisations will improve business value and consumer confidence in the service oriented environments. In a composed services context, a number of trust-related threats arise where several individual services are put together in a composed service. This makes it difficult to have complete control over composite services and thus predict their behavior, and eventually their trustworthiness. For example, the trust level of service components related to the travel assistance service can change over time due to several reasons, such as decreasing reputation, and this compromises the trust level of the whole composition. Overtrust is somewhat related to *elevation of privilege, information disclosure*, and *spoofing*.

[**TC-6**] **Usability:** A bad user interface may result in user frustration that can lead them to make errors or compromise their own data. Sometimes it may occur that user interaction with the interfaces or tools in a composite service can increase the likelihood of data being compromised. For example, a lack of user notification or, indeed a large volume of unnecessary notifications could frustrate the end user to such an extent that they inadvertently make bad decisions, compromising their own data. Consequently, it is necessary to have a friendly and easy-to-use user interface. Usability relates with *information disclosure*.

[**TC-7**] **Unavailability**: Unavailability is closely related to *denial of service*, and is especially critical for composite services as the unavailability of any service components can easily make the composite service useless. Unavailability as such is typically a consequence or results of other threats, as a provider may be forced to take down the service if it is not trustworthy enough.

3.2 Threat Classes

1. **Incompatible Laws:** When services are geographically distributed, legal incompatibilities may arise and pose a security threat (e.g., an adequate level of data confidentiality is not ensured by law in all involved countries). A composite service is perceived as a unique entity by its users. Such a threat occurs because users are typically unaware of the identity of individual providers, of their geographic distribution, and of the laws that apply in the countries where the service component resides. In some business areas, regulations and laws might forbid transferring sensitive data, and may require the consent of the data owner or may result in undesirable legal liabilities for service providers. For example; to exchange a confidential electronic document with the company's vice-president, who is currently on a business trip in country B, the financial manager (who is in country A) assembles a composition based on a secure service S_1 that provides Microsoft Word to

Adobe PDF conversion (to make sure the rendering of the document is preserved regardless of the specific document reader/editor), and a file sharing service S_2 used to share the PDF document with the vice-president. S_1 is deployed in country A, S_2 in country B. The law of country B does not ensure data confidentiality over the Internet, as service providers are obliged to introduce lawful intercept facilities. This generates a confidentiality concern for the composite service. In most countries data confidentiality norms exist. The risk could be low/medium if all parties are within EU. However, the risk could be high if parties involved are more globally (e.g., US and EU).
table top

- *Threat Category: TC-1, TC-2*
- *Impact: High - Incompatible laws may put data confidentiality at risk.*

2. **Incompatible Access Control Models:** Access control of a composition is dependent on the access control capabilities of the individual services. Where different component services use different access control models, the result could be a violation of any of the models. As a simple example, consider a travel assistance service composition where the POI service applies Bell-LaPadula ("no read up, no write down" for confidentiality), while the the route service applies Biba ("no read down, no write up" for integrity), is liable to result in a confused system with both models partially implemented.
- *Threat Category: TC-1, TC-2*
- *Impact: High - The impact of such a attack can be high as confidential and private data may be leaked to unauthorized users or, potentially, attackers. This could be, in fact, worse than having no access control as the users would be completely unaware of the issue and think they are operating in a secure environment.*

3. **Privacy Violation via Composition:** When some services are composed together, it is possible that although every one of them has its own security policy, the interaction between them or the data shared in the composition can lead to vulnerabilities and privacy violation. In isolation, none of the services in the composition is a threat to privacy; however, when in a composition, privacy is endangered. For example, an organisation relies on services to let employees collect needed data for their job. The administration uses service "Tax" to retrieve the tax number of an employee, given her name and surname, and birth date. The statistics department uses service "Real Properties" to gather anonymous data about real properties of employees. If employees of the statistics department gain access to the "Tax" service and compose it with "Real Properties", they violate the privacy of employees, for they can associate real properties to specific employees.
- *Threat Category TC-1, TC-2, TC-3*
- *Impact: High - Privacy data confidentiality and integrity are very sensitive security issues, and pose as potential show-stopper for compositions.*

4. **Exploitable Interaction:** An important characteristic in dynamic service re-composition is the increased, and potentially unplanned, interactions between services. Such interactions are themselves a potential source of vulnerabilities and threats. Problems often arise from existing vulnerabilities.

Table 1. The taxonomy of threats to composite services

Threat Categories	Threats Classes	Threat Impact
TC-1: Incompatibility	Incompatible laws	High
	Incompatible access control models	High
	Degraded policy negotiation	High
	Privacy violation via composition	High
	Exploitable interaction	High
	Unwanted recomposition and reconfiguration	High
	Synchronisation threats	High
	Degraded security interface	High
	Insecure interfaces and API's	High
TC-2: Constrains	Incompatible laws	High
	Incompatible access control models	High
	Degrade policy negotiation	High
	Privacy violation via composition	High
	Security guidelines compromised	Medium
	Dissolved redundancy	High
TC-3: Unaccountability	Extracting information from logs	High
	Information and accountability lost	Medium
	Insecure interfaces and API's	High
	Privacy violation via composition	High
	Security guidelines compromised	Medium
	Malicious service provider	High
	Lack of trust between providers	Low
TC-4: Malicious activity	Insufficient automated security evaluation	High
	DDoS attack occurs on service composition	High
	Malicious service provider	High
	Failure to sanitize special element	High
	Embedded malicious code	High
	Protection mechanism failure	High
	Insecure interfaces and API's	High
	Exploitable interaction	High
	Degrade policy negotiation	High
	Extracting information from logs	High
	Manipulation of trust properties	High
TC-5: Overtrust	Manipulation of trust properties	High
	Untrusted outsourcing/delegation	High
	False perception of trust for end user	High
	Reliance on untrusted inputs in a security decision	High
	Inclusion of functionality from untrusted control sphere	High
	Degraded security interface	High
	Degrade policy negotiation	High
	Failure to sanitize special element	High
	Embedded malicious code	High
	Trustworthiness level variability	Medium
TC-6: Usability	Missing end user notification	Medium
	End user gets annoyed by confirmations	Medium
	Lack of usability in secure composition	Medium
	False perception of trust for end use	High
TC-7: Unavailability	Lack of trust between providers	Low
	DDoS attack occurs on service composition	High
	Corrupt load-balancing	Medium
	Recomposition corrupts response time	Medium
	Synchronisation threats	High
	Cascade failure	High

These might exist in individual services, but can be exacerbated or exploited through dynamic interactions across multiple services. Data validation vulnerabilities are a well-understood and widely-exploited type of vulnerability present in a large number of existing systems. The class encompasses any security threat arising from a failure to validate the syntactic or semantic integrity of data passed between services before the data is used.

- *Threat Category TC-1, TC-4*
- *Impact: High - Confidential and private data may be leaked to unauthorized users or, potentially, attackers.*

5. **Degraded Security Interface:** Service compositions might be long-lived. However, not all services are invoked together. Some are invoked after previous providers deliver the service. During this time, security service interfaces might change, and this could be a threat for the service composition. For example, consider a service composition that determines the salary of a company's employees. Among the various services, there are two subsequent services: "Analyse timesheets" determines the amount of work, while "Compute gross salary" takes the timesheet data and determines the gross salary. In such composition, the provider of "Compute gross salary" commits to confidentiality and not to further delegate the task. However, service "Analyse timesheets" takes time, for human verification is needed. During this time, the service "Compute gross salary" changed its interface, which does not guarantee non-delegation anymore.

- *Threat Category TC-1, TC-5*
- *Impact: High - Changes in the security interfaces might affect the effectiveness of the composition and may not meet the security needs of the user.*

6. **Unwanted Recomposition and Reconfiguration:** A system adaptation may involve replacing existing services with new ones or re-structuring the services. The resulting composition may introduce some functionality that might not be desirable for the user or the new functionality may not support the existing compositions. This may leads to a number of problems, for instance incompatible compositions which could prevent the correct delivery of composite service; compromise on security requirements and degrade the efficiency of the system.

- *Threat Category TC-1*
- *Impact: High - This may leads to a number of problems, i.e., incompatible compositions which could prevent the correct delivery of composite service; compromise on security requirements and degrade system efficiency.*

7. **Insecure Interfaces and APIs:** Service providers typically expose a set of software interfaces or APIs that service consumers use to manage and interact with their services. Reliance on a weak set of interfaces can expose an organisation to a variety of security issues related to confidentiality, availability, and password integrity. For example, anonymous access or reusable passwords, clear-text authentication or transmission of content, inflexible access controls or improper authorizations, limited monitoring and logging capabilities, unknown service or API dependencies. Consider a small company that uses a cloud service for daily business management such as online

sale and order management. An insecure interface is exploited by attackers causing financial losses and damage of company's reputation.

- *Threat Category TC-1, TC-3, TC-4*
- *Impact: High - Using services with insecure interfaces and APIs may result in an incompatible composition thereby introducing a threat to the overall security of the composite service.*

8. **Degraded Policy Negotiation:** Different services may have different policies and often multiple policies cannot be reconciled. This leads to negotiation between service providers. A malicious service provider might use this opportunity to try to affect the security policies of a service to make them weaker in order to attack the service at a later time. A weaker security policy can make a system vulnerable to various attacks.
   - *Threat Category: TC-1, TC-2, TC-4, TC-5*
   - *Impact: High - A weaker security policy can make a system vulnerable to various attacks.*

9. **Security Guidelines Compromised:** The process of matching security requirements (security guidelines defined by a security specialist) with security capabilities of the services can be a notoriously complex and technical process. In general, developers concentrate more on the functional aspects of a system and may not have extensive experience dealing with security considerations. In some cases, it may be impossible to fulfil all of the required security requirements, such as where security ease-of-use must be balanced against security restrictions. If a developer is unable to create a system that fulfils the requirements, problems are likely to arise. Such problems could take the form of inadequate security, or of failure to deploy a service. The source of the threat comes from lack of security expertise or intractable security requirements.
   - *Threat Category TC-2, TC-3*
   - *Impact: Medium - This could lead to all sort of security issues.*

10. **Dissolved Redundancy:** Service compositions often involve redundant provision of a certain service. Sometimes, service providers further delegate service provision to third-party providers. If they delegate the service to the same third-party, then the redundancy principle is violated. For example, an air traffic controller needs accurate weather forecasts. According to the flight regulations, he assembles a service composition that includes two providers for rain/snow real-time data. However, both providers outsource the provision to the same third-party. This way, redundancy is not guaranteed any more and the redundancy policy has been violated.
    - *Threat Category TC-2*
    - *Impact: High - Redundant provision of a service is mandatory for critical tasks. When redundancy dissolves, the critical task is at risk (its failure is more likely).*

11. **Information and Accountability Lost:** In a decentralized system each end point is responsible for collecting and storing information usage events (logs) that may be relevant to current or future assessment of accountability

to some sets of rules/policies. These logs become the major source of assessing policy accountability either in real time or in the future when such an assessment is needed. Therefore, it is important to securely maintain these logs in the system. For example, Alice tries to sign up for a subscription to the newspaper from a foreign country, making use of a SoA comprised of a series of services. For delivery reasons it is not possible to send the newspaper to that country, so one of the services cancels the order. However this is a rare event and the service does not pass the information back to other services with which it is composed. In fact one service sends an email to Alice saying that her subscription was successful. The newspaper has no record of Alice's details.

- *Threat Category TC-3*
- *Impact: Medium – Information and accountability lost may damage the company reputation.*

12. **Extracting Information from Logs:** Logging information is an essential part of maintaining composite services. These logs capture an extreme amount of data, including sensitive information (e.g., personal information, authentication data, bank details) that must be protected. By adequately securing the logged information, the risk of releasing confidential information to untrusted parties from both inside and outside the organisation can be reduced.

- *Threat Category TC-3, TC-4*
- *Impact: High - Confidential and private data may be leaked to unauthorized users or attackers.*

13. **Malicious Service Provider:** A malicious service provider could ask for unnecessary private or confidential information and store all the gained data in order to assemble and sell a detailed costumer profile. Consider a use case of "travel reservation". In the use case, a user would like to reserve a complete travel package from a composition of loosely-coupled web services. First, the user finds a travel agent service on the web and provides the travel agent with destination and preferred dates. Based on the customer's requirements, the travel agent searches and contracts many airline and hotel services, in order to obtain information on the flights and hotel rooms. The travel agent service then assembles a list of travel alternatives and presents them to the user. The user makes his/her choices and provides the travel agent service with personal information for reservation. The travel agent service then asks for the credit card details and confirms the reservation. During the travel booking process, personal data such as name, date of birth, address, phone no and credit card number are exchanged. However a question arises how to ensure that the requested user's personal data is only used for the stated purpose. A user giving personal identifiable information to an organisation may result in the data being used in ways the user never intended. For example, the credit card details could be passed on to persons intending to commit fraud.

- *Threat Category TC-3, TC-4*
- *Impact: High - Compromise privacy, confidentiality, integrity and availability depending on the type of information provided.*

14. **Failure to Sanitize Special Element:** Composite services are often involved in receiving inputs from its users. However, a user could inject keystrokes or even code in order to cause an adverse effect on the service behaviour and its integrity. In composite services, a service with such a weakness may put the integrity of the whole composition at risk. Special elements are often important in weaknesses that can be exploited by injection attacks. Therefore, user-controlled input should be properly filtered and intercepted for special elements.
- *Threat Category TC-4, TC-5*
- *Impact: High - In composite services, a service with such a weakness may put the integrity of the whole composition at risk. Further, it can be exploited by service injection attacks.*

15. **Embedded Malicious Code:** A dishonest service developer could insert malicious code within a service to subvert its security. A simple example could be: insert malicious code in a service to send credit card details or any other sensitive information to a particular email address. The malicious code is normally inserted during service implementation. As service developers are often considered trusted, this threat needs consideration.
- *Threat Category TC-4, TC-5*
- *Impact: High - It can compromise privacy, confidentiality, integrity and availability depending on the malicious code and the attacker motivation.*

16. **Protection Mechanism Failure:** Services are often equipped with security mechanisms that provide defence against various attacks. However, a security weakness arises when a service does not use or uses an insufficient protection mechanism. In case of an insufficient protection mechanism, a service could be saved from certain attacks but could not be saved from others. For example, service A is vulnerable to both Distributed Denial of Service (DDoS) attack and service injection attack. However, the security mechanism it uses can only provide defence against the DDoS attack. Thus, service A can do nothing against the service injection attack. A missing security mechanism could expose service A to both types of attack.
- *Threat Category TC-4*
- *Impact: High - A service without any security mechanism or uses an insufficient protection mechanism may expose a service to various attacks.*

17. **Insufficient Automated Security Evaluation:** Without a timely evaluation, services with malicious intent or vulnerabilities can cause all sorts of trouble such as leakage of information or financial losses. This can be compared to traditional viruses in software code. A simple example could be an insider of a bank inserting back-door code into a service component before the security evaluation has been performed, in order to get customers' personal information.
- *Threat Category: TC-4*
- *Impact: High - It could cause serious privacy and data protection issues for an organisation.*

18. **DDoS Attack Occurs on Service Composition:** DDoS attacks are not new for web-based services. Many high-profile companies have been victims of such attacks. A DDoS attack is easy to detect but difficult to prevent. The distributed nature of composite services makes them even more exposed to DDoS, since the attacker can attack any of the service components and inflict damage to the overall service. This broad attack surface is something that makes DDoS attacks even more likely than for isolated systems. A DDoS attack normally targets web services that have public access gateway. By flooding a server with requests, the service can be overwhelmed, thereby preventing valid access to the service.
    - *Threat Category TC-4, TC-7*
    - *Impact: High - This can make a service unavailable.*
19. **Manipulation of Trust Properties:** The role of reputation systems is to facilitate trust. Remote monitoring of fulfilment of a contract relies on trustworthy collection of real data. However, a dishonest service provider could change or manipulate some trust properties of one of the services that are involved in a composite service. This could happen by compromising the monitoring engine either by manipulating trust properties or submitting a fake report to increase the trust level. For example, suppose Johnny is a service provider with limited ethics. By setting up a large number of false composite services using a payment service he provides, he is able to boost the trust level of this payment service.
    - *Threat Category: TC-4, TC-5*
    - *Impact: High - Malicious users could control service reputation according to their goal. The integrity of the overall composition could be at risk.*
20. **Trustworthiness Level Variability:** The trustworthiness of single services and service providers often changes over time. This is also true when a service is used within a service composition. Maintaining trustworthiness helps consumer confidence and provides a safe environment for businesses to dynamically interact and carry out transactions. The trustworthiness of one of the component services can be deteriorated during the execution of a composite service. This may lead to a situation where a single service with low trustworthiness becomes a threat for the entire composition. For example, in a travel assistance composition, the reputation of the map service provider goes down; thus, the integrity of the entire travel assistance is threatened. The composite service cannot be trusted because the map service could impose a huge threat to the entire composition. It could have a major security flaw that may let an attacker launch a denial-of-service attack and damage the overall composition or it may put the data confidentiality at risk. It is therefore necessary to continuously monitor the trustworthiness of the services and decide to replace the deteriorated component service with another service with the same functionality as soon as the trustworthiness value falls below a threshold.
    - *Threat Category: TC-5*
    - *Impact: Medium - It can compromise privacy, confidentiality, integrity and availability depending on the type of an attack.*

21. **Untrusted Outsourcing/Delegation:** To deliver a service, providers might outsource it or delegate specific activities to other service providers. This might be dangerous if the service user does not trust the additional providers. An air traffic controller is relying on a certain composition to obtain accurate weather forecasts. The service provider that delivers rain/snow real-time data delegates this service to another provider that the controller distrusts. Distrust might concern both service delivery (the controller does not rely on that service) or the handling of data (the position of the aeroplanes might be confidential).
    - *Threat Category: TC-5*
    - *Impact: High - Untrusted outsourcing may put data confidential and privacy at risk. Furthermore, the untrusted service may not be adequately secured and may introduce several vulnerabilities. It could be a weak spot for the attackers to attack the overall composition.*

22. **False Perception of Trust for End User:** An untrustworthy composite service could boost its overall trustworthiness by including highly trustworthy service components. Most of these components do not have an active role in the composition; they are just there to contribute to the calculation of the trustworthiness level of the composition as a whole. This can occur if the mechanism for calculating trustworthiness is simply based on the average trustworthiness of included components. For example, Gary is a customer who is looking looking to buy a product online. The WrongWeb shop uses his preferred and trusted provider, SafePay, so he trusts the WrongWeb shop implicitly (false sense of security). However, when he makes a purchase, the received product is of a terrible quality and worse yet, the WrongWeb shop sells his contact information to spammers. The transaction itself goes without problems.
    - *Threat Category: TC-5, TC-6*
    - *Impact: High - Exploiting the reputation of others can give a service false credibility, enabling a large number of attacks. This credibility can be used to exploit assets from end users, and make trustworthiness/reputation mechanisms less trustworthy.*

23. **Reliance on Untrusted Inputs in a Security Decision:** In some protection mechanisms, security decisions such as authentication and authorisation are made based on the values of input such as cookies, environment variables, and hidden form fields. However, an attacker could change these inputs using customized client applications and bypass the protection mechanism. For example, a web-based email list manager may allow attackers to gain admin privileges by setting a login cookie to 'admin'.
    - *Threat Category: TC-5*
    - *Impact: High - This may lead to the exposure or modification of sensitive data or damaging service availability.*

24. **Inclusion of Functionality from Untrusted Control Sphere:** Services using or importing executable functionalities (a library or a widget) from an untrusted source could introduce several security issues. The functionality could be malicious in nature, outdated or contain other vulnerabilities.

- *Threat Category: TC-5*
- *Impact: High - This might lead to many different consequences depending on the included functionality, but some examples include injection of malware, damaging service availability or gaining access to sensitive data. In a composite service, malicious functionality could inflict damage to the overall composition. It depends on how often a service imports or uses functionalities from other services that are not evaluated for trustworthiness. Furthermore, the impact increases if there are insufficient protection mechanisms in place to check the functionalities that are borrowed and does not belong in the same domain.*

25. **Missing End User Notification:** In a composite service, a recomposition may consist of replacing existing services with new ones. It is possible that the new composition fulfils user requirements but compromises some important properties. By not giving this information to the end user may, it my lead to severe or unintended consequences. For example, Donald is a business man who uses a stock quote service to see the current stock prices for certain important stocks. When Donald sets his preferences about which stock exchange service to use, he only sets the minimum required trustworthiness level and the maximum price of the service. When the initial web service is no longer usable due to the lowering of the services trust level, a free stock exchange service, now at the highest trustworthiness level, is inadvertently recommended to Donald's client. Unfortunately the free service has a 15-minute built-in delay for stock market data. Donald is not notified about this and loses money.
    - *Threat Category TC-6*
    - *Impact: Medium - A service may not deliver as expected.*

26. **End User Gets Annoyed by Confirmations:** This is largely a usability problem, arising from the tension between the need to ensure users to consider the consequences of changes to a system (and their actions) and the desire of the user to focus on functional rather than non-functional aspects of the system. Although most users acknowledge the importance of security, it nonetheless often represents a hindrance to them achieving their intended aims. This is especially true in relation to notifications. The threat is therefore that an overabundance of notifications frustrates the user and makes him choose to fulfil functional desires over security. This can be mitigated to some extent by considerate approaches towards notifications (e.g., providing non-modal notifications, and avoiding repeated notifications), but achieving a suitable balance is a difficult technical problem.
    - *Threat Category TC-6*
    - *Impact: Medium - A user may agree to a reduced security policy unintentionally. This may lead to several security issues, i.e., a threat to data confidentiality.*

27. **Lack of Usability in Secure Composition:** Breadth, depth and flexibility of provided features in a development tool can often lead to compromises in terms of usability. Creating an interface that is both technically rich and easy to use is a difficult proposition. One of the goals of the Future Internet

is to provide flexibility through the use of services, however this often means that complexity management is simply transferred from the end user to the service developer. This is particularly true in the development of generic services, for a developer may have to consider a variety of scenarios, and is therefore unable to make assumptions on how the deployed service will be used. Designing tools and techniques for dealing with this complexity introduces difficult usability challenges. Usability can be measured, but the process of determining the resulting threats is an uncertain process.

- *Threat Category TC-6*
- *Impact: Medium - A service developer may find the development environment too difficult to understand and eventually give up on using it.*

28. **Cascade Failures:** In cascade failures, a failure in one system has an impact on the activities of other systems it interacts with. A real-world example of a cascade failure is the electrical blackout that affected much of Italy on 28 September 2003: the shutdown of power stations directly led to the failure of nodes in the internet communication network, which in return caused further breakdown of power stations [8] [9]. In terms of systems-of-systems (e.g., power stations attached to the national grid), the threat applies equally to composed software services and the Future Internet more widely.

- *Threat Category TC-7*
- *Impact: High - Cascade failures result in some of these other systems failing, which in turn have a cumulative impact on the remaining systems, and so on. Ironically the situation arises especially where back-ups and fail-safes have been put in place, but with the potential consequence that the cascade failures result in a complete failure of the entire composition of systems.*

29. **Corrupt Load-Balancing:** If one system fails due to an attack (e.g., denial-of-service), the remaining systems have to handle the load from the failed system. This may result in an additional backlog transferred from the failed system that pushes the remaining services over their capabilities. If one of these systems fails, even more load is transferred the remaining systems, and a further backlog, with the process repeating to cause a cascade of failures. Such cascade of failures can be attributed to the dynamic reassignment of services resulting from an attempt to address an existing failure.

- *Threat Category TC-7*
- *Impact: Medium - Dynamic system re-composition may be required to address an existing failure, which may affect the overall system operation.*

30. **Recomposition Corrupts Response Time:** When a composite service reconfigures, its component services are rearranged and/or replaced. However, it is possible that some services of the composition are unable to effectively participate in the process of recomposition due to their availability/response time. For example, consider the case where one of the components of Service X is a storage service. Replacing this storage service would require a time-consuming migration task, since large data volumes are stored there. Unfortunately, the composite service is recomposing too frequently, thereby spending significant time on changing the storage service component.

- *Threat Category TC-7*
- *Impact: Medium - Access to data could be restricted or may cause delay in accessing critical information.*

31. **Synchronisation Threats:** In a composite services environment, services may suffer from synchronisation/timing issues that prevent the correct delivery of composite services. These synchronisation/timing issues might cause deadlock, race conditions and prevent the services to interact with each other. For example, the parallel execution of services means that deadlock might occur between two services if they both reach a state whereby they are waiting for input from the other.
    - *Threat Category TC-1,TC-7*
    - *Impact: High - This can cause severe interaction flaws.*

32. **Lack of Trust between Providers:** Assembling a service composition is not sufficient to ensure it works. Given their autonomy, service providers might refuse to collaborate when they do not trust each other. This may cause an unreliable composition which may fail to achieve its objectives. For example, a service composition is established to compute income taxes for a company's employees. Within this composition, service "Incomes" returns the income for employees, whereas service "Tax computation" determines the taxes to pay on the basis of the income. However, "Incomes" does not trust "Tax computation", for it does not guarantee an adequate level of confidentiality. Perhaps, "Tax computation" preserves it but has an incompatible trust certificate. Thus, a service that would be an excellent choice for a composition is unavailable due to the fact that it does not trust other candidate services that would participate in the composition.
    - *Threat Category TC-3, TC-7*
    - *Impact: Low - This may cause an unreliable composition which may fail to achieve its objectives.*

4   Countermeasure Methods for the Threats

From the scenario descriptions, we have devised a set of countermeasure methods for the threats to composite services described in Section 3.

Issues related to incompatible policies and laws can be tackled via design-time verification techniques (*M1*). This requires the interface of both individual and composite services to specify (i) allowed deployment locations, and (ii) the laws/policies that apply. Automated verification checks if the expected exchange of data between services complies with the laws/policies about, e.g., data privacy.

When design-time verification is inapplicable, the information flow has to be monitored and/or enforced at run-time (*M2*). This requires the service infrastructure to monitor data exchange through observable channels. Access control enforcement mechanisms ensure that confidential information is not accessed by unauthorized users. The distinction between data and information is fundamental here: while data exchange can be observed, there is always a risk that information flows in a way that cannot be directly observed.

If the policies of consumers and providers are incompatible, negotiation techniques (*M3*) can help to identify a trade-off that satisfies both parties. Policy federation patterns can be studied in this context.

Identity management systems (*M4*) can prevent (or at least make it more difficult) providers from assuming fake identities. These systems require each service to be bound to a legal entity (a human or an organisation). Trustworthiness/reputation mechanisms will be key for services to successfully operate in a volatile environment. However, these mechanisms have to be robust, both in terms of their computation algorithms (*M5*)—the computed value shall be as realistic as possible—and of their monitoring techniques (*M6*)—resistance to fake reports and attacks to integrity.

Notification mechanisms (*M7*) enable actors to get up-to-date information concerning consumers' and providers' trustworthiness (especially in case of relevant changes, either negative or positive). A possible way to implement notification is via publish/subscribe [11]. In addition to notification, service re-composition algorithms (*M8*) enable responding to decreasing trustworthiness levels. Re-composition should balance quality and stability, i.e. it should not disrupt the current composite service. A particular type of re-composition pattern involves relying on redundant service providers (*M9*). Though more expensive, this avoids the scenario where failure of a component service affects the composite service. Service re-composition shall take into account that services are not controllable agents; rather, their providers are autonomous in choosing when, how, and if to deliver a specific service (*M10*). Thus, while assembling composite services, such autonomy cannot be neglected.

A possible way to prevent composite services from including untrusted services is to provide explicit support to outsourcing (*M11*). This means that service interfaces have to specify whether such operation is allowed to be outsourced as well as providers and services that can/cannot be involved. Such method also requires that, at run-time, actual outsourcing can be observed.

Services can be certified at deployment-time (*M12*) to verify whether a service operates as declared by its interface. Relying on certified services prevents malicious providers from injecting their services in compositions. However, such technique requires access to the source code (or the availability of inspectable binaries). Certification is not sufficient to analyse all possible interactions a service may engage in. Consequently, it should be complemented by runtime interaction monitoring techniques (*M13*) to keep track of actual interactions services participate in. A different yet fundamental approach is to devise secure service development methods (*M14*) that, if followed by developers, prevents or significantly reduces the likelihood of attacks from insiders. Such methods may include pair programming, automated validation techniques, and the establishment of traceability links from requirements to code.

Service interfaces shall be expressive enough to represent fine-grained access control rules about the confidential data a service provides and needs (*M15*). This way, composite service designers can check which data will be disclosed (possibly to whom) and they can verify need-to-know properties, i.e., if data is disclosed to some actor that does not need it. Another technique is to give service interfaces a contractual validity (*M16*): violations lead to penalties (e.g., negative feedback or economic loss). In service-level agreements, penalties are referred to as credits. Necessary condition to make *M16* applicable is that services are deployed in an environment where penalties can be enforced.

In order to overcome changes in security interfaces, partial planning techniques (*M17*) are a helpful technique. A partial plan is defined beforehand and, while the composite service is in place, and depending on the results of the execution, the plan might be incrementally refined in order to timely include services that are appropriate to deliver the expected outcome. Though sub-optimal, partial planning is more robust to unexpected circumstances than planning from scratch. An alternative approach is to define security interfaces that manifest temporal validity (*M18*). This would allow for composition to be defined having a temporal horizon in mind (the provider commits to the validity of the interface till a certain point in time). Such technique can be combined with partial planning to create robust compositions. A third way to cope with changes is to perform early binding of services before their actual usage (*M19*). Such solution works if providers are committed to deliver the services that have already been bound. Combining *M19* with *M18* allows service providers to avoid indefinite allocation of resources.

To reduce the effect of DDoS attacks, efficient and scalable access control engines are a possible solution (*M20*). Cloud computing techniques might be adopted to physically distribute the infrastructure over multiple computational nodes, still providing a unique logical interface. To help consumers in service selection, security interfaces can incorporate information about scalability (*M21*). For instance, the maximum amount of requests the provider can deal with or a distribution curve showing how performance and response time degrade with an increasing the number of users. Such details may be either informative or have contractual validity. A way to early detect DDoS attacks is to monitor service performance to detect degradations (*M22*). Upon detection, response mechanisms can be applied, e.g., migration/redeployment of existing services on different servers, refusal of all new requests, usage of existing techniques to filter out attackers.

Mechanisms should be put in place so that the functionality of the composite service is not endangered by continuous re-compositions needed to improve security performance (*M23*). This might include using utility functions that balance traditional quality-of-service factors and security properties. Monitoring service interconnections (*M24*) allows for preventing cascade failures. Indeed, a single service is often used by multiple consumers, and the effects of a failure (and also of a response) shall take such factor into account.

In order to ensure a throughput and response time, load balancing techniques (*M25*) can be exploited at service deployment-time. Composition techniques should therefore give priority to services with better resource availability. In order to guarantee redundancy in service provision, services shall be enriched with information that allows for specifying and monitoring redundancy constraints

(*M26*). If a service commits to redundant provision, its interaction with third-party services shall be monitored to verify that redundancy does not dissolve. Timing and synchronisation issues—that may affect timely delivery of a composite service—can be tackled by conducting test cases (*M27*). If the set of test cases is defined systematically, the tests can dramatically reduce the likelihood of incurring in such issues at run-time.

Providers can specify, in service interfaces, information concerning what type of log information will be kept, which policies will be applied, and how such policies will be enforced (*M28*). The inherent limitation of such technique is that it requires information about how specific service providers work, which organisations are typically unwilling to disclose.

The design of composite services should take that into account, and minimize the risk of frequent re-composition requests that might lead to users carelessly pressing a "confirm re-composition" button (*M29*). More generally, interaction design aspects shall be seriously taken into account when designing composite services and composition mechanisms. The results of formal verification techniques can be abstracted using higher-level models (*M30*), so to ensure designers consider such results to improve the composite service. For example, this means interpreting issues at the organisational level or showing which are the risks that affect the interactions between services. In order to improve the way service designers/composers assemble services in a secure and trustworthy way, training sessions can be foreseen and organised (*M31*). These sessions provide designers with a methodological approach and with knowledge about the verification techniques that are performed by design-time tools.

Most security problems are continuously reoccurring and with known solutions/mitigation strategies. However, developers are not always aware of the available mitigation strategies. By providing the relevant information for a composition the developer will receive definitive advice and will have the knowledge to make more informed decisions (*M32*). If a specific composite service is attacked, similar services or services using some of the same components are likely to be threatened. An early warning system (*M33*) would notify these other services in advance so that they are able to prepare themselves (e.g., via recomposition).

Table 2 summarises the countermeasure methods. The "type" column classifies the methods according to their main function: (i) Prevention (P) methods avoid the occurrence of a threat; (ii) Monitoring (M) refers to observing relevant events that might suggest a threat; (iii) Verification (V) collects analysis techniques that check whether some security/trustworthiness property is guaranteed; (iv) Diagnosis (D) means correlating monitoring data to determine if a threat exists and to identify the root cause of such threat; (v) Response (R) methods mitigate the threat impact after it occurs. The "phase" column describes at which stage of the service engineering process the method applies: design-time (Des), deployment-time (Dep), and run-time (Run).

Table 2. Taxonomy of the countermeasure methods

Method	Type	Phase
M1 : Design-time security verification takes into account policies/law	V	Des
M2 : Monitor information flow and enforce it using access control rules	M, R	Run
M3 : Policy negotiation automatically performed	D, R	Run
M4 : Detect fake services by keeping track of the identity of the provider	M, D	Run
M5 : Robust trustworthiness/reputation computation mechanisms	D	Des, Run
M6 : Robust trustworthiness/reputation monitoring mechanisms	M	Run
M7 : Monitor and notify changes in reputation/trustworthiness	M	Run
M8 : Recompose when trustworthiness and reputation are decreasing	R	Run
M9 : Create (re)compositions that rely on redundant service providers	P, R	Dep, Run
M10 : Consider providers' autonomy while composing services	P	Des, Dep, Run
M11 : Explicit support to outsourcing (sub-contracting)	P, M	Des, Run
M12 : Deployment-time service certification	V, P	Dep
M13 : Run-time interaction monitoring	M, D	Run
M14 : Secure service development method to prevent insiders attacks	P	Des
M15 : Service interfaces specify fine-grained access control	P, M, D	Des, Run
M16 : Contractual service interfaces, violations lead to penalties	M, R	Run
M17 : Partial planning techniques to enable incremental compositions	P, R	Run
M18 : Security contracts manifest temporal validity	P	Des, Run
M19 : Early binding of services before actual invocation	R	Des, Run
M20 : Scalable access control verification engines	P	Run
M21 : Incorporate scalability information in security interfaces	P	Des
M22 : Monitor service performance to early detect DDOS attacks	P, R	Run
M23 : Consider functionality/service to be delivered during adaptation	P	Run
M24 : Predict cascade failures by monitoring service interconnections	P, D	Run
M25 : Load balancing mechanisms while deploying service compositions	P, R	Dep, Run
M26 : Redundancy specification and monitoring	M, D	Des, Run
M27 : Test cases to check synchronisation/timing issues in compositions	V, P	Des
M28 : Protect logs using the same policies that apply to services	M, D	Des, Run
M29 : Avoid pressing "confirm re-composition" due to annoyance	P	Des, Run
M30 : Design tools should abstract the results of formal verification	P	Des
M31 : Training sessions to educate designers of service compositions	P	Des
M32 : Provide information about threat/attack method	P	Des
M33 : Early warning	P	Run

5   Research Directions

Our study on threats and countermeasures has helped us identify the following prospective techniques and research directions for designing, building, and operating secure and trustworthy composite services:

– **Trustworthiness/Reputation Management.** In the scenarios where consumers and service providers are unknown at design-time and where the service composition is performed with providers that do not know each other, trustworthiness and reputation management will be essential. We envisage that the challenge will be to provide mechanisms that: (i) enable consumers and service providers to obtain information about the reliability of others; and (ii) enable to monitor and compute trustworthiness and reputation in a robust way free of bootstrapping and malicious attackers. Different factors to evaluate should be considered, such as opinions by peers, information about compliance, and certifications released by trusted third parties.

- **Expressive Security Interfaces for Services.** Whereas current service providers represent both functional and non-functional properties about their offered service through the specification of service interfaces, this seems to be largely inadequate to represent security and trustworthiness properties for service compositions. The development of new future languages shall allow service providers for a comprehensive specification of the security and trustworthiness properties they guarantee. Some of them could be: (i) fine-grained access control policies that indicate which information can be shared and with whom, as well as specific services that can or cannot be included in the composition; (ii) redundancy guarantees to increase the reliability; (iii) the threats that affect the composite service and the countermeasures that are deployed to address them.

- **Early Warning and Response.** Currently, when a threat or security issue that affects a service composition is detected, a reconfiguration or recomposition of the services is performed in response. However, this reactive approach is only a mitigation and does not prevent the occurrence of an event. Early warning and response mechanisms, taking advantage of risk assessment techniques to determine when threats are likely to occur, would enable proactive switching to alternative compositions.

- **Certification at Deployment Time.** Certification techniques (especially if the certificates are issued by trusted third parties) that guarantee the trustworthiness of a new service deployed (and even their providers) will play a fundamental role to be considered in service compositions. We envisage that these certifications might include information about the structure and composition of a service, the development methodology followed at design-time, or a commitment about the responsibility of the certification authority in case of a breach of agreements by the certified service.

- **Service Recomposition Revisited.** Existing techniques for recomposition of services are based on components as established in traditional software engineering methodology. Other mechanisms based on service-oriented settings shall be developed to work better in the new scenarios that arise from the Future Internet. Some of the factors that should be taken into account for these new devised techniques are the following: (i) service providers are autonomous (consequently there is no central overall control and the action of composing services will be based on an interaction protocol among the participating service providers); (ii) threats are recomposition triggers (e.g., a recomposition process might be triggered by lower trustworthiness due to the expiry of a certificate); (iii) countermeasures are based on security patterns (service recompositions will typically consist of applying the most adequate pattern); (iv) service interfaces with contractual validity (the provider is committed to guarantee the declared properties in the socio-legal context where the service is deployed); and (v) incremental compositions (e.g. a service composition is only partially assembled at deployment and necessary services are added on the fly based on the availability and quality of service providers).

- **Representing Laws, Checking and Enforcing Their Compliance.** Currently, there are no techniques to fully capture laws and associate them with the services where they apply to, e.g. to represent data confidentiality restrictions that apply in certain countries. Some of the challenges in the Future Internet will be to find mechanisms to ensure the compliance of a composition of services with respect to specific laws and, thus, the need of devising a representation of laws in a machine-understandable way.
- **Robust Identity Management Systems.** Also related to legal issues, another relevant challenge in the Future Internet will be the development of robust identity management systems. Each entity in this new context shall be characterized by an identity and each service (atomic or composite) shall be unequivocally associated to its service provider, who could be have legal responsibilities about the service offered. This need of ensuring each user is who he says to be, is even more crucial in contexts of single sign-on where a single identity enables accessing to multiple systems.
- **Methodologies and CASE Tools.** A large number of security issues could be produced by insider attacks, sometimes without harmful intention but due to lack of knowledge. There are many methodologies and tools that support the development of secure and trustworthy composite services, but they should be able to provide the results in such way that even non-security-expert developers can understand the risks and threats that can affect the composite service under design. Moreover, training sessions should support these methodologies and tools to guarantee their correct use and application.
- **Automated Policy Negotiation via Flexible Templates.** Static policies, such as "Use cryptography protocol X version Y" will be insufficient in the open environment of the Future Internet. More flexible and dynamic policies are required that allow interoperability between different service consumers and providers, dynamic negotiation of the policies in service composition (e.g., within the ranges that have been specified) or even include optional priorities, preferences and parameters that help perform a better matching.
- **Testing Techniques for Composite Services.** The importance of testing is key not only for software, but also for composite services. The main difficulty will be the opening of an environment where services in a composition can be replaced by others at run-time. Very little attention has been paid to this topic so far, which we envisage will be a crucial challenge in the future.

6   Related Work

In this section we briefly present some of the main research projects and papers related to our work and based on the identification and taxonomy of threats and vulnerabilities and methods to deal with them.

During 2008 and 2009, the EU/FP7 project FORWARD identified possible new research areas and threats that need to be addressed. The main results of the project were presented in the FORWARD Whitebook [3], that contains not only the identified threats but also detailed and concrete scenarios of how potential malicious agents can take advantage of them. The main research areas identified by FORWARD were grouped into the following categories: networking, hardware and virtualisation, weak devices, complexity, data manipulation, attack infrastructure, human factors, and insufficient security requirements. The threats identified in the EU/FP7 project FORWARD were updated during 2011 in the SysSec project [4]. SysSec was a European project included in the Seventh Framework Programme that proposes to create a European Network of Excellence in the field of Systems Security and one of its goals is managing Threats and Vulnerabilities in the Future Internet. They decided to preserve the division of threats focusing on three main areas: malware and fraud, smart environment, and cyberattacks. Other related European projects in this area are: the Think-Trust project [5] that has produced a list of research challenges complementary to the RISEPTIS (Research and Innovation for Security, Privacy and Trustworthiness in the Information Society) Report (generated by a high-level advisory body in ICT research on security and trust), the WOMBAT (Worldwide Observatory of Malicious Behaviors and Attack Threats) project [6] that aimed at providing new means to understand the existing and emerging threats that are targeting the Internet economy and the net citizen.

Early work, such as the taxonomy from Landwehr et al.[13], Wang and Wang [20], Weber et al. [21] and Im and Baskerville [12] categorize security threats, flaws and vulnerabilities in a very broad sense related to computer programs. Mirkovic and Reiher [14] have published more specific taxonomies for attacks and defences related to DDoS attacks, but this is something we only treat as a class in our taxonomy. Babar et al. [7] have published a taxonomy of threats for the Internet of Things (IoT), which is more hardware-oriented than ours. The threats taxonomy from Mármol and Pérez[15] is, to the best of our knowledge, the most similar work to ours. They focus on threats trust and reputation models for distributed systems, which have been central aspects for our work as well.

Finally, important work is done through CAPEC [1] from the National Cyber Security Division of the U.S. Department of Homeland Security. CAPEC, the Common Attack Pattern Enumeration and Classification, is a public, international and community-developed list of common attack patterns along with a comprehensive schema and classification taxonomy.

7   Conclusion

The Future Internet will be an environment in which a diverse range of services are offered by heterogeneous suppliers. In this environment users are likely to unknowingly invoke underlying services in a dynamic and ad hoc manner. The dynamic environment of service composition carries new security threats. Following a method where scenarios were contributed by seventeen European organisations, we have established a taxonomy of threats, consisting of seven high-level categories and thirty-two classes, and a taxonomy of thirty-three countermeasures that cover the entire life cycle of composite services.

The threats taxonomy is a comprehensive overview of specific dangers for composite services, that was devised through a thorough analysis of existing and potential vulnerabilities, and is clearly focused on trustworthiness aspects. The taxonomy is not meant to be exhaustive, as new threats will inevitably appear in the future. Our identified research directions provide recommendations on how to put countermeasure methods into practical use.

References

1. CAPEC, the Common Attack Pattern Enumeration and Classification, http://capec.mitre.org/
2. CWE (Classified Weakness Enumeration), http://cwe.mitre.org/
3. Forward project, http://www.ict-forward.eu/
4. SysSec project, http://www.syssec-project.eu/
5. Think-Trust project, http://www.think-trust.eu/
6. WOMBAT (Worldwide Observatory of Malicious Behaviors and Attack Threats), http://www.wombat-project.eu/
7. Babar, S., Mahalle, P., Stango, A., Prasad, N., Prasad, R.: Proposed security model and threat taxonomy for the internet of things (IoT). In: Meghanathan, N., Boumerdassi, S., Chaki, N., Nagamalai, D. (eds.) CNSA 2010. CCIS, vol. 89, pp. 420–429. Springer, Heidelberg (2010)
8. Berizzi, A.: The Italian 2003 blackout (June 2004)
9. Corsi, S., Sabelli, C.: General blackout in Italy Sunday September 28, 2003 (June 2004)
10. Hernan, S., Lambert, S., Ostwald, T., Shostack, A.: Uncover Security Design Flaws Using The STRIDE Approach, http://msdn.microsoft.com/en-us/magazine/cc163519.aspx
11. Hoffman, K., Zage, D., Nita-Rotaru, C.: A survey of attack and defense techniques for reputation systems. ACM Comput. Surv. 42, 1:1–1:31 (2009), http://doi.acm.org/10.1145/1592451.1592452
12. Im, G.P., Baskerville, R.L.: A longitudinal study of information system threat categories: The enduring problem of human error. SIGMIS Database 36(4), 68–79 (2005), http://doi.acm.org/10.1145/1104004.1104010
13. Landwehr, C.E., Bull, A.R., McDermott, J.P., Choi, W.S.: A taxonomy of computer program security flaws. ACM Comput. Surv. 26(3), 211–254 (1994), http://doi.acm.org/10.1145/185403.185412
14. Mirkovic, J., Reiher, P.: A taxonomy of ddos attack and ddos defense mechanisms. SIGCOMM Comput. Commun. Rev. 34(2), 39–53 (2004), http://doi.acm.org/10.1145/997150.997156
15. Mármol, F.G., Pérez, G.M.: Security threats scenarios in trust and reputation models for distributed systems. Computers & Security 28(7), 545–556 (2009), http://www.sciencedirect.com/science/article/pii/S0167404809000534
16. CSRC - NIST: Glossary of Key Information Security Terms, http://csrc.nist.gov/publications/nistir/ir7298-rev1/nistir-7298-revision1.pdf
17. Papadimitriou, D.: Future Internet–The Cross-ETP Vision Document (2009), http://www.future-internet.eu/fileadmin/documents/reports/Cross-ETPs_FI_Vision_Document_v1_0.pdf
18. Shirey, R.: Internet Security Glossary, Version 2 (RFC4949) (2007), http://www.rfc-base.org/rfc-4949.html

19. Stoneburner, G., Goguen, A., Feringa, A.: Risk management guide for information technology systems recommendations of the national institute of standards and technology. Nist Special Publication 800(30), 55 (2002), http://csrc.nist.gov/publications/nistpubs/800-30/sp800-30.pdf

20. Wang, H., Wang, C.: Taxonomy of security considerations and software quality. Commun. ACM 46(6), 75–78 (2003), http://doi.acm.org/10.1145/777313.777315

21. Weber, S., Karger, P.A., Paradkar, A.: A software flaw taxonomy: Aiming tools at security. SIGSOFT Softw. Eng. Notes 30(4), 1–7 (2005), http://doi.acm.org/10.1145/1082983.1083209

Adopting Existing Communication Platforms for Security Enabling Technologies

Konstantinos Giannakakis

Athens Technology Center S.A., Halandri, Athens, Greece
k.giannakakis@atc.gr

Abstract. Development of secure solutions requires special care and consideration. In most situations dedicated tools need to be used and strict procedures
must be followed. However, more often than not, secure web services must be
based on existing technologies and interact with the real world, where special
security considerations aren't made. This introduces a big challenge for designers and developers, who need to integrate existing libraries and tools into a
specific secure technology stack. The deployment of the services is equally
challenging, as developers want to benefit from the advantages of state-of-the-
art platforms and deployment in Cloud environments. This chapter is going to
examine how the above mentioned challenges were addressed in the design and
development of the Aniketos Platform.

Keywords: communication platform, cloud, OSGi, secure service development.

1   Introduction

The Aniketos Platform aims to establish and maintain trustworthiness and secure
behaviour in a constantly changing service environment. It aligns existing and develops new technology, methods, tools and security services that support the design-time
creation and run-time dynamic behaviour of composite services, addressing service
developers, service providers and service end users.

The Aniketos Platform consists of many different components, each one offering a
specific functionality. In order to integrate this diverse set of components from various vendors, it was decided that the architecture of the platform would be based on
the OSGi framework. The OSGi framework defines a dynamic module system for
Java. It is a standardised technology and fully documented through the OSGi specifications documents [6]. OSGi is supported both by industry and an active open-source
community. Open source implementations of high quality are available. It is becoming more and more popular and it is the technology of choice for a large number of
projects. The reasons for selecting OSGi and the benefits it brings to the Aniketos
Platform will be presented in detail at section 2 of this chapter.

On top of the OSGi architecture various challenges need to be addressed. The platform aims to integrate existing components with new ones, which have been developed specifically for Aniketos. A wide range of technologies are used. Also the

A.D. Brucker et al. (Eds.): Secure Service Composition, LNCS 8900, pp. 36–49, 2014.

platform should be able to adapt itself, so that it can run in different environments. Integration of such a big system is not an easy task and here we will escribe, how diverse technologies and components can be fit together in a common environment, in order to provide the rich functionality of the platform.

2   Modular Design

A big system with broad functionality is usually designed by separating it into different components that are logically separated. This process is called modular design and it is especially important, when the full system also needs to integrate existing components. Enforcing modularity is essential during the development, deployment and execution of a system. The OSGi framework fosters modularity in all the above phases. In the following sections, we are going to explain the benefits that the adoption of the OSGi architecture brings to the Aniketos Platform.

2.1   Design Time Modularity

Design time modularity refers to splitting the source code of a complex system into various software components. Design time modularity is enforced during the development phase.

The OSGi framework allows the creation of bundles, which encapsulate code that performs a single task. A software module, i.e. a single logical unit that offers a specific functionality, consists of one or more bundles. The separation of source code in different bundles is the module layer of the OSGi architecture. It is the first step towards design time modularity as it allows developers to work on different topics independently.

The communication between bundles is achieved by exporting and importing Java packages. Every bundle defines in a manifest file, which Java packages it needs to import and which packages it can provide to other bundles. Versioning information as well as some other rules that can be used at runtime during dependency resolution are also included in the manifest file. These are beyond standard JVM behaviour, which doesn't provide such granularity. In order to be effective, the bundles, which are actually Java jar files with some extra information, must be deployed and run in an OSGi container.

On top of OSGi's module layer there is the services layer. OSGi has been successfully described as Services Oriented Architecture in JVM. It features a service registry, where a bundle can register a provided service. A service is defined by a Java interface, which can be considered the "contract" between the provider and the consumer. Other bundles discover the provided services in order to consume them. In the runtime there can be more than one implementations of the same service available. This doesn't affect the development, as the OSGi container will do the appropriate linking. The bundles developers only need to worry about properly consuming the interface.

Design time offers additional benefits, when different teams from different vendors work on implementing an integrated solution. A common practice is to create an "interface bundle", which contains all Java interfaces needed by external components. This bundle is used internally for the development of the "implementation bundles". The implementation bundles actually provide the specific functionality of a software module. This functionality needs to be consumed by external components. With OSGi architecture, the external bundles only need the interface bundle to be able to interact with a component. It is the single artefact that must be exchanged between different development teams. The interface bundle also plays the role of documenting the contract of the OSGi services provided.

2.2   Runtime Modularity

Runtime modularity refers to the deployment and execution of different software components that together build a unified system. OSGi bundles are deployed in an OSGi container. An OSGi container is an implementation of the OSGi specification. It is responsible for resolving dependencies between bundles and linking bundles together. The benefits of OSGi's runtime modularity are more than enough for a complex system:

- One module can be uninstalled or updated without affecting the rest of the system. Proper maintenance can be achieved much more easily.
- There can be more than one implementations of the same module. The selection of the most appropriate one is made by the container.
- It is much easier to handle dependency issues. In a big system with a lot of modules, it is very likely that two components require a different version of the same third party library. This situation is close to impossible to handle in a standard JEE container. However, this doesn't constitute a problem for OSGi, as the two different versions can be both be installed at the same time.

3   Integration of Existing Technologies

3.1   Interaction with Enterprise Applications

The term enterprise applications is used to define software applications that aim to solve problems of an organisation.   In Java terminology, enterprise applications refer to applications that need to be distributed, interactive and have to manage security, transactions and persistence.

The Aniketos Platform need to integrate components with enterprise characteristics. These components consume and provide web services – either SOAP or REST. They store information in a database and may use a messaging mechanism. In order to integrate them in a common system the next two different approaches can be followed.

Converting Existing Applications to OSGi

The first approach of integrating an existing component is to convert it to use the OSGi framework. The OSGi Alliance, which is the organisation responsible for OSGi standardisation, has understood the need of enterprise applications and has released the OSGi Enterprise Specification (currently in release 5). This specification defines how OSGi bundles implement characteristics typical to enterprise applications, such as accessing a database or creating a web application. Apache Aries project provides implementations and extensions of most of the Enterprise OSGi specifications.

In the Aniketos Platform, Apache Aries[1] components have been used to implement the database layer. Access to an existing relational database is achieved through the Blueprint, JPA, JNDI and JTA specifications. This is considered the proper way of accessing database servers in an OSGi environment.

Figure 1 depicts the configuration of a blueprint component that declares an EntityManager data source connecting to a MySQL database. In Apache Karaf[2], which is Aniketos OSGi container of choice, one can simply copy this file to the deploy folder in order to instantiate the blueprint component.

```
<blueprint xmlns="http://www.osgi.org/xmlns/blueprint/v1.0.0">

  <bean id="mysqlDataSource"
class="com.mysql.jdbc.jdbc2.optional.MysqlDataSource">
    <property name="url" value="jdbc:mysql://10.1.1.66:3306/aniketos_rt"/>
    <property name="user" value="root"/>
    <property name="password" value="****"/>
  </bean>

  <bean id="mysqlXADataSource"
class="com.mysql.jdbc.jdbc2.optional.MysqlXADataSource">
    <property name="url" value="jdbc:mysql://10.1.1.66:3306/aniketos_rt"/>
    <property name="user" value="root"/>
    <property name="password" value="****"/>
  </bean>

  <service interface="javax.sql.DataSource" ref="mysqlDataSource">
    <service-properties>
      <entry key="osgi.jndi.service.name" value="jdbc/sredb"/>
    </service-properties>
  </service>

  <service interface="javax.sql.XADataSource" ref="mysqlXADataSource">
    <service-properties>
      <entry key="osgi.jndi.service.name" value="jdbc/xasredb" />
    </service-properties>
  </service>

</blueprint>
```

Fig. 1. Blueprint Data Source Configuration

The consumption of the above data source can be performed inside another blueprint component, as depicted in Figure 2.

---

[1] http://aries.apache.org
[2] http://karaf.apache.org/

```
<bean id="dataAdapter"
class="eu.aniketos.serviceruntime.data.DataAdapterImpl">
  <jpa:context unitname="sredb" property="entityManager"/>
  <tx:transaction method="*" value="Required"/>
</bean>
```

Fig. 2. Blueprint connection to data source

The above configuration injects the data source inside the DataAdapter class. The DataAdapter class can later use JPA to work with the database. Although the DataAdapter and the Data Source are Blueprint components, the use of the Blueprint component framework in other parts isn't mandatory. The DataAdapter bundle can register OSGi services, which can be discovered with other means (Declarative Services, Service Tracker).

Since OSGi is based on the Java language, migrating an existing JEE application to OSGi is entirely possible. However, OSGi has a special class loading mechanism that allows every bundle to be isolated from every other. This has many technical implications for third-party libraries commonly used in JEE (database drivers, ORM frameworks and all libraries using reflection are affected). For these libraries a special OSGi version is needed. Luckily, many vendors provide OSGi versions of their libraries. For legacy libraries and components that do not provide an OSGi version, special considerations must be taken in order to perform the migration. This usually involves creating a single bundle, which includes all required dependencies. This is of course against OSGi principles and breaks modularity, however it proved to be the only solution in some cases. (In Aniketos we were forced to follow this practice in the case of Drools Rule Engine[3]).

Communication with Web Services
Migrating an existing component to OSGi is not always possible, not only due to technical constraints, but also due to licensing issues. Some components provide their functionality through a service and not through a binary or a source code package that can be redeployed. OSGi can leverage web services in order to interact with these components.

3.2   Security Considerations

Integration of secure components in a complete solution can be achieved almost effortlessly in an OSGi environment. In OSGi every bundle is completely isolated from one other. This allows including security sensitive operations in separate components. Also, OSGi supports Java Platform Security and can fully take advantage of the provided API.

4   Cloud Deployment

In today's world more and more applications find their way to the Cloud. A Cloud deployment offers many advantages and any newly developed application needs to make the necessary considerations in order for it to be possible to deploy to a Cloud environment.

---

[3] http://drools.jboss.org/

The Aniketos Platform is a modern system that aims to be installed in as many environments as possible in the near future. As such it must be flexible enough to be deployable effortlessly in both Cloud and non-Cloud infrastructure. The modular architecture of OSGi really helps in this direction.

An addition to the OSGi Specification is the OSGi Remote Services specification. OSGi Remote Services define how bundles deployed in different containers can discover and consume services between them. This is achieved by exposing an OSGi through a SOAP or a REST interface. Popular open source implementations of the OSGi Remote Services include Apache CXF DOSGi[4] and Eclipse Communication Framework (ECF)[5].

OSGi Remote Services allow Aniketos Platform modules to be installed in remote containers. These modules can still interact with one another, providing and consuming OSGi services, the same way as if they were installed in a single container. There is no need at all for code changes. These OSGi containers can be deployed in any infrastructure that supports invocation of a JVM. Currently there are containers running in proprietary infrastructure as well as in Amazon Web Services. A sample architecture is depicted in Figure 3.

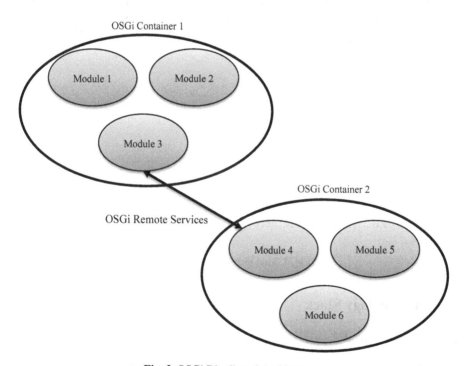

Fig. 3. OSGi Distributed Architecture

---

[4] http://cxf.apache.org/distributed-osgi.html
[5] http://www.eclipse.org/ecf/

4.1   Discovery

The architecture described above presents the problem of node discovery. Although every container can contain different modules, in order for these modules to be able to communicate, it must be possible for one container to discover each other. In Apache CXF DOSGi this is achieved through Apache ZooKeeper[6].

Apache ZooKeeper is an open-source server, which enables highly reliable distributed coordination. The OSGi containers aren't connected directly to each other. Instead they all connect to the ZooKeeper service. The ZooKeeper service allows the containers to discover each other and exchange messages. This allows the addition of new containers to the system, without having to re-configure the old ones.

4.2   Deployment

Apache CXF DOSGi exposes web services through non-standard HTTP web ports. An example endpoint of a web service is http://localhost:9090/marketplace?wsdl. The usage of non-standard ports in problematic in enterprise environments, which have very strict firewall settings. This issue can be resolved by using Apache Web Server and mod_proxy module to redirect the web service to a standard port. The required configuration of httpd.conf is depicted in Figure 4 (For simplicity the configuration allows proxying from all locations. This should be changed in a production environment).

```
<IfModule proxy_module>
    ProxyRequests Off
    ProxyPreserveHost On
    <Proxy *>
        Order deny,allow
        Allow from all
    </Proxy>

    ProxyPassReverse /marketplace http://localhost:9090/marketplace
    ProxyPass /marketplace http://localhost:9090/marketplace
</IfModule>
```

Fig. 4. Mod proxy configuration

5   Technology Stack

5.1   Apache Karaf

OSGi in an open technology and there are many open source implementations available. The Aniketos Platform is using Apache Karaf for deployment. Apache Karaf offers many unique characteristics that make it ideal for OSGi applications:

---

[6] http://zookeeper.apache.org/

- It is very easy to customise and configure.
- It provides many ways for the bundles provisioning. Bundles can be installed from a command shell or by copying them directly to the deploy folder. Most importantly Karaf offers a features characteristic that allows bundles to be grouped in logical units which can then be installed all together in a single go.
- It is a very lightweight container that out of the box only offers the absolutely necessary functionality. This contributes to fast start-up times and to a cleaner environment. Common third-party libraries can be easily installed as features.
- It supports the Maven protocol. It can connect to Maven repositories and install bundles from them. This is a very convenient way of bridging development and deployment.
- It offers an advanced command shell that can be easily extended.
- It has all the necessary characteristics of a production environment container: It can be installed as an OS service; it offers a centralised logging mechanism that can easily be configured; the command shell can be accessed remotely by any SSH client.

For the Aniketos Platform a special distribution of Apache Karaf has been created. This distribution has been customised and configured according to the needs of the platform. It has been proved helpful both for development and deployment. Developers had an easy way to replicate the deployment environment and test their modules. For deployment, the Aniketos Karaf distribution made it easy to deploy the container in different servers.

5.2   Activiti

Activiti is a workflow and Business Process Management Platform. It features a BPMN 2 process engine that is used to execute business processes. It is an open source solution released under the Apache license. Activiti can be installed as a standard WAR file in Tomcat or any other Java Web container. It offers a graphical interface for deploying and managing services. However, a REST API is also available. This REST API can be used to integrate Activiti with external components.

6   Aniketos Service Runtime Environment

The Aniketos Service Runtime Environment (SRE) is the Aniketos mechanism for executing secure composite services. SRE as well as other Aniketos components are presented in [1]. Although it isn't an internal Aniketos component, it is tightly integrated with the Aniketos platform with respect to the following aspects:

- Security and trust in recomposition/adaptation of composite services. [2]
- Monitoring and evaluation of trustworthiness and security violations of service contracts, also considering contextual information such as change in operation conditions and users' behaviour.
- Runtime validation of secure service behaviour.

The Aniketos SRE is implemented with the aid of the OSGi and Activiti technologies presented above.

6.1   Architecture

Figure 5 depicts the architecture of the Aniketos Service Runtime Environment.

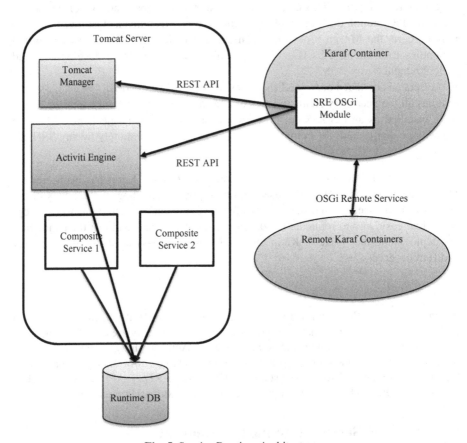

Fig. 5. Service Runtime Architecture

The Service Runtime Environment consists of two main components:

- A Tomcat server, which hosts an Activiti v5.11 engine responsible for executing the BPMN composition plans and the composite services deployed through SCF and SRE.

- Aniketos and environment modules deployed as OSGi bundles in Apache Karaf containers

The bridge between these two components is the SRE OSGi Module. This is a set of OSGi bundles, which also has the responsibility of connecting the Runtime Environment with the Design Tools. The main tasks of this module are:

- Exposes a Web Service that is consumed from the Service Composition Framework (SCF) for the deployment of composite services.

- Deploys composition plans (BPMN) to the Activiti Engine making use of the REST API provided.

- Dynamically generates the composite services WAR files and deploys them to Tomcat through a REST interface.

- Subscribes to notification events for composite and atomic services and triggers re-composition and re-configuration, whenever it is required

The SRE OSGi Module needs to communicate directly or indirectly with numerous other Aniketos modules: Marketplace, Notification, SCPM, NCVM, CMM, Trustworthiness. Some of them are installed in the same OSGi container, while some others in remote ones. The communication between OSGi bundles that reside in different OSGi containers is performed with the aid of CXF DOSGi Remote Services implementation.

6.2   Deployment of Composite Services

An Aniketos Composite Service is created with the Service Composition Framework (SCF) tool. A service designer uses SCF to combine one or more atomic services, discovered in the Aniketos Marketplace, into a BPMN diagram, attach security requirements and configure the rules for re-configuration and re-composition. The SCF tool is described in detail in the Aniketos Design Time Tools section. SCF connects to the SRE OSGi module to physically deploy a composite service.

Currently the SRE module supports BPMN diagrams with service tasks only. Diagrams with user tasks are not supported and will fail to deploy. The reason for this will become evident, when the process of executing a composite service is described.

The following sequence diagram presents the actions taken during a composite service deployment.

The process of the deployment is initiated by the SCF. The SRE OSGi module exposes a Web Service interface for deployment processes. SCF provides all the necessary information for the deployment:

- The main composition plan and the list of alternatives.
- Agreement template.
- Consumer policy.
- Rules to follow for re-configuration and re-composition, when a notification alert for the composite service or one of its atomic services is received.
- Deployment details. This is a set of service designer's preferences. They are used for the registration of the composite service to the Marketplace and for the creation of the composite service's interface.

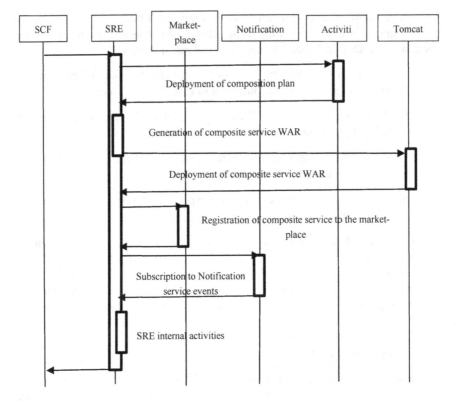

Fig. 6. Composite Service Deployment

When a valid deployment request is received by the SRE, it will first try to deploy the composition plan (BPMN) to the Activiti engine. It will then generate a WAR file that will expose the composite service interface and deploy it to Tomcat. The next step is to register the composite service to the Marketplace. The registration uses information from the deployment details. The tags to characterize the service are available there. This information is important in order to be able to discover the composite service and re-use it as an atomic service in a different scenario.

After the service registration the SRE subscribes to events from the Notification service for the composite service itself and for the atomic services used in the service tasks. This will allow the SRE to re-act in case of an alert and trigger re-composition or re-configuration. Finally SRE performs some internal required actions and responds to the SCF.

6.3   Execution of a Composite Service

All composite services expose a similar interface:

```
String [] operationName(String [] arg0, String [] arg1);
```

The operation name is included in the deployment details and it is up to the service designer to select it. Every service accepts as input two String arrays of equal size. The first is the parameter names and the second one the parameter values. Only simple types (string, numeric, Boolean) are accepted. These are the input parameters needed by the composition plan in order to be executed. The caller of the service must be aware of the required parameters. An example SOAP envelope is presented below.

```
<soapenv:Envelope
xmlns:soapenv="http://schemas.xmlsoap.org/soap/envelope/"
xmlns:com="http://compositeService.aniketos.eu/">
    <soapenv:Header/>
    <soapenv:Body>
        <com:getMap>
            <arg0>LotInfo</arg0>
            <arg1>3</arg1>
        </com:getMap>
    </soapenv:Body>
</soapenv:Envelope>
```

The output of the service is a String array with the results of the composition plan execution. An example SOAP response follows.

```
<S:Envelope xmlns:S="http://schemas.xmlsoap.org/soap/envelope/">
    <S:Body>
        <ns2:getMapResponse
xmlns:ns2="http://compositeService.aniketos.eu/">
            <return>LotInformation=37.99411,23.75631</return>
            <re-
turn>MapView=http://dev.virtualearth.net/REST/v1/Imagery/Map/Road/
37.99411,23.75631/15?pushpin=37.99411,23.75631&amp;dcl=1&amp;mapSi
ze=600,600&amp;key=AkMqtYXkW6HV1CDW7GNF712mrntdCnEe9Qv_eXHESYdOFCq
IuW9Tc7Kh2oo9rYWq</return>
        </ns2:getMapResponse>
    </S:Body>
</S:Envelope>
```

The required actions for the execution of a composite service are presented in the following sequence diagram.

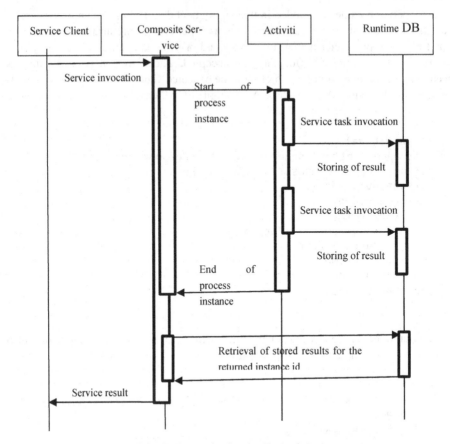

Fig. 7. Composite Service Execution

When a composite service is invoked it makes use of Activiti Engine's REST interface in order to start a process instance. A process instance executes the BPMN workflow of the composition plan. The BPMN workflow includes one or more service tasks. The service task is executed through an Activiti extension that has been developed in the context of the Aniketos project. This extension is called "Aniketos Delegation" and is based on the Execution Listeners technology provided by Activiti. The tasks of Aniketos Delegation are:

- Communicate with Security Policy Monitoring Module (SPMM) before a service task is executed
- Store the result of the service task in the Service Runtime Engine database. The results are stored alongside the process id that was allocated to the execution from Activiti

After the process has finished executing, Activiti returns through the REST interface the process id used. The composite service uses this process id to read the results from the database and return them to the caller.

From the above diagram it becomes evident the reason why only service tasks are supported in the composition plan. Composite services are normal SOAP services and must respond to clients in a timely manner. In case of user tasks the process execution is stalled until some human interactions takes place. This can take an arbitrary amount of time and the service call would most probably timeout before a response is received. A solution would be to devise an asynchronous mechanism for receiving the results. In that case however the composite service wouldn't be a simple SOAP service and could only be used in compatible environments.

7   Conclusions

Designing, developing and deploying security enabling components is far from trivial. However, one can leverage existing technologies to achieve this task. The OSGi framework offers a lot of advantages to this end. The communication between the components can be based on standard solutions (SOAP and REST web services). Finally, the Activiti Business Process Management Platform offers a suitable way for executing secure business processes. The Activiti REST API can be used to automate the deployment and execution of services.

OSGi and Activiti technologies are used to implement the Aniketos Service Runtime Environment. The Aniketos Service Runtime Environment allows the deployment and execution of secure Aniketos composite services.

References

1. Meland, P.H., Rios, E., Tountopoulos, V., Brucker, A.D.: The aniketos platform. In: Brucker, A.D., Dalpiaz, F., Giorgini, P., Meland, P.H., Rios, E. (eds.) Secure and Trustworthy Service Composition. LNCS, vol. 8900, pp. 50–62. Springer, Heidelberg (2014)
2. Meland, P.H., et al.: Security and trustworthiness threats to composite services: Taxonomy, countermeasures, and research directions. In: Brucker, A.D., Dalpiaz, F., Giorgini, P., Meland, P.H., Rios, E. (eds.) Secure and Trustworthy Service Composition. LNCS, vol. 8900, pp. 10–35. Springer, Heidelberg (2014)
3. OSGi in Action - Richard S. Hall, Karl Pauls, Stuart McCulloch, and David Savage - Manning Publications Co. (April 2011)
4. Enterprise OSGi in Action - Holly Cummins and Timothy Ward - Manning Publications Co. (March 2013)
5. Building Modular Cloud Apps with OSGi - Paul Bakker, Bert Ertman - O'Reilly Media (September 2013)
6. OSGi Alliance Specifications, http://www.osgi.org/Specifications/HomePage
7. Activiti Web Site, http://activiti.org/
8. Apache Karaf Web Site, http://karaf.apache.org/
9. Zookeper Web Site, http://zookeeper.apache.org/

The Aniketos Platform

Per Håkon Meland[1], Erkuden Rios[2], Vasilis Tountopoulos[3], and Achim D. Brucker[4]

[1] SINTEF ICT, N-7465, Norway
per.h.meland@sintef.no
[2] TECNALIA Research and Innovation, Parque Tecnológico de Bizkaia 700, Spain
erkuden.rios@tecnalia.com
[3] Athens Technology Center S.A., Halandri, Athens, Greece
v.tountopoulos@atc.gr
[4] SAP SE, Vincenz-Priessnitz-Str. 1, 76131 Karlsruhe, Germany
achim.brucker@sap.com

Abstract. The overall objective of Aniketos has been to help establish and maintain trustworthiness and secure behaviour in a constantly changing service environment. The resulting Aniketos platform contains existing and newly developed technology, methods, tools and security services that support the design-time creation and run-time dynamic behaviour of composite services, addressing service developers, service providers and service end users. This chapter gives and overview of the Aniketos platform as a whole and its software packages.

Keywords: Aniketos, platform, service composition, components.

1 Introduction

The Future Internet will provide an environment in which a diverse range of services are offered by a diverse range of suppliers, and users are likely to unknowingly invoke underlying services in a dynamic and ad hoc manner. Moving from today's static services, we will see service consumers that transparently mix and match service components depending on service availability, quality, price and security attributes. Thus, the applications end users see may be composed of multiple services from many different providers, and the end users do not have much of a guarantee that a particular service or service supplier will actually offer the claimed security.

We can illustrate service composition through a practical service example: Let's say a service developer wants to create a travel agency service, MyPerfectTravel, which lets the end user read about various destinations, check the weather forecast and book a trip containing flights, hotel, a hire car and tickets to leisure activities. Under the hood of such a composite service there will be a range of services from independent providers, but the end users only has to relate to MyPerfectTravel. There are many services like this already today, but these are largely static affairs, and require redesign once there is some sort of change. New and emerging technologies for

A.D. Brucker et al. (Eds.): Secure Service Composition, LNCS 8900, pp. 50–62, 2014.

dynamic service composition allow a more autonomous and ad-hoc approach, so that a service can adapt to another configuration at runtime. Let's say that MyPerfectTravel ordinarily uses a service from the Amadeus reservation system to handle the flight bookings, but this service becomes exposed to a threat, lowering its assurance level or availability. MyPerfectTravel should consequently react to this, and for instance replace this service component with a similar one from e.g. Galileo, Worldspan or Sabre without the end user ever noticing it.

The main objective of Aniketos is to establish and maintain trustworthiness and secure behaviour in a constantly changing service environment. Aniketos provides methods for analysing, solving, and sharing information on how new threats and vulnerabilities can be mitigated. We have constructed a platform for creating and maintaining secure and trusted composite services that:

- Complements state-of-the-art service composition technology. The platform provides methods, tools and community services to support service implementation, discovery, composition, adaptation and management through the concept of full life-cycle security engineering.
- Allows definition, validation and monitoring of trustworthiness and security properties of composed and dynamically evolving services through models for requirements specification and business-processes enhanced with security policies and metrics.
- Makes it possible to efficiently analyse, solve and share information on how new threats and vulnerabilities affect the composition and can be mitigated, so that composed services can automatically adapt to them without loosing availability and end user trust.
- Manages to handle trustworthiness and security of adapted/recomposed services from a socio-technical perspective. Security and trust are not only a technical issue for the heterogeneous nature of composite services, but rather an interleaving problem between technical and social aspects that cannot be considered in isolation.

In section 2 we give a high level overview of the Aniketos platform, the processes, activities and stakeholders it supports. Section 3 gives more detail on the component structure and explains how they are grouped in different packages. Concluding remarks are given in section 4.

2   The Aniketos Platform at a Glance

The Aniketos platform complements existing state-of-the-art Service Oriented Architecture (SOA) frameworks by connecting emerging technological solutions with the human practices that are needed to create and maintain secure and trusted composite services. Figure 1 shows how Aniketos supports activities within the composite service life cycle. Service developers compose services at design-time by discovering and including available service components from external service providers. A service component needs to provide an abstraction of its behaviour and security guarantees. Consuming composite services require a specific behaviour and impose their own policies that the service components have to respect. Aniketos is used to make sure that service providers can be trusted and that service components do not unintentionally violate security policies.

At runtime, the service provider offers the composite service to a service end user. Due to the Aniketos capabilities, this end user is able to put his trust in one party instead of relating to all of the service providers involved. He would like to have stable level of trust, being indifferent to whether service components are changed or service providers come and go. Aniketos uses monitoring and notifications to help the service providers perform intelligent adaptation or recomposition of the services, triggered by changes in component behaviour, change in the trustworthiness of a service provider, new threat information, and also changes in the operating environment (e.g. a service is being used for a purpose it was not originally intended for or the end user relocates to a more hostile environment).

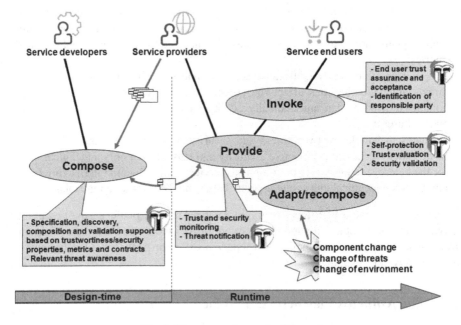

Fig. 1. The composite service life cycle

As shown in Figure 2, the Aniketos platform itself can be structured into the three areas related to design-time support, runtime support and community support. These are explained in the text below in relation to different stakeholders.

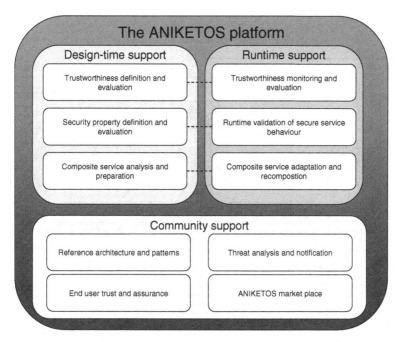

Fig. 2. Overview of the Aniketos Platform

2.1   Design-Time Support

This area consists of methodologies and tools that define and evaluate trustworthiness and security properties over and between external service components. This allows a service developer to perform service discovery and composition based on security properties and metrics, not just functional descriptors. He is also able to choose service providers and service components according to trustworthiness aspects. Composite services are analysed and prepared through automated on-line mechanisms that gather data concerning both individual components and service compositions as a whole, and the developer is informed about known threats to these through the threat notification from the community.

Aniketos did not set out to create a whole new process of developing composite services; a lot of work has already been done in this field and should therefore be exploited. Figure 3 shows typical work processes related to design-time service composition and how Aniketos complements these. The generic part may of course have other variations, with more/fewer process boxes (e.g. testing has been omitted since we focus on validation at design-time) and where the order might be a little bit different (e.g. contracts can be established after service assemble), but we think this one is a fairly generic version to which we can relate to. Note that loops have been omitted (e.g. if validation fails it will be necessary to go back one or several steps).

Only the service developer stakeholder has been included here, but this one can represent other more specific roles, such as service composer, service designer and service implementer. Additionally, the service owner and the service end user would typically be involved in giving high-level requirements input to the service specification process.

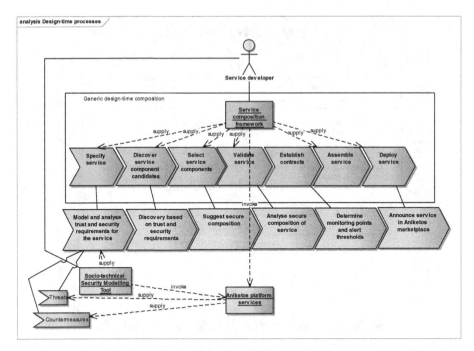

Fig. 3. Typical processes related to design-time service composition

2.2 Runtime Support

Any service provider must expect changes related to external dependencies, such as updates or alterations of service components, or unwanted circumstances that influence the service compositions. The design-time definitions are used to monitor threats that cannot be mitigated at design-time, evaluate the trustworthiness and look for potential security violations of the service components. The platform allows a proactive increase in trustworthiness by asking for more credentials and tries to control the damages in case of attack by selecting the appropriate security level on which the service can run. A runtime threat alert-and-adapt mechanism is able to receive emerging threat notifications from the community. All these are possible triggers to dynamic adaptation or recomposition of the service.

Figure 4 gives a generic overview of the runtime domain. The Provide service process is continuously running, and will at some point in time receive an alert from the Aniketos platform. This will indicate to the service provider that a service validation would be a wise thing to do. The service validation can have three outcomes:

1. The service is OK and the alert was nothing to care about, go back to regular provision.
2. The service is not OK, try and adapt with a reconfiguration (meaning keep the same service components but with some modifications).
3. The service is not OK, try to recompose (replace service components).

In the two latter cases the service provider would normally do a new validation since there has been a change.

In the lowermost part of the figure we have showed that monitoring is also something that is continuously done by the service provider. If something out of the ordinary is detected, an alert can be sent to the Aniketos platform, which would route this message to the relevant receivers. For instance, if a service provider detects an intrusion he would have to notify consuming composite services if this is a contract requirement.

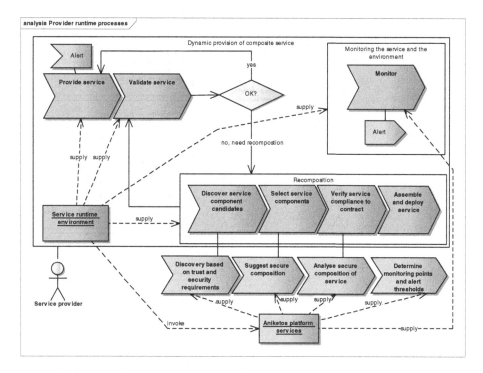

Fig. 4. General processes related to runtime reaction to changes and monitoring

2.3   Community Support

Service developers can find information on how to apply Aniketos as a part of the community support, which also includes example services, demonstration material, tutorials, process descriptions, development patterns and guidelines. Threat/countermeasure information and notifications are provided to both service developers and service providers in order to guide design-time composition or trigger runtime adaptation/recomposition based security goals or service components included in the composite service. The service end user will only need to relate to one entity that she can place her trust to and keep responsible in case something goes wrong, though a composite service has many underlying service providers. The Aniketos marketplace offers a way of requesting/offering service components with defined security and trustworthiness properties.

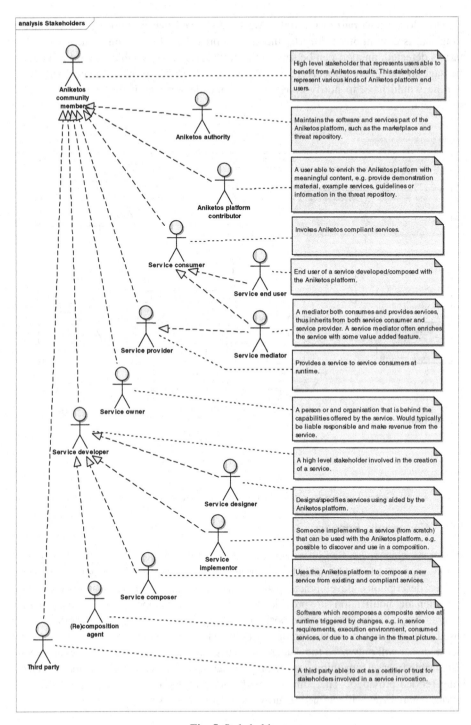

Fig. 5. Stakeholders

2.4   Overview of Stakeholders

As already shown in the process diagrams, Aniketos supports several types of stake-holders who in one way or another are influenced by the platform. Figure 5 presents a more complete stakeholder breakdown (the arrow relationship between stakeholders is always inheritance/specialisation) along with a brief comment explaining the typical characteristics. At the most abstract level we have defined the "Aniketos community member", which all other stakeholders inherit from. The specialisations give more detail on their particular role and how they benefit from the Aniketos platform. Note that these stakeholders are not mutually exclusive, for example a service provider might also be a service owner.

3   Aniketos Components and Packaging

The Aniketos platform has been realised by a set of loosely coupled components that can be glued together based on what type of support is needed. Figure 6 gives a three-layered overview of these components. Some of these are environment components, which are basically reference implementation of something that interacts with Aniketos, and can be replaced by other tools that perform similar tasks. These tasks are the design and deployment of composite services (done with the Service Composition Framework - SCF), the execution and adaptation of service compositions (performed by Service Runtime Environment – SRE), the detection of deviations (through the Service Monitoring Module – SMM) and management of identity identification (through the Identity Management Service – IdM).

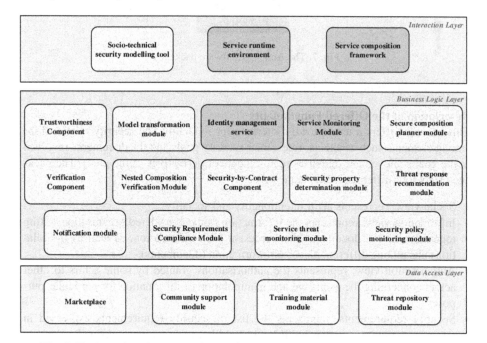

Fig. 6. The layer-based conceptual representation of the Aniketos architectural design

The Aniketos Platform and Environment components have been grouped into four software packages shown in Figure 7, which better facilitate the delivery of the Aniketos platform functionalities to the target user groups. The Socio-technical Security Requirements package can be used standalone and is a pure design-time package that is used to analyse the system as a whole on an organisational level. The Secure Service Specification and Deployment package is relevant both at design-time and runtime. It is also stand-alone, but can be enhanced with the Security Validation and Verification package and Security Monitoring and Notification package.

Below we describe the components from Figure 6 in relation to these software packages. Many of the components are part of more than software package, and all packages are able to interact with each other in order to take advantage of the full spectrum of the Aniketos platform.

Fig. 7. The Aniketos software packages

3.1   Socio-technical Security Requirements Package

Description of the Offered Functionality
This package offers a user friendly interface for modelling the security relationships among elements such as agents, roles, their security goals and the documents involved in the goal achievement (either as requirements or derivatives of the goal). The package offers four different views, namely:

- Social view: represents actor intentionality and sociality;
- Information view: represents the information in the considered organisation/setting together with the documents that represent such information, as well as the relationships among different pieces of information (documents).
- Authorisation view: represents the authorisations granted by some actors to other actors concerning the exchange and manipulation of information for particular purposes.
- Security requirements: represents the list of security requirements expressed in terms of commitments that hold/should hold between actors to cover the security needs expressed in the above three views.

It also enables users to associate model elements with potential threats, which can be fetched from a threat repository. These threats can again be used to find suitable countermeasures for effectively addressing the risks they impose.

Involved Aniketos Components

This package consists of the following Aniketos components and modules:

- The Socio-Technical Security Modelling Tool (STS), which offers the main tool to model security requirements.
- The STS Threats Plugin, which enables attach threats and respective countermeasures to the security goals of a composite service.
- The Threat Repository Module (TRM), which exposes the list of registered threats and countermeasures encountered in various domains.

Main Outcome

- A document (in pdf) of the security relationships among the agents, the roles, the goals and the involved documents.
- An XML file with the set of security requirements specifications applied to the defined goals, expressed as commitments between the actors.

3.2   Secure Service Specification and Deployment Package

Description of the Offered Functionality

This package enables the service developer to create the composite service process model and configure the security requirements on a more detailed level. It also enables easy deployment of the composite service specification to the runtime environment that will offer the service to the end user. The specification includes operational instructions for the composition as a whole and for each service component, such as functional specification with security characteristics, detailing the level of security that should be supported by the specific service.

The package offers the possibility to publish Aniketos compliant services to a service registry and searching in this registry to discover the most appropriate service descriptions. The current set of supported security properties are trustworthiness, separation and binding of duty, confidentiality, non-repudiation and integrity.

Involved Aniketos Components

This package consists of the following Aniketos components:

- The Service Composition Framework (SCF), which is a process modelling tool and is used to model the composite service processes. This component acts as an orchestrator between the various components of this package.
- The Conspec Editor, which is a flexible UI tool to help security experts defining properties for their services in Conspec format.
- The Model Transformation Module (MTM), which can be optionally used for transformation between the socio-technical security requirements, as expressed (with STS package) in the form of commitments, and the formal service specification.

This module can also create the template for the consumer's security policy (in Conspec format), based on the commitments.

- The Identity Management Service (IdM), which offers authentication and authorisation services and feeds the package tools with the roles, which should be defined in the service design.
- The Security Requirements Compliance Module (SRCM), which can be optionally used to compare the service specification created from MTM and the security requirements specifications and verify that these two are compliant with each other.
- The Threat Repository Module (TRM), which exposes the list of registered threats and countermeasures encountered in ICT systems.
- The Threat Response Recommendation Module (TRRM), which provides suggestions on the countermeasures, which should be applied during service composition in order to deal with those threats related to the development and deployment of a composite service.
- The Composition Security Validation Module (CSVM), which enables define security properties with respect to the separation or binding of duty and provides static analysis of the defined security requirements with respect to the specified composite service processes.
- The Marketplace, which acts as an enriched service registry maintaining both the functional and security characteristics of individual service components.
- The Contract Manager Module (CMM), which manages the overall security checking process and checks the compliance of the offered service security level from a service provider with the consumer's security policy.
- The Trustworthiness Module (TM), which offers prediction over the trustworthiness value of a service component.
- The Security Property Determination Module (SPDM), which manages the security properties associated with a service.
- The Service Runtime Environment (SRE), which orchestrates the deployment of the composite service process.

Main Outcome

- The specification of the composite service process, enriched with security requirements (consumer policy), expressed in Conspec format.
- A list of service specifications, which satisfy the consumer's security policy.
- A Web-based implementation of a selected composite service process, which complies with specific security requirements.
- A Boolean response on whether an announcement of an Aniketos compliant service is successful or not (this step might need an additional verification check, as it is described in next Section).

3.3   Security Service Validation and Verification Package

Description of the Offered Functionality

This package offers verification and validation checks to the design, registration and execution of secure composite services. The service validation process is invoked when a composite service when the service developer needs to check the security characteristics of the involved services. The same check can be performed at runtime to validate that the offered security level of the composite service complies with the consumer's security policy.

Involved Aniketos Components

This package consists of the following Aniketos components:

- The Secure Composition Planner Module (SCPM), which suggests the most secure composite service specifications based on certain security features.
- The Contract Manager Module (CMM), which manages the overall security checking process and checks the compliance of the offered service security level from a service provider with the consumer's security policy.
- The Nested Composition Verification Module (NCVM), which verifies the compliance of a service specification with the offered security level from a service provider.
- The Trustworthiness Module (TM), which offers prediction over the trustworthiness value of a service component.
- The Security Property Determination Module (SPDM), which manages the security properties associated with a service.
- The Composition Security Validation Module (CSVM), which verifies the compliance of a service composition to the offered security properties.
- The Property Verification Module (PVM), which analyses a service implementation (e.g., based on its source code) for compliance with required security properties (e.g., absence of certain vulnerabilities, enforcement of access control, ensuring data privacy) as expressed in a service contract.
- The Composite Service Security Testing Module (CSSTM), which is used to detect vulnerabilities in a service specification.
- The Threat Repository Module (TRM), which exposes the list of registered threats and countermeasures encountered in ICT systems.
- The Service Threat Monitoring Module (STMM), which analyses an event referring to a change in the threat level of an offered composite service.
- The Notification Module, which compiles the proper alert and notification messages to be communicated to the application and other involved Aniketos components.

Main Outcome

- A Boolean response that the security properties of a service specification have been verified.
- A list with the security checks performed and the respective result.

3.4   Security Monitoring and Notification Package

Description of the Offered Functionality

This package enables an operational environment to monitor the execution of composite services and generating alerts when any malfunction is identified. Such malfunctions can refer to the violation of a service contract and/or the change in the trustworthiness and/or threat level of the offered composite service.

The other main element is the functionality for subscriptions to service notifications for different types of events, so that information about data breaches, vulnerabilities and changes is sent to the relevant subscribers in both a human and machine-readable format.

Involved Aniketos Components

This package consists of the following Aniketos components:

- The Service Composition Framework (SCF), which is a process modelling tool and is used to define rules to an existing composite service process for handling incidents identified during the execution of the service process.
- The Service Runtime Environment (SRE), which orchestrates the subscription to monitors and generates the events during the composite service execution.
- The Service Monitoring Module (SMM), which captures the events generated by the SRE and classifies them according to their type for further use.
- The Service Threat Monitoring Module (STMM), which receives subscriptions of service components to threats and analyses an event referring to a change in the threat level of an offered composite service.
- The Threat Repository Module (TRM), which exposes the list of registered threats and countermeasures encountered in ICT systems.
- The Security Policy Monitoring Module (SPMM), which is notified of the composite service contract and analyses an event referring to a service contract violation.
- The Security Property Determination Module (SPDM), which manages the security properties associated with a service.
- The Trustworthiness Component (TM), which is notified on the requirement for monitoring the trustworthiness values of the composite service and analyses an event referring to a change in the trustworthiness level of an offered composite service.
- The Notification Module (NM), which receives subscriptions for notifications to specific security events (i.e. contract change, trust level change, security property change, threat level change, etc.) and compiles the proper alert and notification messages to be communicated to the application and other involved Aniketos components.

Main Outcome

- A set of alerts and notification messages, stating the type of malfunction that was identified.
- A set of rules to guide on the proper incident handling at runtime.

4   Conclusion

This chapter presented the Aniketos platform as-a-whole and is intended to be a starting point for anyone interested in its usage and technology behind. The following chapters in this book give more detailed explanations on how the various components work and interact with each other and the environment.

The Socio-technical Security Requirements Modelling Language for Secure Composite Services

Elda Paja[1], Fabiano Dalpiaz[2], and Paolo Giorgini[1]

[1] University of Trento – DISI, Via Sommarive 5, 38123, Povo, Trento, Italy
{elda.paja,paolo.giorgini}@unitn.it
[2] Utrecht University – Department of Information and Computing Sciences, Princetonplein 5,
De Uithof, 3584 CC Utrecht, The Netherlands
f.dalpiaz@uu.nl

Abstract. Composite services foster reuse and efficiency in providing consumers with different functionalities (services). However, security aspects are a major concern, considering that both service consumers and providers are autonomous and heterogeneous—thus, loosely controllable entities. When consumers provide information in order to be furnished some service, what happens to that information? Do service consumers trust service providers? In order to tackle the design of secure and trustworthy composite services, we should consider the security requirements such a composition must satisfy. We propose STS-ml, a security requirements modelling language that allows modelling security requirements over participants' (consumers and providers) interactions. These security requirements are expressed in terms of social contracts the various parties shall comply with while interacting (consuming/furnishing some service). Most importantly, STS-ml considers social and organisational threats that might affect the said composite services. In this chapter, we give an overview of STS-ml, introducing its modelling and reasoning capabilities while building models from the Aniketos eGovernment case study and verifying that the composite service complies with the specification, as well as checking whether a recomposition is needed.

1 Introduction

The Future Internet aims at digitalising many aspects of our lives, in particular offering online a great deal of services we are used since ages to have/obtain on the basis of face-to-face communication and interaction. This new system surpasses geographical limitations and confines, for it allows a wide range of organisations and individuals to offer (provide) a plethora of services to a wide variety of users (consumers). Everyone is free to join or leave this system and be in any of the roles, provider or consumer. Thus, the system exists because of the interaction among participants, a black-box interaction among autonomous actors based on service interfaces.

As much as this new environment facilitates interaction and communication, often increasing the quality of services (because of competition—now with all providers of the same types of services), it opens up many new challenges and issues with respect to trust, security and privacy. Typically consumers need to provide or exchange information with service providers to be able to access and use the offered services. But, in

A.D. Brucker et al. (Eds.): Secure Service Composition, LNCS 8900, pp. 63–78, 2014.

many cases consumers have little or no information about the providers, so can they really trust them with their information? Can the consumers trust providers not to misuse their information? Can consumers trust providers not to disclose their data to unauthorised parties? These are some of the questions we need to consider in engineering a system that offers the desired services while respecting users' needs on protecting their information (maintaining user trust and an adequate level of security).

The analysis of security aspects is of utmost importance, since information is disclosed (and tasks are executed) beyond the "safe" boundaries of a single organisation, and due to the autonomy of the participants, users have no control whatsoever over providers (with respect to what might happen to their information). The lack of control makes the design of composite services a challenging task. Such design should not consider technical details alone, but the bigger picture comprising the participants interacting to get and provide services, which stand at the basis of service-oriented applications. We need a way to capture and represent participants' needs when interacting with others, either to consume a service or to exchange information, in order to understand what are their concerns with respect to security over the said interaction. Moreover, in such a dynamic environment, the participants may be subject to security threats affecting their important assets. These threats are not necessarily technical, rather they are *social*, as they originate from the interactions between social actors (humans and organisations).

As in any engineering discipline, early awareness and analysis of potential problems is beneficial to system design, resulting in the development of more robust systems. For this, we have proposed a security requirements engineering modelling language that supports the specification of security requirements for service-oriented applications. The modelling language, STS-ml (Socio-Technical Security modelling language), allows to represent service-oriented settings in terms of goal-oriented actors that interact with one another to obtain (consume) services and exchange information. The key idea is to relate security requirements to *interaction*. This means adding constraints to the way actors exchange information, and to the delegation of goals (services). These constraints help specify the security requirements the actors shall comply with while interacting. STS-ml specifies security requirements as *social commitments* [6], promises with contractual validity made by an actor to another. One actor commits to another that, while delivering some service, it will comply with the required security needs. For example, a service provider might need to respect (commit for) the non-disclosure of the consumer's personal data, which is required as input to the provided service. Similarly, the same service provider may commit not to redelegate its offered services to other actors (providers), which might be not trusted by the consumer. As any approach to security, for a thorough security analysis, STS-ml does not overlook threats, and considers social and organisational threats that might affect the well-functioning of the systems. In our case, threats might affect the services under operation and the threats' impact might require a service recomposition (considering alternative services already known at design time) so that the required functionalities are maintained for the consumers.

Security requirements are integrated within the service interface, so that the provider makes a commitment to prospective service consumers to satisfy the given security needs. In this way, security requirements can be effectively used to specify the service under development. Expressing security requirements within service interfaces ensures that the security needs expressed by the consumers result in actual commitments the provider makes to the consumer to satisfy the imposed constraints (the security needs) while delivering the service. For instance, if consumers are concerned with the disclosure of personal data, the service interface may declare that the data will not be disclosed to other actors. Irrespective of the service implementation, such interface makes the provider committed for non-disclosure.

These specifications guide the design of composite services that satisfy the security requirements. However, in certain cases, the specification may be *inconsistent*, i.e., one or more requirements might be conflicting. If not effectively managed, inconsistencies result in the implementation of a system that violates one or more requirements. We propose to rely on automated reasoning to identify and resolve these conflicts. This choice is justified by our gathered evidence [8] that requirements models are large and that even skilled analysts would be unable to identify all the conflicts in a model.

Analysis results over security requirements are intended to improve the created models, so that the final security requirements specification is consistent and can serve as a basis for the implementation of the considered composite services. An analysis of threats impact, on the other hand, determines whether a service recomposition is required or not, should any of the composing services be threatened (become unavailable).

2   STS-ml: An Overview

STS-ml has been first proposed in [2], here we present the current version of STS-ml. STS-ml includes high-level organisational concepts such as actor, goal, delegation, etc. Security requirements in STS-ml models are mapped to *social commitments* [6]—contracts among actors—that actors (participants) shall comply with at runtime. STS-ml modelling consists of three complementary views of the same model, namely *social*, *information*, and *authorisation view* (see Fig. 1, 3, and 4), so that different interactions among actors can be analysed by concentrating on a specific view at a time. Inter-view consistency is ensured by STS-Tool[1] (see Chapter 7).

We consider a scenario from the eGovernment case study (Chapter 15) as a running example to illustrate STS-ml.

Example 1 (Lot Searching). The Department of Urban Planning (DoUP) wants to build an application which integrates the existing back-office system with the available commercial services to facilitate the interaction of involved parties when searching for a lot. The *Lot Owner* wants to sell the lot, he defines the lot location and may rely on a Real Estate Agency (*REA*) to sell the lot. *REA* then creates the lot record with all the lot details, and has the responsibility to publish the lot record together with additional legal information arising from the current Legal Framework. *Ministry of Law* publishes the accompanying law on building terms for the lot. The *Interested Party* is searching for a lot and: (i) accesses the DoUP application to invoke services offered by the various REAs; (ii) defines a trustworthiness requirement to allow only trusted REAs to contact him; (iii) sets a criteria to search and select a *Solicitor* and a *Civil Engineer* (CE) to

---

[1] http://www.sts-tool.eu

asses the conditions of the lot; (iv) assigns solicitor and CE to act on his behalf so that the lot information is available for evaluation; and (v) populates the lot selection for the chosen CE and Solicitor. *Aggregated REA* defines the list of trusted sources to be used to search candidate lots, it collects candidate lots from trusted sources, and ranks them to visualize to the user. *The Chambers* provide the list of creditable professionals (CE and Solicitors).

2.1 Multi-view Modelling

STS-ml relies on multiple views of the same model, each representing a specific perspective on the analysed setting. Multi-view modelling promotes modularity and separation of concerns. Currently, STS-ml includes three views: *social view*, *information view*, and *authorisation view*.

Social View. The *social view* (see Fig. 1)—a variant of *i** [9]–based modelling languages, such as SI* [5]—, represents participants of a socio-technical system as *intentional* and *social* actors. These actors are intentional for they enter the system in order to fulfil their objectives (goals), and they are social, for they interact with others to fulfill their objectives (by *delegating goals*) and obtain information (by *exchanging/transmitting documents*). STS-ml supports two types of actors: agents— representing concrete participants, and roles—abstract actors, used when the actual participant is unknown. In our example, (Example 1), the identified roles are *Lot owner*, *REA*, *Map Service Provider*, *Interested Party*, *Solicitor*, *CE Chambers*, and *Solicitor Chambers*, while the represented agents are: *DoUP Application*, *Aggregated REA*, and *Ministry of Law*, see Fig 1. The reason for this is that *roles* refer to general actors that are instantiated at run time, while *agents* refer to concrete entities already known at design time. That is, we do not know who *Lot owner* or *Interested Party* is going to be, but we consider that there is only one *Aggregated REA* and one *Ministry of Law* in this scenario, which are known already at design time.

Actors may achieve their goals on their own by decomposing (further refining goals) via: (i) and-decompositions: all subgoals must be achieved for the goal to be achieved; and (ii) or-decompositions: at least one subgoal must be achieved for the goal to be achieved. For instance, in Fig 1, *Lot Owner* has goal *lot sold*. He could sell the lot either privately or through an agency. Therefore, *Lot Owner* or-decomposes *lot sold* into *lot sold privately* and *lot sold via agency*. In the Lot searching scenario, we consider that the *Lot Owner* interacts with a real estate agency (REA), hence we further refine how this is achieved. To sell the lot through an agency: a lot record should be created, lot information needs to be provided, the lot location needs to be defined and finally the lot price needs to be approved. Thus, this is represented through the and-decomposition of goal *lot sold via agency* into goals *lot record created*, *lot info provided*, *lot price approved*, and *lot location defined*.

Actors can delegate goals when they cannot achieve them on their own or it is more convienient to rely on others. Note that delegation is possible if the delegator actor has the said goal[2]. For instance, in Fig 1, *Lot Owner* wants to have the lot sold via agency, for which he delegates goal *lot record created* to the *Real Estate Agency*.

---

[2] Note that in STS-ml only leaf goals can be delegated!

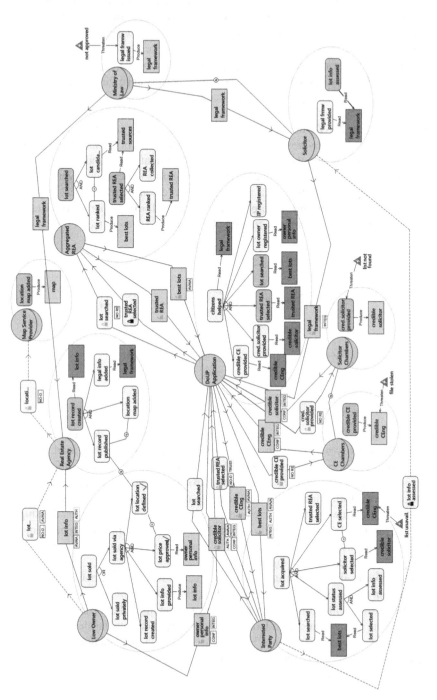

Fig. 1. Lot Searching scenario—Social View

Actors may possess documents (containing information); they may read, modify, or produce documents while achieving their goals. For instance, in Fig 1, *Real Estate Agency* reads *lot info* to achieve goal *lot record created* (the owners personal data are needed to create the *lot record*). This document (*lot info*) is produced by the *Lot Owners* while providing lot information (goal *lot info provided*). Actors can transmit documents to others only if they possess the required document. For instance, in Fig 1, *Lot Owner* is the creator of *lot info* (i.e., possesses the document) and he transmits this document to *Real Estate Agency*.

Modelling threats. In STS-ml we represent events threatening stakeholders' assets—*informational assets* and *intentional assets*. However, given that in the social view stakeholders exchange and manipulate information via documents, we model threats over actors' *documents* and *goals* respectively. STS-ml proposes the concept event and the relationship threaten relating the event to the asset it threatens. For instance, in Fig. 1, we represent the events identified to threaten actors' assets for Example 1. For instance, event *file stolen* threatens document *credible CE* of *CE Chambers* (see Fig. 2 which zooms over Fig. 1).

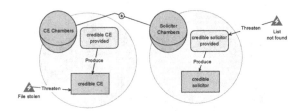

Fig. 2. Modelling threats

Information View. This view (Fig. 3) shows how information and documents are interconnected to identify which information actors manipulate, when they read, modify, produce, or transmit documents to achieve their goals in the social view. Information can be represented by one or more documents (through Tangible By), and on the other hand one or more information entities can be made tangible of the same document.

Importantly, this view relates information to their owners through own relationships. For instance, *Lot Owner* provides information about the lot, and thus we identify information *lot info details*, which is owned by the *Lot Owner* himself and is represented (made tangible) by document *lot info* (see Fig. 3).

Information view gives a structured representation of actors' information and documents via part of relationships. These relationships can result in information hierarchies (relating information with information) or document hierarchy (relating documents with documents). This means that such relationship holds only between entities of the same type, either information or documents. For instance, in Fig. 3, information *lot geo location* is part of information *lot info details*, while documents *trusted REA* and *best lots* are part of document *trusted sources*.

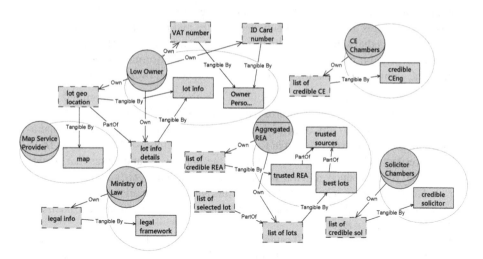

Fig. 3. Lot Searching scenario—Information View

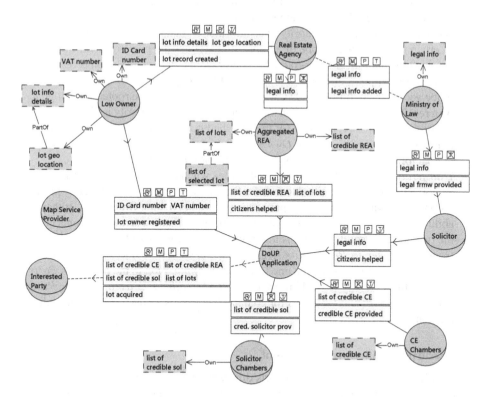

Fig. 4. Lot Searching scenario—Authorisation View

Authorisation View. STS-ml includes the primitive authorisation, see Fig. 4, to capture two key concepts in security, namely *permissions* and *prohibitions*. The main idea behind this view, is that actors (typically information owners) may want to specify what they allow or prohibit others to do over their proprietary information. Following this intuition, the authorisation relationship in STS-ml is specified over four dimensions:

- *Allowed/Prohibited Operations*: they define whether the actor is permitted (green tick symbol) or prohibited (red cross symbol) to Read (R), Modify (M), Produce (P), and Trasnmit (T) any document that makes tangible the information (operations are graphically represented in four boxes with distinguishable labels, R, M, P, and T respectively). For instance, in Fig. 4, the *Lot Owner* authorises *Real Estate Agency* to read, produce, and transmit information *lot info details* and *lot geo location*. No prohibitions are specified through this authorisation relationship. Instead a prohibition on modifying information *legal info* is expressed from the *Ministry of Law* to *Real Estate Agency*.
- *Information*: authorisation is granted over at least one information entity. Given the structuring of information in terms of part-of relationships, authorising some actor over some information means that the actor is authorised over parts of information as well, because ownership of information propagates top-down through part-of relationships. The information entities over which authorisation is specified is represented right below the allowed/prohibited operations.
- *Scope of Authorisation*: authority over information can be limited to the scope of a certain goal. As such, scope of authorisation defines the goals for the fulfillment of which the authorisation is granted. In other words, the authorisation is restricted to a certain purpose, and does not apply to different purposes. Our notion of goal scope adopts the definition in [1], which includes the goal tree rooted by that goal. As a result, if a goal is specified in the scope of authority, authority is given to make use of the information not only for the specified goal, but also for all its sub-goals. For instance, in Fig. 4, the *Lot Owner* authorises *Real Estate Agency* in the scope of goal *lot record created*, not for every goal of *Real Estate Agency*.
- *Transferability of the Permissions*: it specifies whether the actor that receives the authorisation is in turn entitled to transfer the received permissions or specify prohibitions (concerning the received permissions) to other actors. Graphically, transferability of the authorisation is allowed when the authorisation arrow line connecting the two actors is solid, while it is not granted when it is dashed. The authorisation from *Lot Owner* to *Real Estate Agency* is a transferable authorisation (continuous/solid arrow line), while the one from *DoUP Application* to the *Interested Party* granting the authority to read information *list of credible CE*, *list of credible REA*, *list of credible sol* and *list of lots* for goal *lot acquired*, is a non-transferrable authorisation (dashed arrow line).

2.2 Security Requirements in STS-ml

Through its three views, STS-ml supports different types of security requirements. In the social view security requirements are specified over the social relationships in which actors take part, such as goal delegation and document transmission. Moreover, a number of supported security requirements is imposed by the regulatory framework and laws in place, which restrict responsibility uptake and role adoptions. The information view serves as a brigde between the social and authorisation view, for a richer set of security requirements. As such, no security requirements are expressed in the information view. In the authorisation view, security requirements are expressed through the authorisation relationships themselves.

The following is the list of security requirements supported by the social view:

1. *Over Goal Delegations:*
   (a) *No-redelegation*—the re-delegation of the fulfilment of a goal is forbidden; in Fig. 5 *Lot Owner* requires the *Real Estate Agency* not to redelegate the goal *lot record created*.
   (b) *Non-repudiation*—the delegator cannot repudiate he/she delegated (*non-repudiation of delegation*); and the delegatee cannot repudiate he/she accepted the delegation (*non-repudiation of acceptance*); for instance, in Example 1, *DoUP Application* requires *CE Chambers* the *non-repudiation of the acceptance* of goal *credible CE provided*, see Fig. 1.
   (c) *Redundancy*—the delegatee has to employ alternative ways of achieving a goal; We consider two types of redundancy: *True* and *Fallback*. *True redundancy*: at least two or more different strategies are considered to fulfil the goal, and they are executed simultaneously to ensure goal fulfillment. *Fallback redundancy*: a primary strategy is selected to fulfill the goal, and at the same time a number of other strategies is considered and maintained as backup to fulfill the goal. None of the backup strategies is used as long as the first strategy successfully fulfils the goal. Within these two categories of redundancy, two sub-cases exist: (i) only one actor employs different strategies to ensure redundancy: single actor redundancy; and (ii) multiple actors employ different strategies to ensure redundancy: multi actor redundancy. In total, we can distinguish four types of redundancy, which are all mutually exclusive, so we can consider them as four different security requirements, namely, (i) *fallback redundancy single*, (ii) *fallback redundancy multi*, (iii) *true redundancy single*, and (iv) *true redundancy multi*. In Fig. 6, *Interested Party* imposes on the *DoUP Application* a *true redundancy single* security requirement for goal *trusted REA selected*.
   (d) *Trustworthiness*—the delegation of the goal will take place only if the delegatee is trustworthy; for instance, the delegation of goal *trusted REA selected* from *Interested Party* to *DoUP Application* will take place only to trustworthy application providers, see Fig. 5.
   (e) *Goal Availability*—the delegatee should ensure a minim availability level for the delegated goal; for instance, *Lot Owner* requires *Real Estate Agency* 90% availability for goal *lot record created*, see Fig. 5.
   Note that security requirements over goal delegations are expressed through annotations over these relationships, graphically represented through a padlock symbol, and made explicitly visible under the goal itself, when selected. Different labels and colours are used to distinguish them.
2. *Over Document Transmissions:*
   (a) *Non-repudiation*—the sender cannot repudiate he/she transmitted (*non-repudia- tion of transmission*); and the delegatee cannot repudiate he/she received (accepted) the transmission (*non-repudiation of acceptance*);

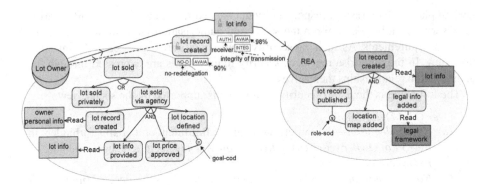

Fig. 5. Capturing security requirements from security needs for REA

(b) *Integrity of transmission*—the sender should ensure that the document shall not be altered while transmitting it (*sender integrity*); the receiver shall ensure the integrity of transmission for the given document is preserved (*receiver integrity*); and the system shall ensure that the integrity of transmission of a document in transit is preserved (*system integrity*). For instance, in Fig. 6, *DoUP Application* shall ensure sender integrity on the transmission of document *best lots* to *Interested Party*.

(c) *Confidentiality of transmission*—the sender should ensure the confidentiality of transmission for the given document (*sender confidentiality*); the receiver shall ensure the confidentiality of transmission for the given document is preserved (*receiver confidentiality*); and the system shall ensure that the confidentiality of transmission of a document in transit is preserved (*system confidentiality*). For instance, in Fig. 6, *DoUP Application* shall ensure sender confidentiality on the transmission of document *credible solicitor* to *Interested Party*.

(d) *Document Availability*—the sender should ensure a minimal availability level (in percentage) for the transmitted document. In Fig. 6, *DoUP Application* should ensure an availability level of 94% for the document *best lots* and an availability level of 90% for the document *credible solicitor*, when transmitting both these documents to *Interested Party*.

Note that security requirements over document transmissions are expressed through annotations over these relationships, graphically represented through a padlock symbol, and made explicitly visible under the document itself, when selected. Different labels and colours are used to distinguish the various supported security requirements over document transmissions.

3. *Over responsibility uptake*[3]:

(a) *Separation of duties* (SoD)—defines incompatible roles and incompatible goals, so we define two types: *role-SoD*—two roles are incompatible, i.e., cannot be played by the same agent, and *goal-SoD*—two goals shall be achieved by different actors; for instance, the goals *lot record published* and *location map added* are defined as incompatible (unequals sign, see Fig. 5). An example of

---

[3] Imposed either by the rules and regulations of the organisation, or by law.

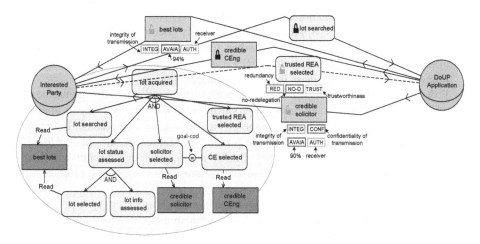

Fig. 6. Capturing security requirements from security needs for Interested Party

role-SoD is shown in Fig. 1 among roles *CE Chambers* and *Solicitor Chambers*.

(b) *Combination of duties* (CoD)—defines combinable roles and combinable goals, so we distinguish between *role-CoD*—two roles are combinable, i.e., shall be played by the same agent; and *goal-CoD*—two goals shall be achieved by the same actor. For instance, in Fig. 5, there is a *goal-CoD* expressed among goals *solicitor selected* and *CE selected* of *Interested Party*. Note that these security requirements from organisational constraints are captured through a set of relationships, namely *incompatible* (represented as a circle with the unequal sign within) and *combines* (represented as a circle with the equals sign within) respectively. This is related to the fact that they are not directly expressed over a social relationship, but constrain the uptake of responsibilities of stakeholders. Both relationships are symmetric, therefore there are no arrows pointing to the concepts they relate.

Security requirements over authorisations are captured implicitly by prohibiting certain operations and limiting the scope of the authorisation:

- Limiting the **scope** of the authorisation expresses a *need-to-know* security requirement, which requires that information is read, modified, produced only for the specified scope; for instance, *Lot Owner* authorises *DoUP Application* to read information *ID Card number* and *VAT number* only for the purpose of being registered (goal *lot owner registered*), expressing a need-to-know security requirement to *DoUP Application*, on reading this information only for *lot owner registered*, see Fig. 4.
- Prohibiting the **read** operation expresses a *non-reading* security requirement, which requires the information is not read in an unauthorised way; it implies that the authorisee should not read any documents making tangible the specified information. There are no examples of the *non-reading* security requiremet in Example 1.
- Prohibiting the **modify** operation expresses a *non-modification* security requirement, which requires the information is not modified in an unauthorised way; it implies

that the authorisee should not modify any documents making tangible this information. For instance, *DoUP Application* cannot modify documents representing information *ID Card number* and *VAT number*, for the authorisation from *Lot Owner* grants the right to read information *ID Card number* and *VAT number*, but prohibits the right to modify these information entities, see Fig. 4.

- Prohibiting the **produce** operation expresses a *non-production* security requirement, which requires the information is not produced in an unauthorised way; it implies that no new document, representing the given information, is produced. In Fig. 4, *DoUP Application* cannot produce documents that represent information *list of credible solicitors* or information *list of credible CE*, given that the authorisations from *Solicitor Chambers* and *CE Chambers* prohibit the operation to produce the respective information entities.
- Prohibiting the **transmit** operation expresses a *non-disclosure* security requirement, which requires the information is not disclosed in an unauthorised way; it implies that no document, representing the given information, is transmitted to other actors. In Fig. 4, *Solicitor* cannot transmit documents representing information *legal info*.
- Setting the **transferrability** dimension to false expresses a *non-reauthorisation* security requirement, which requires the authorisation is not transferrable, i.e., the authorisee shall not further transfer rights either for operations not granted to him (implicitly) or when the transferability of the authorisation is set to false (explicitly). This means that any non-usage, non-modification, non-production or non-disclosure security requirement implies a not-reauthorise security requirement for the operations that are not allowed. An example of explicit *non-reauthorisation* in Fig. 4 is expressed by *Ministry of Law* to the *Real Estate Agency*, given that the authorisation coming from the first on information *legal info* is non-transferable (dashed arrow line).

3   Security Requirements Specification for Composite Services with STS-ml

With the help of Example 1, we showed the interactions among the various actors in the eGovernment Lot searching scenario, in particular the interactions with the *DoUP Application*, which is in fact an application that helps citizens making use of a number of services (services that compose *DoUP Application*'s main service), such as: providing the list of credible civil engineers (for which it relies, via a goal delegation, on the *CE Chambers*), providing the list of credible solicitors (for which it relies on the *Solicitor Chambers*), searching for a lot (for which it relies on the *Aggregated REA*), etc. In the same spirit, to offer the best service to citizens, the *DoUP Application* makes use of information such as the *legal framework* (obtained from *Solicitor*, who received it from the *Ministry of Law*).

Notice that the social relationships supported by STS-ml reflect rigorously the service-oriented paradigm, capturing the interactions among a service consumer and a service provider via goal delegations and document transmissions. The interaction between a delegator and a delegatee is similar to that of a service consumer (represented by the delegator) and a service provider (represented by the delegatee) on consuming/furnishing a service (represented by the goal). The same stands for document transmissions too, the sender is the service provider, while the receiver is the service consumer.

Security requirements, on the other hand, reflect the constraints to be integrated and implemented by service interfaces. Think for instance about *non-repudiation*. This security requirements is at the basis of the contracting that occurs among various service providers: a service provider (acting as a consumer in this case) interacts with another provider for a particular service. Non-repudiation is required to ensure that collaborating parties are legally bound when an agreement is reached [7]. The satisfaction of non-repudiation mechanisms such as proof of fulfilment could be employed.

A security requirement for *not-redelegation* imposes limitations to service providers, for they are required not to rely on third parties for offering the required services.

Authentication is typically concerned with who exactly is trying to use the service [7]. This involves confirming a claim that two references to identities are the same, for example, that the sender of a message is the same person. In STS-ml, we extend this to support dual authentication given that any actor could act both as a service consumer and as a service provider.

Notice that *goal availability* (similarly *document availability*) is highly related to the notion of service availability, where a provider specifies an uptime level for the service. In service-oriented settings, availability levels often become integral part of service-level agreements between providers and consumers.

Authorisations capture what service consumers are allowed to do. Typically consumers are permitted to use the requested service, however they cannot read the internal policies of the service provider.

Similarly, the rest of the supported set of STS-ml security requirements is to be translated to a service interface specification. But, can these specifications be satisfied by the said services and their respective providers? We aim at providing an answer to this question through automated analysis, to avoid inconsistencies and conflicts before going towards service deployment that might lead to a service not satisfying all security requirements.

4 Automated Analysis

STS-ml supports different automated analyses types. Firstly, given that we are dealing with requirements models that tend to become large and complex, an analysis of the well-formedness is required, to ensure that the created models are syntactically correct, see Section 4.1. Secondly, we verify whether there are any conflicts among the specified security requirements that might lead to a composite service not to be able to satisfy them all at the same time, see Section 4.2. Finally, considering the social and organisational threats affecting either services (represented via goals) or the information they might need to provide the required functionality (be fulfilled), we calculate the impact these threats have on the rest of the system, see Section 4.3.

After constructing the STS-ml model for Example 1, we can run the automated analyses to verify its consistency, the satisfaction (or possible violation) of security requirements, and the threat propagation over actors' assets.

4.1 Well-Formedness Analysis

The purpose of this analysis is to verify whether the diagram built by the security requirements engineer is consistent and valid. It is also referred to as *offline well-formedness analysis*: some well-formedness rules of STS-ml are computationally too expensive for online verification, or their continuous analysis would limit the flexibility of the modelling activities. Thus, some analyses about well-formedness are performed upon explicit user request. Examples of verifications include delegation cycles, part-of cycles, inconsistent or duplicate authorisations, etc. The well-formedness analysis for the scenario of Example 1 did not find any warnings or errors.

4.2 Security Analysis: Reasoning over Security Requirements

Security analysis is concerned with verifying: (i) if the security requirements specification is consistent—no requirements are potentially conflicting; (ii) if the STS-ml model allows the satisfaction of the specified security requirements. Under the hood, this analysis is implemented in disjunctive Datalog [3] and consists of comparing the possible actor behaviors that the model describes against the behavior mandated by the security requirements. Principally, requirements define actions that actors must do (or must not do). Conflicts are then identified whenever: (i) actors do actions that security requirements specify they must not do, (ii) actors do not do actions that the security requirements they should comply with mandate doing.

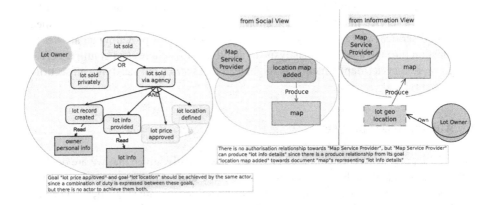

Fig. 7. Executing security analysis: visualisation of results

The security analysis found several violations (errors) of the specified security requirements, such as for instance the violation of non-production by the *Map Service Provider*. As it can be seen by the diagram in Fig. 4 showing authorisation relations, there is no authorisation relationship towards *Map Service Provider* on information *lot geo location* which, following the semantics of STS-ml, is translated into an authorisation from the owner of this information, namely *Lot Owner*, prohibiting all operations over this information. This means that the *Map Service Provider* is required all security requirements derived from an authorisation relationship over the given information (i.e., *non-reading, non-modification, non-production, non-disclosure, not-reauthorisation*). But, from Fig. 1, we see that *Map Service Provider* can produce *lot geo location* since there is a produce relationship from its goal *location map added* towards document *map* representing (making tangible) information *lot geo location*, owned by the *Lot Owner* who requires non-production of this information. Thus, we identify a conflict that results in the violation of the non-production security requirement.

Similarly, there is a possible violation of a combination of duties between the goals *lot price approved* and *lot location defined* of *Lot Owner*. A combination of duties requires that the same actor pursues both goals, but there is no single actor achieving both these goals, see Fig. 7. However, this could change during runtime, and is to be verified through monitoring techniques. At the design level, we verify throughout the models whether any strategies are undertaken to fulfil the imposed security requirement. Therefore, this conflict is considered a warning, differently from the previous one which is considered an error. Warnings may be skipped, while errors need to be resolved before implementation. Resolution techniques might, however, require negotiation among service consumers and providers, as well as trade-off analysis [4].

4.3 Threat Analysis

Threat analysis is concerned with calculating the propagation of threatening events over actors' assets. It answers the question: "*How does the specification of events threatening actors' assets affect their other assets?*"

We consider the threats shown in Fig. 2 and calculate their impact. We present the results of this analysis for the event *list not found* threatening goal *credible solicitor provided* in Fig. 8.

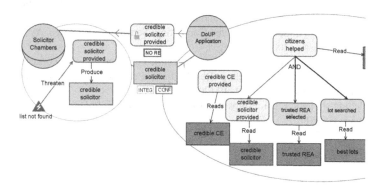

Fig. 8. Executing threat analysis

Considering the results of the threat analysis, we may need to consider a service recomposition, which does not account on *Solicitor Chambers* for offering service *credible solicitor provided*, since from our information on this provider there are no other alternatives to provide the said service.

5   Conclusions

We discussed the need for early awareness and analysis of security issues (requirements) compositive services should take into account already at design time, before they are implemented.

We presented STS-ml, a security requirements modelling language that relates security to interaction, which makes it suitable to identify security problematics strongly related to the interactions among service consumers and service providers.

We demonstrated how the reasoning techniques offered by STS-ml help designers identify possible conflicts and violations of security requirements for composite services. In particular, social threats putting at risk the well-functioning of the composite service are considered, together with the impact they have on the rest of the system.

References

1. Dalpiaz, F., Chopra, A.K., Giorgini, P., Mylopoulos, J.: Adaptation in open systems: Giving interaction its rightful place. In: Parsons, J., Saeki, M., Shoval, P., Woo, C., Wand, Y. (eds.) ER 2010. LNCS, vol. 6412, pp. 31–45. Springer, Heidelberg (2010)
2. Dalpiaz, F., Paja, E., Giorgini, P.: Security requirements engineering via commitments. In: Proceedings of STAST 2011, pp. 1–8 (2011)
3. Eiter, T., Gottlob, G., Mannila, H.: Disjunctive datalog. ACM Transactions on Database Systems (TODS) 22(3), 364–418 (1997)
4. Elahi, G., Yu, E.: A Goal Oriented Approach for Modeling and Analyzing Security Trade-Offs. In: Parent, C., Schewe, K.-D., Storey, V.C., Thalheim, B. (eds.) ER 2007. LNCS, vol. 4801, pp. 375–390. Springer, Heidelberg (2007)
5. Giorgini, P., Massacci, F., Mylopoulos, J., Zannone, N.: Modeling security requirements through ownership, permission and delegation. In: Proc. of RE 2005, pp. 167–176 (2005)
6. Singh, M.P.: An ontology for commitments in multiagent systems: Toward a unification of normative concepts. Artificial Intelligence and Law 7(1), 97–113 (1999)
7. Singh, M.P., Huhns, M.N.: Service-Oriented Computing: Semantics, Processes, Agents. John Wiley & Sons, Chichester (2005)
8. Trösterer, S., Beck, E., Dalpiaz, F., Paja, E., Giorgini, P., Tscheligi, M.: Formative user-centered evaluation of security modeling: Results from a case study. International Journal of Secure Software Engineering 3(1), 1–19 (2012)
9. Yu, E.: Modelling strategic relationships for process reengineering. PhD thesis, University of Toronto, Canada (1996)

From Consumer Requirements
to Policies in Secure Services

Erkuden Rios[1], Francesco Malmignati[2], Eider Iturbe[1],
Michela D'Errico[2], and Mattia Salnitri[3]

[1] TECNALIA Research and Innovation,
Parque Tecnológico de Bizkaia 700, Derio, Spain
[2] SELEX, Selex ES S.p.A, A Finmeccanica Company,
via Laurentina 760, 00143, Rome, Italy
[3] UNITN, University of Trento, via Belenzani 12, 38122, Trento, Italy

Abstract. Automatic translation of elicited consumer security requirements at high level (problem space) into application or service level security requirements (solution space) has been traditionally the Achilles'
heel of security requirements engineering. Such automated translation
would result in significant failure and cost reduction in application development and maintenance, particularly in those complex applications
based on compositions and choreographies of services. In this paper we
present a framework which makes a step forward to solve this dilemma.
The framework supports the engineering of composite service security
and trust requirements directly derived from the organisational needs
expressed for such service. The followed approach starts with the modelling of organisation actors' objectives and commitments among these
actors, and follows with the transformation of such commitments into
security elements in the service business process specification and into
a consumer security policy which the service will need to be compliant
with.

Keywords: security, requirements, transformation, service composition,
BPMN, consumer policy.

1   Introduction

The alignment of organizational requirements with requirements for a software
architecture is a well known problem in requirements engineering [23,27]. This
alignment is essential to keep architectures satisfy requirements when they evolve,
and is particularly important for embedding and tracking security requirements
compliance in the application lifetime.

The existing goal-based modelling languages as Tropos [4], Secure Tropos [15]
and SI* [12] are adequate to consider organizational (business) requirements in
Socio Technical Systems (STSs) [13].

The abstract level used in such languages for expressing the requirements is
not suitable for expressing implementation level security requirements of loosely

A.D. Brucker et al. (Eds.): Secure Service Composition, LNCS 8900, pp. 79–94, 2014.

coupled service based applications. These Service-Oriented Applications (SOA) are usually described using business process modelling languages, such as Business Process Model and Notation (BPMN) [19]. Our work considers a BPMN extension that allows the incorporation of security requirements into a business process. Rodriguez et al. [26], in 2007, introduced a BPMN extension for the inclusion of five different security requirements: non-repudiation, attack harm detection, integrity, privacy and access control. In 2011, Mulle et al. [16] proposed a language for the formulation of security constraints embedded in BPMN. In all these approaches the security requirements are incorporated into a BPMN process from the perspective of a business process analyst and there is not much rationale about where these requirements were originated from.

To tackle the problem of high level and low level security requirements misalignment, as part of the work in the Aniketos project [2] we have developed a framework to analyse and capture security needs from the organizational point of view and derive application or service level security and trust requirements through the use of a model transformation tool. This transformation tool offers two main transformations: (i) from organizational security requirements to service level requirements as BPMN extensions, and (ii) from socio-technical security requirements to consumer policies in ConSpec [1] format. Therefore, the tool allows also the alignment with machine readable consumer policies which compliance can be verified at run-time.

The chapter structure is as follows. Section 2 introduces our modelling framework. First, in subsection 2.1, we explain the modelling of socio-technical security requirements at organizational level, which will be the input for the transformations. Then, we describe the modelling of the two outputs: section 2.2 for service BPMN level security extensions and section 2.3 for consumer security policies specification. Section 3 shows our approach for transforming security requirements specified as commitments into BPMN elements. Section 4 explains how commitments are transformed to composable consumer security policies. Finally, Section 5 concludes with main remarks and discussion about our contribution compared to related work.

2   A Framework for Modelling Security Requirements and Contracts

2.1   Modelling of Socio-technical Security Requirements

The initial step of our framework for modelling service security requirements and contracts, is the use of the Socio-Technical Security modelling language (STS-ml) [7] (see chapter 5) to analyse and model the consumer organization needs, and express them in terms social interactions among the involved stakeholders. This will serve to derive business security requirements in the form of commitments reached among the participants for the achievement of their goals.

The STS-ml is a goal based security requirements engineering language. It allows characterising organizational security requirements of Socio-Technical

Systems (STSs): information systems that involve complex interactions among humans, technological components and the environment [3,9]. In STSs actors are autonomous entities that interact and collaborate with each other in order to reach common objectives. Examples of STSs are health care systems, smart cities/homes, air traffic management systems, eCommerce and eGovernment applications, etc.

STS-ml adopts a multi-view modelling approach to characterise the different perspectives of an organizational setting and therefore it supports the multi faceted analysis of a business. The three views are: *social view, information view* and *authorization view.* Figure 1 shows an excerpt of a case study of a telecommunication company where two actors, the *Store locator* and the *Map provider*, interact in order to find the closest shops in a given area.

The *social view* represents actors as intentional social entities [20], which strategic interests are called *goals.* Every goal can be decomposed in sub-goals which, if achieved, contribute in achieving the top goal. There are two types of decompositions, AND-decomposition and OR-decomposition. The former means that all sub-goals must be achieved in order to achieve the top goal, while the latter means that the top goal is achieved if at least one of the sub-goals is achieved. For example, the actor *Store locator* has one top goal called *Closest stores found* which is AND-decomposed in two sub-goals called *Map created* and *Location retrieved.* Consequently, both sub-goals must be achieved in order to achieve the top goal. The goal *Location retrieved* is marked with a capability tick which means that the actor is able to individually achieve the goal.

In STS-ml models, actors can be *agents* or *roles.* *Agents* represent actual participants at runtime while *roles* represent abstract participants, when the specific participant is unknown. This avoids mandating the existence of specific agents, but specifying the business at role level, which can later be played by concrete agents. In the example showed in Figure 1, *Store locator* is an concrete agent while *Map provider* is a role, so it can be played by unspecified agents.

In social view goals are linked to *documents* which represent physical objects that actors may *Need* (read), *Modify,* or *Produce* (create from scratch) in order to achieve their goals.

The interactions among actors are represented in **social view** as delegation of goals (a delegator actor transfers the responsibility of goal achievement to another actor) and provision of documents (a delegator actor transfers a document to another actor). In the example of Figure 1 the *Store locator* delegates to the *Map provider* the goal *Map created,* and the *Store locator* provides to *Map provider* the document *Position* needed to achieve the goal *Map created* .

The **information view** represents the ownership and structure of the resources involved in the business under study. A piece of information is owned by one actor (represented with a double arrow) and is made tangible by one or more documents (represented with *Tangible by* arrow), as shown in Figure 1 (this relation is represented with an arrow labelled).

The **authorization view** represents how authorizations over the resources are granted to actors. An authorization relation expresses the permissions an

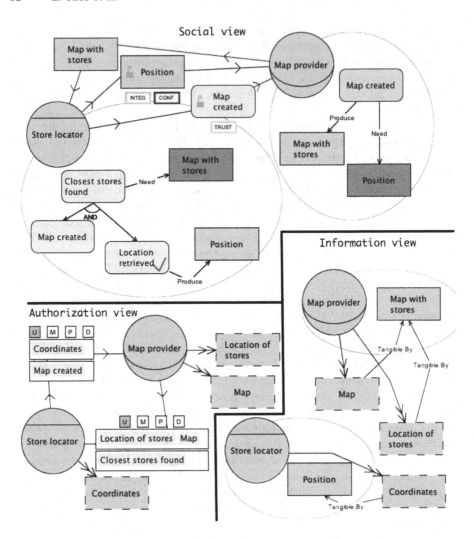

Fig. 1. Example STS-ml model

actor allows to another actor over particular resources and it specifies: (i) the set of operations granted, i.e., use, modify, produce and distribution (represented with marked U,M,P or D letters in the authorization arrow); (ii) the set of information for which the authorization is granted, represented in the upper box of the authorization arrow; (iii) the set of objectives for which is legal to use the information, represented in the lower box of the authorization arrow. For example in Figure 1 the *Store locator* authorize the *Map provider* to use the information *Coordinates* for achieving the goal *Map created*.

STS-ml can represent a number of security requirements such as *Separation of Duty* [23], *Trustworthiness, Integrity of transmission* and *Confidentiality of transmission.* All these security requirements can be expressed in the social view. In this chapter we focus only in the last three.

Trustworthiness is something that can be computed, measured or cognitively estimated in order to evaluate to what degree an entity should be trusted. Trustworthiness is associated to metrics, measuring one or a set of properties [25]. In STS-ml trustworthiness is represented with a *TRUST* tag attached to a goal delegation. Figure 1 shows an example of trustworthiness requirement modelled using STS-ml. The *TRUST* tag attached to the delegation of the goal *Map created* means that the *Store locator* may delegate the goal *Map created* to *Map provider* only if the actor who plays the *Map provider* role has a trustworthiness level higher than a value specified by the designer.

Integrity of transmission concerns the protection of information that is exchanged either from unauthorized writing or inadvertent corruption. Integrity refers to the assurance that exchanged information has not been altered [18]. In STS-ml the *Integrity* is represented with an *INTEG* tag attached to document provision relationship. In the example in Figure 1, the *INTEG* tag attached to the provision of *Position* document means that the *Store locator* is responsible for providing the document to *Map provider* without any modification by unauthorized users.

Confidentiality of transmission concerns the protection of documents during their provision: the document must not be accessed by unauthorized stakeholders. In STS-ml this security requirement is represented with the *CONF* tag associated to document provision. In the example in Figure 1 the confidentiality requirement is modelled on the provision of document *Position*, meaning that, during the document transmission, only authorized actors, in this case only *Map provider*, are allowed to access it.

Once the social interactions of the organization participants are modelled in STS-ml, the security requirements are derived in the form of social *commitments*. Social *commitments* express the promises taken by the actors when a security need is specified over their interaction. The commitments are expressed as a ternary relation $C(x,y,p)$, where a debtor actor x commits to a creditor actor y that p will be brought about. In STS-ml the p is about the satisfaction of security requirements. An example of commitment is the one generated from the security requirements of *integrity* on the document *Position*:

$$C(Store\,locator, Map\,provider, integrity(Position))$$

which means that the *Store locator* commits to the *Map provider* to guarantee the integrity of the provided document *Position*.

STS-ml is supported by a modelling and analysis support tool called STS-tool (see chapter 7). It has been developed as an Eclipse Rich Client Platform application written in Java, distributed for multiple platforms (Win 32/64, Linux and Mac OS X), and it is freely available for download from http://www.sts-tool.eu [21]. Besides model well-formedness analysis, the STS-tool supports the designer with security analysis to verify the satisfaction or violation of the security needs specified in the STS-ml models [21].

STS-tool offers the possibility to export commitments in a machine-readable Security Requirement Specification (SRS) in Extensible Markup Language (XML) format, which will be used by the transformation module to generate service level security requirements and policies.

2.2 Modelling Security Properties in BPMN with Aniketos Extensions

The Aniketos Service Composition Framework (SCF) (see chapter 9) allows a service designer to create a business process specification that represents a composite service along with a set of security properties (*Integrity*, *Confidentiality*, *Trustworthiness*, *Separation of Duty* [6] and *Binding of Duty* [6]) that the generated service needs to be compliant with.

The Service Composition Framework has been developed as an Eclipse RCP application and is based on Activiti Designer which is an Eclipse plugin that allows the modelling of BPMN 2.0 processes. Since BPMN 2.0 does not support naturally the definition of the security properties, we have defined the Security Extended BPMN which extends the original BPMN 2.0 model with security and trust properties.

By exploiting the SCF workbench a service designer creates the composite service following desired functional requirements. The result is a composition plan which is the BPMN process modelling the execution of the atomic services involved into the composition. The atomic services, modelled in BPMN as *service tasks*, are bound to web services by performing service discovery in an external service marketplace.

Considering that the *Trustworthiness* level of a service, which denotes to what degree the service can be trusted, can be evaluated over a set of properties such as the reputation of the service provider and that it can be expressed as a numerical value, a service designer can desire to bind to a service task only the web services having a certain level of *Trustworthiness*. To support the specification of this property the BPMN 2.0 XML specification has been extended by adding a new tag element called *security* into the *service task* tag element and by adding a new *Trustworthiness* tag element inside the *security* tag element.

The requirement of a *Trustworthiness* threshold of 99 is then specified as follows:

```
<serviceTask id="servicetask1" name="Service Task">
    <extensionElements>
        <aniketos:security>
            <aniketos:trustworthiness value="99"/>
        </aniketos:security>
    </extensionElements>
</serviceTask>
```

The service designer may also want to specify the *Integrity* property between two atomic services linked through a BPMN sequence flow. The objective of *Integrity* property is to allow a service A being sure about the integrity of the data received from the service B. The fulfilment of this property requires that the service B, linked to the service A through the sequence flow, implements a mechanism enabling the interested party to perform an integrity check. Through the user interface of the SCF the designer can further specify the requirements for the implementation of the *Integrity* property. By selecting the *service task* element in the BPMN model the designer has to enter the type of the integrity mechanism (*Message Integrity Code* for example) and the specific algorithm to be used to implement the mechanism.

The requirement that the data sent by *servicetask1* to *servicetask2* need to be checked with MIC and algorithm SHA1 is specified as follows:

```
<serviceTask id="servicetask1" name="Service Task">
    <extensionElements>
        <aniketos:security>
            <aniketos:integrity type="MIC" with="servicetask2"
            algorithm="SHA1"/>
        </aniketos:security>
    </extensionElements>
</serviceTask>
```

The framework also allows the designer to specify *Confidentiality* property if the communication among the services is required to be kept confidential. The fulfilment of *Confidentiality* property will be achieved by applying cryptography at message level. This choice is reflected in the possibility offered to the designer who can decide to cipher the input, the output or both data. To complete the *Confidentiality* property specification the designer has to select the desired strength for the encryption mechanism (low, medium, high) which will be translated in the application of a suitable encryption algorithm and key length.

The requirement that the data sent by *servicetask1* need to be cipherred with algorithm RSA and key length of 128 bits is specified as follows:

```
<serviceTask id="servicetask1" name="Service Task">
    <extensionElements>
        <aniketos:security>
            <aniketos:confidentiality type="output"
            algorithm="RSA128"/>
        </aniketos:security>
    </extensionElements>
</serviceTask>
```

2.3   Modelling of Security Policies

Modelling security properties in consumer policies requires a deontic contract language [1] which enables software applications to parse and process contract obligations to determine state information about matters governed by the contract. This way, the modelled security policies allow verifying compliance of service execution. In Aniketos we address this need with ConSpec, a policy language that serves to describe both (composite) consumer policies and service agreement templates or contracts. For example, in [8] mobile application contracts were specified using ConSpec. For our approach, the main feature of ConSpec is its support to formal proofs of policy adherence.

ConSpec was developed mainly for mobile code (e.g., Java mobile) execution verification and it is an automata-based language inspired by the policy specification language PSLang [11]. Conspec is specific for expressing security relevant behaviour of the systems, and although more restricted than PSLang, it is expressive enough to define policies that apply to multiple executions of a service as well as interactions with other services.

The formal specification of ConSpec encodes a security automaton representing the contract that shall be guaranteed by the service or the policy that is desired by the consumer. We assume that the consumer security policy is built upon non-interleaving rules (expressed in ConSpec) that concern different matters (e.g., connections or files). This way, the rules can be verified separately, which simplifies the monitoring of the policy compliance. Each rule consists of three parts: *Scope* definition, *Security state* declaration, and *Event* clauses.

The policy starts with the definition of the limit on values of the type int and the maximum length of strings. And then the *Security state* specifies the initial values of the set of variables which ensure a safe state.

The *Scope* allows expressing security requirements on single or multiple executions of the same application (*scope* Session or Multisession, respectively), on executions of all applications of a system (*scope* Global) and on lifetimes of objects of a certain class (*scope* Object).

The *Scope* declaration is followed by a list of security relevant events. An *Event* clause describes a security relevant action (i.e. a method invocation) and its modifier (BEFORE, EXCEPTIONAL, AFTER). That is, the *Event* clause specifies under which conditions and how the security state variables should be updated in case the event is detected in the current state.

```
MAXINT m
MAXLEN n
SCOPE <Object ClassName | Session | Global | MultiSession>
SECURITY STATE
    <bool | int | string> SecVarName1 = <InitValue1>
    ...
    <bool | int | string> SecVarNameN = <InitValueN>
<BEFORE | EXCEPTIONAL | AFTER> EVENT MethodSignature1 PERFORM
    condition1 -> updateBlock1
    ...
    conditionM -> updateBlockM
[ELSE -> updateBlock]
    ...
<BEFORE | EXCEPTIONAL | AFTER> EVENT MethodSignatureK PERFORM
    ...
```

3 Transforming SRS to Security Properties in Service BPMN Process

The Model Transformation Module (MTM) is the responsible module for connecting the high-level (business) requirements with the low-level security requirements for the implementation of the composite services and their correspondent contracts. Thus, the aim of the MTM is to connect two spaces: (1) the problem space, where the organizational security and trust requirements are defined in the STS model, and (2) the solution space, where they are transformed into security and trust properties to be included in the business process specification as well as in the consumer policy.

The tool has been developed as an Eclipse plugin that integrates with the SCF. The MTM transformations are based on GEMDE [17], a generic executable framework for Model Driven Engineering. GEMDE serves for both model correctness verification and model transformation rules definition and execution.

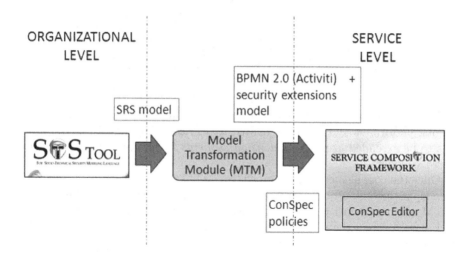

Fig. 2. Transformation of SRS model with Model Transformation Module

As shown in Figure 2, the input for the MTM is the Security Requirements Specification (SRS), which describes the list of security requirements, expressed as commitments, needed by the organisation stakeholders. During the transformation process, the MTM first identifies the SRS elements (socio-technical actors, assets and goals) to be mapped into elements of the business process. The next step is to transform as much as possible these elements into business process level elements. In order to connect both dimensions, the MTM needs the service developer involvement during the transformation process. Therefore, the MTM provides a GUI for the service developer to support him or her in the mapping between both spaces. Finally, as a result of the transformation, the MTM generates a skeleton of the business process model of the composite service in BPMN 2.0[1] [19].

The MTM identifies the elements from the SRS to be transformed during the mapping process: the core elements (the organizational actors, their goals, and the documents involved in the commitments) and the security requirements such as *Trustworthiness* and *Integrity of transmission*.

We use the mapping proposed by Salnitri et al.[23], to link STS-ml elements with core BPMN elements. The actors' goals are mapped to tasks at business process level. The actors, both the agents and the roles, included in the security commitments are mapped to task performers. And the documents are linked to variables of the tasks. The table 2 shows the relationship between the SRS core elements and the business process elements.

Table 1. Mapping between the SRS core elements and the BPPMN 2.0 elements

SRS core element	Relationship	Mapping type	BPMN 2.0 element
Goal	1..* -> 1	Relates-to	Task
Actor (agent or role)	1 -> 1..*	Plays / is-a	Performer
Document	1 -> 1..*	Represents	Variable

In order to transform both actors and documents into business process elements, performers and variables related to service tasks, the BPMN 2.0 model has to be extended using the *Extension elements* feature provided by Activiti's BPMN model.

Once the core elements are mapped, the MTM transforms with the aid of the developer the high-level security requirements. In order to perform this step, the MTM uses the Security Extended BPMN model (Section 2.2).

Figure 3 shows the result of the transformation using the MTM (integrated in the SCF) of the STS-ml model example in Figure 1. The aim of the generated composite service is to find the closest stores in a given area; the first service, called *Get list of stores*, returns the list of the closest stores taking as input the actual position of the user invoking the composite service; the second service, called *Create Map*, creates a map containing the previously obtained list of closest stores.

The MTM currently allows the transformation of the following security and trust properties: *Trustworthiness, Integrity, Confidentiality, Separation of Duty* [6] and *Binding of Duty* [6]. In the following, the first three transformations are explained.

---

[1] The BPMN 2.0 specification used by the MTM to generate the service specification can be found in http://www.activiti.org

Fig. 3. Example of a transformed BPMN process

Table 2. Example of the mapping between the SRS core elements and the BPPMN 2.0 elements

SRS core element	Relationship	Mapping type	BPMN 2.0 element
Closes Stores found	1 -> 1	Relates-to	Get list of stores (Service task)
Map created	1 -> 1	Relates-to	Create map (Service task)
Store locator	1 -> 1	Plays / is-a	StoreLocatorProviderName (Performer)
Map provider	1 -> 1	Plays / is-a	MapProviderName (Performer)
Position	1 -> 1	Represents	List of stores (Variable)

The commitment related to the Trustworthiness property is expressed as follows:

C(Store locator, Store locator, delegatedTo(Map provider, trustworthiness level 99), true)

The MTM translates this trustworthiness requirement in SRS into an element defined in Security Extended BPMN metamodel associated with a service task:

```
<serviceTask id="Create map" name="Service Task">
    <extensionElements>
        <activiti:field name="ServiceProvider">
            <activiti:string/>MapProvider</activiti:string/>
        </activiti:field>
        <aniketos:security>
            <aniketos:trustworthiness value="99"/>
        </aniketos:security>
    </extensionElements>
</serviceTask>
```

The commitment related to the *Integrity of transmission* property is expressed as follows:

C(Store locator, Map provider, integrity(provided(Map provider, Store locator, Position)), true)

The integrity in Security Extended BPMN is defined as a relationship between two service tasks: the transmitter service task (*Get list of stores* in the example above) and the recipient service task (*Create map*). The *List of stores* is an output variable (that contains the position) of the transmitter for which integrity should be maintained when this variable is passed as input to the recipient task. The MTM translates the integrity requirement as follows:

```
<serviceTask id="Get list of stores" name="Service Task"
activiti:class="org.aniketos.runtime.AniketosClientDelegation">
    <extensionElements>
        <activiti:field name="ServiceProvider">
            <activiti:string/>StoreLocatorProvider</activiti:string/>
        </activiti:field>
        <activiti:field name="resultVariable">
            <activiti:string>List of stores</activiti:string>
        </activiti:field>
        <aniketos:security>
            <aniketos:integrity type="MIC" with="Create map"
            algorithm="AES"/>
        </aniketos:security>
    </extensionElements>
</serviceTask>
```

The commitment related to the *Integrity* property is expressed as follows:

C(Store locator, Map provider, confidentiality(provided(Map provider, Store locator, Position)), true)

Following the specification of the Security Extended BPMN explained in Section 2.2 the confidentiality property is translated as follows:

```
<serviceTask id="Get list of stores" name="Service Task"
activiti:class="org.aniketos.runtime.AniketosClientDelegation">
    <extensionElements>
        <activiti:field name="ServiceProvider">
            <activiti:string/>StoreLocatorProvider</activiti:string/>
        </activiti:field>
        <activiti:field name="resultVariable">
            <activiti:string>List of stores</activiti:string>
        </activiti:field>
        <aniketos:security>
            <aniketos:confidentiality type="output"
            algorithm="RSA128"/>
        </aniketos:security>
    </extensionElements>
</serviceTask>
```

4   Transforming SRS to Consumer Security Policies

As previously mentioned, in addition to transforming the organizational security requirements (SRS) into security elements of a business process specification, the MTM is in charge of transforming consumer needs into security properties for the consumer policy. The generated consumer security policies are machine-readable and are expressed in the same format used for the definition of the service *security agreement templates* (which describe the offered set of security properties of the service) and the service security *contracts* themselves. This allows both the creation of the security agreement template and the automatic matching of the policy with the contract for run-time monitoring of the policy compliance.

Once the MTM has transformed the security requirements into security elements at business process level using the Security Extended BPMN 2.0, the MTM can further translate the service specification into a service consumer security policy, written in Conspec language (see Figure 2).

In a similar way as the previous transformation, the MTM provides a user-friendly GUI to the service developer to perform this transformation. For each security requirement specified in the SRS (*Trustworthiness*, *Non-repudiation*, *Integrity*, etc.) the MTM offers a policy pattern automatically fulfilled as much as possible with the already transformed security elements in the business process. As a result, the MTM generates a draft of the consumer security policy that can be finalised by the developer with an editor integrated in the SCF. The MTM sets also default values for the limits for int and string types and the initial values of the variables in the Security State. The developer can edit the policy and modify these values or add more variables or *Event* clauses, if needed. At all times, the MTM guides the developer in what information is missing for the policy to be complete enough. The Aniketos SCF offers an integrated ConSpec editor in order to facilitate the edition of the ConSpec policies.

The result of the transformation of *Trustworthiness* and *Integrity* properties of our example are shown below.

```
RULE Trustworthiness
MAXINT 32000
MAXLEN 1000
SCOPE Session
SECURITY STATE
   string guardedTask = Create map;
BEFORE v#activity.start(string id, string name, string type, int time,
int date, string exec) PERFORM
   i#Trustworthiness(id)<99 && guardedTask==name -> skip
   !(guardedTask==name) -> skip

RULE Integrity
MAXINT 32000
MAXLEN 1000
SCOPE Session
SECURITY STATE
```

```
string hash = _;
   string guardedSender = StoreLocatorProvider;
   string processingService = Create map;
   string generatingService = Get list of stores;
BEFORE v#activity.end(string id, string name,string type, int time,
int date, string exec, string output) PERFORM
   exec == guardedSender && generatingService==name ->
      hash = s#SHA1Hash(output);
   !(exec == guardedSender) ||!(generatingService==name) -> skip
BEFORE v#activity.start(string id, string name, string type, int time,
int date, string exec, string input) PERFORM
   name == processingService && hash == s#SHA1Hash(input) -> skip
   !(name == processingService) -> skip
```

5   Conclusions

There exist a number of approaches that address the extension of BPMN with annotations to specify security requirements [22] [14] [5]. However, these approaches do not put the focus on the roots in the consumer needs that such security requirements have or in the automatic mapping of such service level requirements with elicited socio-technical security requirements at high level.

In this chapter we presented our framework for building secure and trustworthy composite services, which really puts the focus in the alignment between the modelled security requirements at organizational level and the security requirements at service level, as well as the corresponding service policies.

The framework starts with the analysis and modelling of organization participants' objectives and their relationships in the achievement of such business goals. The social commitments in such interactions are gathered in a Security Requirements Specification that is automatically transformed into trust and security information added to the service low level specification, as well as into consumer security policy. This allows the three perspectives being continuously aligned, and eases the end-to-end development and maintenance of compliant secure and trustworthy service compositions.

When the considered organisation stakeholders change their security needs, or when the considered scope for the requirements analysis is broadened to include more stakeholders, changes in the social, resource, and authorisation views of the corresponding STS-ml model are triggered. Since our SRS is derived from the STS-ml model, this results in an evolution of the SRS. In particular, differences in the SRS may be due to a different set of commitments or/and differences in the involved information resources relationships. In order to keep the consumer needs in SRS aligned with security elements in service specification, our approach is complemented with the Security Requirements Compliance Module (SRCM) of Aniketos which is in charge of verifying the compliance of an existing Security Extended BPMN with respect to the requirements in the SRS. In cases when the compliance does not keep, the developer can execute again the MTM in order to perform a new transformation.

The lines of future work include the extension of our framework with other socio-technical requirements, for example those related to time constraints (data retention, etc.), as well as the automatic transformation of task execution flows.

Moreover, we are interested in enriching our framework with cloud relevant security and trust properties (data location, accountability, etc.) [10] and cloud contract compliance monitoring techniques through the use of formal verification of ConSpec policies at runtime.

References

1. Aktug, I., Naliuka, K.: ConSpec — a formal language for policy specification. Electronic Notes in Theoretical Computer Science 197(1), 45–58 (2008)
2. Aniketos Website, http://www.aniketos.eu
3. Baxter, G., Sommerville, I.: Socio-technical systems: From design methods to systems engineering. Interacting with Computers 23(1), 4–17 (2011)
4. Bresciani, P., Perini, A., Giorgini, P., Giunchiglia, F., Mylopoulos, J.: Tropos: An agent-oriented software development methodology. Autonomous Agents and Multi-Agent Systems 8(3), 203–236 (2004)
5. Brucker, A.D., Hang, I., Lückemeyer, G., Ruparel, R.: SecureBPMN: Modeling and enforcing access control requirements in business processes. In: Proceedings of the 17th ACM symposium on Access Control Models and Technologies, pp. 123–126. ACM (June 2012)
6. Brucker, A.D., Malmignati, F., Merabti, M., Shi, Q., Zhou, B.: A Framework for Secure Service Composition. In: International Conference on Information Privacy, Security, Risk and Trust (PASSAT), pp. 1–6. IEEE (September 2013)
7. Dalpiaz, F., Paja, E., Giorgini, P.: Security requirements engineering via commitments. In: 2011 1st Workshop on Socio-Technical Aspects in Security and Trust (STAST), pp. 1–8 (September 2011)
8. Dragoni, N., Massacci, F., Naliuka, K., Siahaan, I.: Security-by-contract: Toward a semantics for digital signatures on mobile code. In: López, J., Samarati, P., Ferrer, J.L. (eds.) EuroPKI 2007. LNCS, vol. 4582, pp. 297–312. Springer, Heidelberg (2007)
9. Emery, F.E., Trist, E.L.: Socio-Technical Systems. Management Science, Models and Techniques 2, 83–97 (1960)
10. ENISA. Procure Secure: A guide to monitoring of security service levels in cloud contracts (April 2012),
http://www.enisa.europa.eu/activities/Resilience-and-CIIP/
cloud-computing/procure-secure-a-guide-to-monitoring-
of-security-service-levels-in-cloud-contracts
(Cited on September 10, 2013)
11. Erlingsson, U.: The inlined reference monitor approach to security policy enforcement. Cornell University (2003)
12. Giorgini, P., Massacci, F., Mylopoulos, J., Zannone, N.: Modeling security requirements through ownership, permission and delegation. In: Proceedings of the 13th IEEE International Conference on Requirements Engineering, pp. 167–176. IEEE (August 2005)
13. Trist, E.L.: On socio-technical systems. Sociotechnical systems: A sourcebook, 43-57 (1978)

14. Menzel, M., Thomas, I., Meinel, C.: Security requirements specification in service-oriented business process management. In: International Conference on Availability, Reliability and Security, ARES 2009, pp. 41–48. IEEE (March 2009)
15. Mouratidis, H., Giorgini, P.: Secure tropos: A security-oriented extension of the tropos methodology. International Journal of Software Engineering and Knowledge Engineering 17(02), 285–309 (2007)
16. Mulle, J., Stackelberg, S., Bohm, K.: A Security Language for BPMN Process Models. Karlsruhe Reports in Informatics (September 2011)
17. Noguero, A., Espinoza, H.: A generic executable framework for model-driven engineering. In: 2012 7th Iberian Conference on Information Systems and Technologies (CISTI), pp. 1–6. IEEE (June 2012)
18. OASIS, Reference Model for Service Oriented Architecture 1.0 (2009), http://docs.oasis-open.org/soa-rm/soa-ra/v1.0/soa-ra.pdf (cited September 12, 2013)
19. OMG. Business Process Model and Notation (BPMN) Version 2.0 (2011), http://www.omg.org/spec/BPMN/2.0/ (Cited on September 10, 2013)
20. Paja, E., Dalpiaz, F., Giorgini, P.: Identifying Conflicts in Security Requirements with STS-ml. University of Trento. Technical report (2012)
21. Paja, E., Dalpiaz, F., Poggianella, M., Roberti, P., Giorgini, P.: STS-Tool: Specifying and Reasoning over Socio-Technical Security Requirements. In: iStar 2013, pp. 131–133 (2013)
22. Rodríguez, A., Fernández-Medina, E., Piattini, M.: A bpmn extension for the modeling of security requirements in business processes. IEICE Transactions on Information and Systems 90(4), 745–752 (2007)
23. Salnitri, M., Dalpiaz, F., Giorgini, P.: Aligning Service-Oriented Architectures with Security Requirements. In: Meersman, R., Panetto, H., Dillon, T., Rinderle-Ma, S., Dadam, P., Zhou, X., Pearson, S., Ferscha, A., Bergamaschi, S., Cruz, I.F. (eds.) OTM 2012, Part I. LNCS, vol. 7565, pp. 232–249. Springer, Heidelberg (2012)
24. Singh, M.P.: An ontology for commitments in multiagent systems. Artificial Intelligence and Law 7(1), 97–113 (1999)
25. University of trento, STS-ml manual (2013), http://www.sts-tool.eu/doc/STS-ModelingLanguage_ver1.3.2.pdf (cited September 12, 2013)
26. Wolter, C., Menzel, M., Meinel, C.: Modelling Security Goals in Business Processes. Modellierung 127, 201–216 (2008)
27. van Lamsweerde, A.: Requirements engineering in the year 00: a research perspective. In: Proceedings of the 22nd International Conference on Software Engineering, pp. 5–19 (2000)

Security Requirements Engineering with STS-Tool

Elda Paja[1], Mauro Poggianella[1], Fabiano Dalpiaz[2],
Pierluigi Roberti[1], and Paolo Giorgini[1]

[1] University of Trento – Department of Information Engineering and Computer Science,
Via Sommarive 5, 38123, Povo, Trento, Italy
{elda.paja,mauro.poggianella,
pierluigi.roberti,paolo.giorgini}@unitn.it
[2] Utrecht University – Department of Information and Computing Sciences,
Princetonplein 5, De Uithof, 3584 CC Utrecht, The Netherlands
f.dalpiaz@uu.nl

Abstract. In this chapter, we present STS-Tool, the modelling and analysis support tool for STS-ml, an actor- and goal-oriented security requirements modelling language for socio-technical systems. STS-Tool is a standalone application written in Java and based on the Eclipse RCP Framework. It supports modelling a socio-technical system in terms of high-level primitives such as actor, goal delegation, and document exchange; to express security constraints over the interactions between the actors; and to derive security requirements once the modelling is done. It also supports analysing the created STS-ml models in terms of (i) well-formedness, (ii) violation of security requirements, and (iii) threats impact over actors' assets. We also present the architecture of STS-Tool together with its main features and provide technical details of the modelling and analysis capabilities.

1 Introduction

STS-Tool [6,7] is the graphical modelling and analysis support tool for STS-ml (Chapter 5). STS-ml [1] (Socio-Technical Security modelling language), an actor- and goal-oriented security requirements modelling language for socio-technical systems, which relies on the idea of relating security requirements to interaction. STS-ml allows stakeholders (reified as actors) to express *security needs* over interactions to constrain the way interaction is to take place, and uses the concept of *social commitment* [9] among actors to specify security requirements. For example, if a buyer sends its personal data to a seller, the buyer may require the data not to be disclosed to third parties. Commitments [9] are a pure social abstraction used to model interaction, and in STS-ml they are used to capture security requirements, in terms of promises (social contracts) for the satisfaction of *security needs*. This means that, in STS-ml security requirements are specified as follows: one actor (*responsible*) commits to another (*requestor*) that it will comply with the required *security need*. In the previous example, the seller commits not to disclose personal data to other parties.

In previous work [7] we have shown the use of *social commitments* in specifying security requirements; we have explained how STS-Tool supports modelling and the automated derivation of commitments; we have presented the automated analysis techniques in [5], and illustrated their integration and implementation in STS-Tool to detect

A.D. Brucker et al. (Eds.): Secure Service Composition, LNCS 8900, pp. 95–109, 2014.

violations of security requirements in [8]. We present details on the underlying modelling language, STS-ml in Chapter 5. Here, we provide the technical details behind the features supported by STS-Tool.

2 Overall Features of STS-Tool

STS-Tool offers the following features:

- *Specification of Projects*: STS-ml models are created within the scope of project containers. A project refers to a certain scenario, and contains a set of models. Typical operations on projects are supported: create, rename, import, and export.
- *Project Explorer*: a feature of STS-Tool developed as a customization of the Eclipse RNF (Resource Navigator Framework). Since it is not designed to be used inside an RCP application, the integration was a bit challenging. The project explorer allows the user to manage files better, organising them into folders and projects.
- *Diagrammatic Modelling*: the tool enables the creation (drawing) of diagrams (models). Diagrams are created only within a project and typical create/modify/ save/ load/ undo/redo operations are supported. In particular, STS-Tool supports *multi-view modelling*—different tabs are provided in the tool to allow modelling the various models of a socio-technical system diagram, namely *social*, *information*, and *authorisation model*, following STS-ml's multi-view feature. Each tab (referred to as view) shows specific elements and hides others, while keeping always visible elements that serve as connection points between the models (e.g. roles and agents). Inter-model consistency is ensured by for instance propagating insertion (deletion) of certain elements to all models (social, information, and authorisation) composing the overall STS-ml model.
- *Export Diagram to Different File Formats*: STS-ml models (or parts of models, i.e., specific elements), as well as analysis results, can be exported to various formats, such as jpg, png, pdf, svg, eps, etc.
- *Derivation of Security Requirements*: the tool allows the automatic derivation of security requirements in terms of relationships between a *requestor* and a *responsible* actor for the satisfaction of a *requirement*.
- *Automated Reasoning*: two automated reasoning techniques (*security analysis* and *threat analysis*) are integrated in and supported by STS-Tool. Note that the execution of automated reasoning is to be performed over well-formed models. We verify well-formedness in two steps, depending on the complexity of the check: (i) online or on-the-fly, while the model is being drawn, or (ii) offline, upon user explicit request for computationally expensive checks (embedded within *well-formedness analysis*). *Security Analysis* and *threat analysis* are performed upon request of the end-user (security requirements engineer).
- *Visulisation of analyses' results*: the tool visualises the results of the analyses (per each analysis) and provides details of the findings.
- *Generation of Requirements Documents*: the tool allows the generation of a security requirements document that contains the list of security requirements derived from the model. This document contains information describing the models, information that is customisable by the designer (by choosing which model features to include).

It is good practice to generate the requirements document at the end of the modelling, and after refining the models in order to fix eventual errors detected by the automated analyses. This document is helpful especially when communicating with stakeholders, for it provides details about the different elements of the diagram.

3 Architecture

STS-Tool was developed using the Java programming language, and built on top of different frameworks produced by the Eclipse community. The overall architecture for STS-Tool is depicted in Fig. 1. As shown in this figure, the architecture of STS-Tool is composed of three macro blocks. Starting from the bottom, we find the *System Component* block that contains the underlying operating system (Windows, Linux or OsX) and the Java virtual machine that executes the Java code.

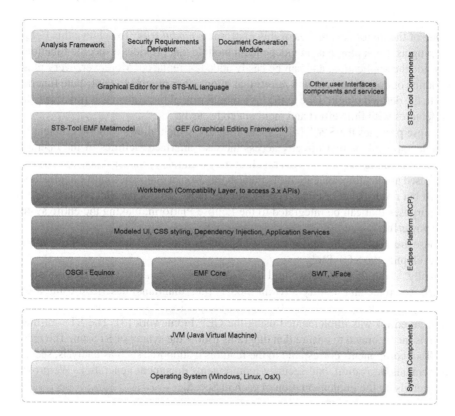

Fig. 1. STS-Tool architecture

At the second layer, we find the *Eclipse Platform*, also known as Eclipse Rich Client Platform (RCP). The Eclipse Platform is developed and maintained by the Eclipse community[1] and is a powerful framework for building multi-platform standalone

---

[1] https://www.eclipse.org/

applications. An Eclipse application consists of individual software components. According to Vogel in [11], the most important components are:

- OSGi: a specification that describes a modular approach for Java application. The programming model of OSGi allows defining dynamic software components, namely OSGi services.
- Equinox: one implementation of the OSGi specification and is used by the Eclipse platform. The Equinox runtime provides the necessary framework to run a modular Eclipse application.
- SWT: the standard user interface component library used by Eclipse. JFace [12] provides some convenient APIs on top of SWT, while the workbench provides the framework for the application. It is responsible for displaying all other UI components.
- Eclipse 4: provides a compatibility layer which allows that plug-ins using the Eclipse 3.x programming model can be used unmodified in an Eclipse based application.

One of the major advantages of this platform is *modularity*. To achieve this Eclipse uses plugins. Each plugin is an independent module that provides a specific functionality inside the application, and can be easily added or replaced. Moreover, every plugin can define or consume *extension points* that allow other plugins to contribute functionality to the defined plugin. Due to the high modularity of the system it is possible to add new features with little effort and maintain code easily.

Eclipse provides the SWT [4] graphical library, which allows to build efficient and portable applications that directly access the user-interface facilities of the operating systems it is implemented on. This revolutionary technology makes it possible to create Java-based applications that are indistinguishable from a platform's native applications.

Last but not least, the Eclipse community develops a lot of parallel projects for various purposes that can be integrated to the Eclipse Platform, making the entire system more powerful.

These are some of the reasons that Eclipse was chosen as the underlying platform for developing the STS-Tool.

Finally, at the third layer, we find the *STS-Tool Components*. The STS-Tool allows the user to create and modify STS-ml models (i.e., diagrams) described using a specific language, namely STS-ml. To support the particular specification of STS-ml, a graphical editor was implemented using the GEF Framework [3]. The STS-ml metamodel is incorporated to ensure that diagrams follow the syntax of STS-ml. The rest of STS-Tool components correspond to the features it supports, such as analysis, security requirements derivation, and security requirements document generation. We provide more details on the implementation of each in Sec. 5.

4   Installation Details

The STS-Tool is distributed as a compressed archive for multiple platforms and it is free to download from the STS-Tool website[2]. The tool is available in both source and

---

[2] http://www.sts-tool.eu/

binary form, and the license is APGL (Affere General Public License). As prerequisite, at least version 6.26 of the Java Virtual Machine is needed. Previous versions of the tool are also available online in Archive[3].

The installation of STS-Tool requires no setup, it is enough to download the version suitable for the machine and operating system under consideration, extract the content of the archive containing the tool, to finally run the launcher file.

The STS-Tool comes with *Online Help*. Help is produced by the Eclipse project, we provide only the content of the help.

To obtain updates of the STS-Tool, one does not need to download the latest version from the website, rather an *update system* is already integrated in the tool. The update system is a customization of the Eclipse P2 (Eclipse update system). A public web site was expressly created in order to update the new versions of the tool automatically. The STS-Tool checks for updates and if any are found, it asks the user to install them. However, the user has the choice of activating this feature (configuring updates from the menu: Windows – Preferences – Updates) or getting updates manually.

5   Technical Implementation Details of STS-Tool

We provide technical details on how the STS-Tool supports modelling (Sec. 5.1), security requirements derivation (Sec 5.2), analysis (Sec 5.3), and security requirements document generation (Sec 5.4).

5.1   Modelling with STS-Tool

To implement the graphical editor for the STS-ml language, the GEF Framework [3] was chosen. The GEF Framework is an interactive Model-View-Controller (MVC) framework, which fosters the implementation of SWT–based tree editors [11], and Draw2d–based [3] graphical editors for the Eclipse Workbench UI [13]. One of the challenges faced in the development of the graphical editor was related to the fact that the GEF framework is a single view editor, while the STS-Tool editor had to be a multi-view editor in order to support the multi-view modelling of STS-ml models. The problem was solved by implementing a custom multi-view editor starting from the class MultiPageEditorPart (org.eclipse.ui.part.MultiPageEditorPart) [4].

Currently, STS-ml supports three views. However, considering a possible evolution of the language and tool, we took advantage of the modular nature of the platform to create a new extension point in order to allow the automatic addition (insertion) of new views (should there be any in the future). The MultiPageEditor reads the extension point and creates the required objects to then allow their initialization.

The extension point id is it.unitn.disi.ststool.editor.subparts and can have an infinite number of children (one for each view) of 2 different types: *Subeditor* or *View*, see Fig. 2. The difference between them is the type of interface they must implement. The two

---

[3] http://www.sts-tool.eu/Archive/

[4] http://help.eclipse.org/indigo/index.jsp?topic=%2Forg.eclipse.
platform.doc.isv%2Freference%2Fapi%2Forg%2Feclipse%2Fui%
2Fpart%2FMultiPageEditorPart.html

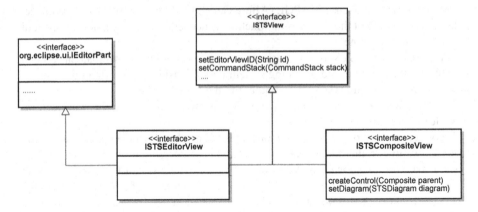

Fig. 2. STS-Tool Graphical Editor Support via Extension Points

interfaces are similar. They both extend the common interface ISTSView, which defines the common methods each view must have, but the editor interface the ISTSEditorView extends also from the org.eclipse.ui.IEditorPart allowing to add Eclipse editors as view (as the GEF Editor), while the ISTSCompositeView allows to add simple composites as views, useful to create a textual view. Each view must declare a unique id to make one view distinguishable from the others. This id is subsequently used in the code to identify the correct objects GraphicalConstraint (see Sec. 5.1–**The Model**).

After implementing the multi-view feature, we concentrated on the fundamental modelling features of the editor. As already mentioned above, a GEF Editor was extended. Since GEF is a MVC Framework, three main objects should be provided for each, namely *the model*, *the view* and *the controller* (see Fig. 3).

In the following paragraphs, we discuss in detail each and every one of the objects.

The Model. Each diagram the user displays or edits is described by an underlying Java model. Each Java object contains its own properties, and represents a specific element that will be displayed on a graphical canvas. The STS-Metamodel was implemented using the EMF Framework [2]—a modelling framework and code generation facility for building tools and applications based on a structured data model. It provides tools and runtime support to produce a set of Java classes for the model, along with a set of adapter classes that enable viewing and command-based editing of the model.

Apart from the Java code creation facility, EMF provides a powerful notification system that is necessary when working with MVC frameworks. The notification system notifies all the registered listeners when a property of one object changes so a graphical update can occur. The STS-Metamodel (see Fig. 1) was created using this framework, and was adapted to reflect the STS-ml language properties. The model was included in the it.unitn.disi.ststool.model plugin.

To avoid mixing model properties with graphical properties the model was logically separated in two parts:

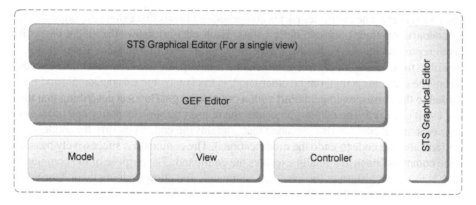

Fig. 3. STS-Tool Graphical Editor

1. The abstract class does not specifically represent an STS-ml element, while the main class from which all other elements derive is the STSElement. This class defines the common element attributes, such as the unique identifier or the description properties, to be inherited by all subclasses[5]. Subsequently, STS-ml elements (Nodes) and relationships (Links) are represented through two dinstinct classes: STSNode and STSLink. The class GraphicalConstraint storer graphical information such as node bounds or link binding points, which is useful to maintain separated the graphical information from the model information. Given that such constraints are specified over different elements and relationships (representing interaction), the class is extended to differentiate among Nodes', Links', and Diagram's GraphicalConstraint. This is useful to avoid continuous casting in the code too. GraphicalConstraint can have multiple properties, GraphicalProperty, in the form of key/value, which facilitates the creation/addition of new non-default properties.
2. The real STS-ml model representation. Each STS-ml model object is reproduced in the STS-EMF model. A plugin was created from the metamodel description: the it.unitn.disi.ststool.edit plugin. This plugin is also generated from the EMF Framework and contains a set of classes that allow to display and edit a model object through the property view (as supported by Eclipse).

The View. The views for the GEF editor are made of simple shapes. These shapes are created using the eclipse draw2d library and each shape extends the org.eclipse.draw2d. IFigure interface. The IFigure was not implemented from scratch, rather the Shapes figure provided by the draw2d library was extended. Views as such do not have any information about the object model they are representing, but they are connected to them through the *Controller*. This is useful to keep the model separated from the view and maintain the code clear and easily reusable.

---

[5] Class STSDiagram is an exception, as it defines the overall diagram. Thus, it is the parent of all other objects in the diagram, serving as a root container so the entire model is represented by this object.

The Controller. The controller part is composed of classes that extend the org.eclipse. gef.editparts.AbstractGraphicalEditPart class. Each editPart knows the *model object* it has to represent and the *figure* associated to it, and is able to *link* them. Editpart is responsible for tracking model (diagram) changes and update the view in which changes occur. The user interaction, on the other hand, is tracked by the EditingDomain and forwarded to the corresponding editPart with a org.eclipse.gef.Request describing that the user event occurred. The editPart processes the request through its policy and produces a org.eclipse.gef.commands.Command that contains the code to modify the model object (and also the code to undo the modifications). The command is successively passed to the commandStack that finally executes the command. The purpose of the command stack is to keep a history of the executed commands and allow undoing them. Once the command is executed the model object is modified, and an event is propagated to the editPart to update the respective view.

Each view editor shares with the other editors two important things: the *diagram model object* and the CommandStack, while each has its own palette that is populated during the construction of the editor. This allows the different views to have distinct palettes. View filtering is made in the EditPart: each EditPart is responsible for listing the children objects and the connections that start and end to the represented model element. Filtering this list supports the filtering of what the editor displays.

5.2 Security Requirements Derivation

In this section, we present how security requirements are generated in STS-Tool starting from security needs (Chapter 5, Section 2.2). Each Element in the STS Metamodel derives from the STSElement class which defines a containment relation (0..*) with an object of type ElementNeed, which keeps track of the security need specified over the element. Therefore, each Element in the model is related to its element need. Each element need has an id that identifies the type of the element need, and a map of $key \rightarrow values$ of properties, used to store specific values of the security need, which allows having multiple values for a single element need. This solution was chosen over the one of binding specific properties on each model object, to make it possible to add requirements through an extension point, without modifying and sequentially regenerating the metamodel code. Moreover, this option supports the automatic creation of menus without modifying the editor code. That is, if a new security need is required to be supported by STS-Tool, it can be added through a new plugin. This is made possible by the it.unitn.disi.ststool.development.model. elementneed extension point. This extension point allows two types of children, an elementNeedGroup and an ElementNeed respectively.

The elementNeedGroup requires 3 parameters:

1. *id*: uniquely identifies the group,
2. *name*: is displayed in the menu, and
3. *parent group id*: an optional id to create submenus.

The ElementNeed ,instead, requires 6 parameters:

1. *id*: uniquely identifies the element need type,
2. *groupId*: points to an elementNeedGroup ID,
3. *name*: is displayed to the user,
4. *short name*: used in the graphical representation,
5. *color*: used in the graphical representation,
6. *applicableTo*: string value that contains a list of comma separated Class names on which the elementNeed will be applied (will be displayed in is context menu).

Furthermore the ElementNeed allows five types of children, which describe the properties of the ElementNeed. Each ElementNeed can have multiple of these children allowing an element need to support multiple properties. These children are:

1. *singlechoice_value*: allow to choose a single value from a list;
2. *int_value*: allow to insert an integer value;
3. *string_value*: allow to insert a text value;
4. *bool_value*: allow to insert a Boolean value;
5. *percent_value*: allow to insert a value in range 0-100.

For now these are the supported values, but in future versions of the STS-Tool, newer value types could be added. In STS-Tool, security requirements are a specialization of the ElementNeed. They are defined in a separate plugin unitn.disi.ststool. securityrequirements. This plugin defines the ElementNeed used in the STS-ml language, and also provides a security requirement generator and a view (the security requirements view) to display the evaluated security requirements. To perform an evaluation, two different components are involved. The first component is the SecurityRequirementsManager singleton. This component tracks the current active editor and if a valid editor is found it retrieves the associated STSDiagram Model object and delegates the evaluation of the security requirements to the second component the SecurityRequirementEvaluator. The Manager also tracks the changes on the model and when they occur it asks the evaluator to perform a new evaluation. When the evaluation completes the result of the evaluation is stored and registered listeners to the manager, as the security Requirements View, are updated with the new evaluation result. The SecurityRequirementEvaluator instead takes an STSDiagram as parameter and when started recursively iterates over the entire model and for each element it evaluates its ElementNeeds and generates one (or multiple) objects of type ISecurityRequirement that describe(s) the security requirements associated to the ElementNeed. When no more elements are found, the complete list of ISecurityRequirement is returned. A possible improvement of this implementation: the SecurityRequirementEvaluator contains an hardcoded set of rules to evaluate and create the correct implementation of the ISecurityRequirement, in the future this could be moved to an extension point. The SRS Generator is another component included in the Security Requirements plugin. When invoked by the user (through a generate SRS button) it retrieves from the SecurityRequirementsManager the list of the security requirements and transform them into an XML file.

5.3 Reasoning about Security Requirements

Here we show the automated reasoning capabilities implemented in STS-Tool.

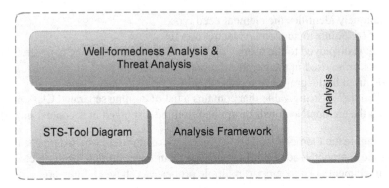

Fig. 4. STS-Tool Automated Analysis

STS-Tool supports analysis activities through a dedicated analysis module, as depicted in Fig. 4. Similarly to the other STS-Tool supported features, the analysis module was developed and integrated through specific plugins. In the following, we describe
each and every plugin used for the analysis module.

1. The it.unitn.disi.ststool.analysis plugin supports the execution of analysis over an
   STSDiagram object. This is achieved through a small framework, which has the
   following main interfaces:
   (a) IAnalysis: describes an analysis and contains a list of ITasks to be executed.
   (b) ITask: defines a generic task in the analysis, and the dependencies to other
       tasks. This interface cannot be directly implemented (see IComposedTask, IEx-
       ecutableTask).
   (c) IComposedTask: defines a composite task that contains subtasks. When this
       task is started the subtasks are executed and the result of the task is the worst
       result of the children. This is useful when a single task is composed of multi-
       ple tasks that have dependencies between them (e.g., in the security analysis,
       the *AuthorityViolations task* is composed of other subtasks. The first subtask
       named *preanalysis'* executes the ViolationAnalysis, but if for some reason this
       fails, the other sibling tasks are skipped because they need the results of the
       preanalysis).
   (d) IExecutableTask: defines a task that will execute a piece of code performing an
       evaluation and returning a result.
   (e) IResult: describes a result.
   (f) IAnalysisEngine: retrieved from the AnalysisEngineFactory singleton is the En-
       gine that will execute the IAnalysis.
   (g) ITaskEvent: the Analysis engine also supports events to notify registered listen-
       ers of the analysis progress. The progress of the analysis is made through this
       event object. The it.unitn.disi.ststool.analysis plugin also provides the graphical
       user interfaces to display the analysis results and other utilities classes, useful
       when performing analysis.
2. The it.unitn.disi.ststool.analysis.wellformedness plugin and the it.unitn.disi.
   ststool.analysis.threat plugin contain respectively the well-formedness analysis

implementation and the threat analysis implementation. These plugins provide the ITask implementation needed to perform the analysis. These analyses are performed completely in Java, analysing the STSDiagram Model object.

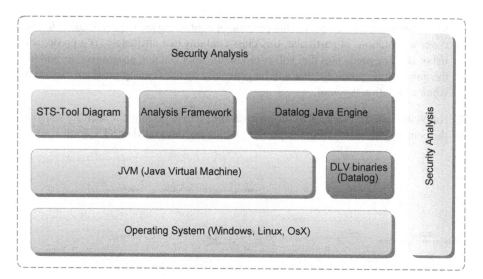

Fig. 5. STS-Tool Security Analysis

3. For the security analysis things get complicated. Since the security analysis is implemented in disjunctive Datalog (see Fig. 5), it requires the use of Datalog program and engine. But, the Datalog program is released only in native OS executables, and thus, a Java wrapper had to be implemented. To make it reusable, this wrapper was developed in a separate plugin, namely it.unitn.disi.ststool.analysis.dlv.

The java DLVEngine class is in charge of recognizing the current operating system in use and selecting the correct executables. It creates the required files on the filesystem and when requested, it executes the program using the Runtime.exec(String params) instructions. To make the DLVEngine more flexible, another class was inserted, namely EngineExecutionParameters, which contains methods to configure the DLVEngine, such as setting the maximum number of models or setting filters, and also contains the Datalog code that has to be executed. The output produced by the DLVEngine is parsed by a provided implementation of the EngineOutputReader class. This set of classes makes the use of the DLV binaries transparent to the Java code. The it.unitn.disi.ststool.analysis.security plugin contains the task that executes the security analysis. The fundamental tasks of the security analysis rely on a particular analysis (that is made internally and not in a separate plugin) called ViolationsAnalysis. This analysis uses the Datalog engine in order to be executed and completed. Some other classes have been added to support this analysis:

- Predicate: this class object represents a Datalog predicate; it has a name and contains parameters that are mapped to a model object.

- Violation: a wrapper for a predicate. This class, apart from containing the predicate, contains also other values derived from the analysis, such as the total number of occurrences of the predicate, and the total number of models generated by the DLV engine.
- ViolationDefinition: while Violation is used to wrap the result of the analysis, the ViolationDefinition class serves the purpose of containing the required values to discover a Violation. In particular, this class contains two attributes: (i) a predefined list of Datalog predicates that will compose the final Datalog program code, and (ii) the name of the predicate that will be generated by the Datalog program execution when a violation is found.

The following schema (see Fig. 6) summarizes the process guiding the security analysis and the components involved in the process, which are integrated in STS-Tool.

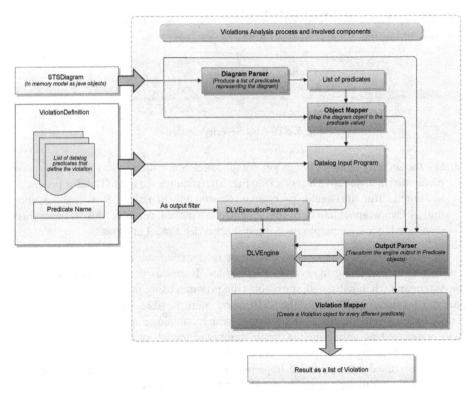

Fig. 6. STS-Tool Security Analysis: Verification of Security Requirements Violations

The ViolationsAnalysis requires two input parameters: an STSDiagram and a ViolationDefinition. When the analysis is started some events occur. First of all, a specific parser containing a set of rules iterates over the entire STSDiagram transforming each element in a Datalog predicate. The generated predicates are transformed one by one into String and the predicate values are mapped in a temporary Map. This allows us to be able to reconstruct the predicates when the DLV output is parsed. At this point the String that represents the predicates derived from the diagram and the predicates provided by the ViolationDefinition are merged together and passed as InputProgram through an instance of a DLVExecutionParameters to the DLVEngine. Afterwards the predicate name, which is retrieved from the ViolationDefinition, is set as the filter option to the DLVEngine. Setting the output filter drastically reduces the output produced by the DLV program and consequently improves memory footprint and efficiency. The engine can be started with the configured parameters. The output parser reads the output produced by the engine, interprets it and creates instances of Predicate. When the DLVEngine completes its execution, all the generated predicates are transformed in Violation instances and returned to the specific Security analysis task that requested them, and are used to produce the analysis results.

Visualising Analysis Results. The visualisation of the analysis results passes through a singleton object, specifically designed to manage the analysis results. Each analysis, once completed, provides to the ResultManager its results. Results are collected, stored, and displayed into the analysis view. Every result object has some properties: a *text* and a *description* that are used in the user interface to describe the result, the gravity of the result (OK,WARNING,ERROR), and a list of elements (or model objects) that have to be highlighted when the user wants to display them over the STS-ml model (diagram). After the results are displayed in the analysis view, the user can select one or more results to show them over the diagram. Once a result is selected, this action causes a ResultManager retrieve from the selected results, which returns the list of objects that need to highlighted and modified over the diagram (by setting a graphical property to each of this object graphical constraint), so the editor can change the displayed colour of the element to highlight it on the diagram.

5.4 Generating the Security Requirements Document

The STS-Tool supports the generation of the security requirements document, which is supported by the *report module*, as shown in Fig. 7. Similarly to the analysis module, the report module was distributed into multiple plugins.

The main plugin is the it.unitn.disi.ststool.documents. This plugin contains only the Java aspose libraries, which allow editing and creating text documents and presentation documents in multiple formats, as well as some UI classes and a set of classes that generate the final documents. While this plugin is involved in managing the creation of the documents, the content of the final document is obtained (contributed) via an extension point it.unitn.disi.ststool.documents.report.contribution that other plugins can use to add their own content. This extension point accepts multiple children of type contribution. A contribution must have a unique id, a priority value (a number) to make contributions sortable and a class that will perform the contribution (add the content of the document). Moreover the contribution type must have at least one child of type part. The part object is used in the graphical selection of the parts that can be generated, to allow customisation of the security requirements document by the analyst. This object has a unique id that can be used later in the code to retrieve the information about the selection, a name that is used in the UI, and

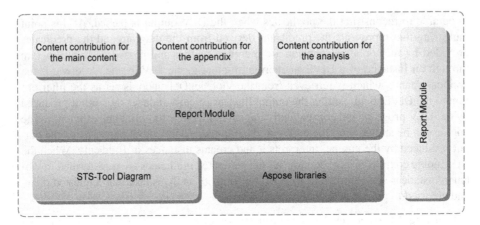

Fig. 7. STS-Tool Security Requirements Document Generation

some Boolean properties. part can also have part children to allow multi-level part-selection. While the it.unitn.disi.ststool.documents plugin contributes only to the report generation functionality, the it.unitn.disi.ststool.documents.report.analysis.security, it.unitn.disi. ststool.documents.report.analysis.wellformedness, it.unitn.disi.ststool. documents.report.securityreqirements, and it.unitn.disi.ststool.documents.report.view contribution plugins contribute to the content providing it through the extension points previously described. The content is generated analysing the STSDiagram; static code retrieves from the model the required information, caches them and at the end generates the content that has to be inserted into the document.

6   Conclusions

The STS-Tool is quite a stable graphical requirements engineering modelling tool. It is based on the Eclipse EMF framework and supports modelling and reasoning over the created models. The latest version of the tool is the result of an iterative development process, having been tested on multiple case studies and evaluated with practitioners [10] in the scope of Aniketos. STS-Tool was proved suitable to model and reason over models of a large size from different domains [5], such as eGovernment (see Chapter 15) or Air Traffic Management Control (see Chapter 14).

References

1. Dalpiaz, F., Paja, E., Giorgini, P.: Security requirements engineering via commitments. In: Proceedings of STAST 2011, pp. 1–8 (2011)
2. The Eclipse Foundation. Eclipse modeling framework project (emf). Lastchecked (March 2014)
3. The Eclipse Foundation. Gef (mvc). Lastchecked (March 2014)
4. Northover, S., Wilson, M.: Swt: the standard widget toolkit, vol. 1. Addison-Wesley Professional (2004)

5. Paja, E., Dalpiaz, F., Giorgini, P.: Managing security requirements conflicts in socio-technical systems. In: Proceedings of ER (2013) (to appear)
6. Paja, E., Dalpiaz, F., Poggianella, M., Roberti, P., Giorgini, P.: STS-Tool: socio-technical security requirements through social commitments. In: Proceedings of RE 2012, pp. 331–332 (2012)
7. Paja, E., Dalpiaz, F., Poggianella, M., Roberti, P., Giorgini, P.: STS-Tool: Using commitments to specify socio-technical security requirements. In: Proceedings of ER 2012 Workshops, pp. 396–399 (2012)
8. Paja, E., Dalpiaz, F., Poggianella, M., Roberti, P., Giorgini, P.: Specifying and reasoning over socio-technical security requirements with sts-tool. In: Proceedings of the 32nd International Conference on Conceptual Modeling, ER Workshops, pp. 504–507 (2013)
9. Singh, M.P.: An ontology for commitments in multiagent systems: Toward a unification of normative concepts. Artificial Intelligence and Law 7(1), 97–113 (1999)
10. Trösterer, S., Beck, E., Dalpiaz, F., Paja, E., Giorgini, P., Tscheligi, M.: Formative user-centered evaluation of security modeling: Results from a case study. International Journal of Secure Software Engineering 3(1), 1–19 (2012)
11. Vogel, L.: Building eclipse rcp applications based on eclipse 4 (2013), Revision history: Revision 0.1 - 6.9 February 14, 2009-July 4, 2013
12. Vogel, L.: Eclipse jface tree - tutorial (2013) Revision history: Revision 0.1-0.1-3.3 August 22, 2010-October 15, 2013
13. Xenos, S.: Inside the workbench a guide to the workbench internals (October 2005) (Lastchecked: March, 2014)

Using SecureBPMN for Modelling
Security-Aware Service Compositions

Achim D. Brucker

SAP SE, Vincenz-Priessnitz-Str. 1, 76131 Karlsruhe, Germany
achim.brucker@sap.com

Abstract. Today, many systems are built by orchestrating existing services, custom developed services, as well as interaction with users. These
orchestrations, also called composition plans, are often described using
high-level modelling languages that allow for simplifying 1) the implementation of systems by using generic execution engines and 2) the adaption of deployed systems to changing business needs. Thus, composition
plans play an important role for both communicating business requirements between domain experts and system experts, and serving as a
basis for the system implementation.

At the same time, ICT systems need to fulfil an increasing number
of security and compliance requirements. Thus, there is a demand for
integrating security and compliance requirements into composition plans.

We present SecureBPMN, a language for modelling security properties
that can easily be integrated into languages used for describing service
orchestrations. Moreover, we integrate SecureBPMN into BPMN and,
thus, present a common language for describing service orchestration
(in terms of business process models) together with their security and
compliance requirements.

Keywords: SecureBPMN, BPMN, Access Control, Confidentiality.

1 Introduction

Today, many systems are built by orchestrating existing service offerings, custom developed services, as well as human-centred tasks. These orchestration
models, also called composition plans, are often described using high-level modelling languages, such as the Business Process Modelling Language and Notation
(BPMN) [21] or the Business Process Execution Language (BPEL) [20]. Using
such high-level description languages allows for simplifying:

1. the implementation of systems by using generic execution engines and
2. the adaption of deployed systems to changing business needs.

Thus, high-level composition plans play an important role both for communicating business requirements between domain experts and system experts as well
as a basis for the system implementation.

Since several years, enterprise systems need to fulfil an increasing number of
security and compliance requirements. One reason for this is that the number

A.D. Brucker et al. (Eds.): Secure Service Composition, LNCS 8900, pp. 110–120, 2014.

of businesses that operate in regulated markets, i.e., that need to comply to regulations such as HIPAA [15] in the health care sector or Basel III [4] in the financial sector, is increasing. Such compliance regulations along with the increased awareness of IT security result in need for modelling, analysis, an d execution techniques that treat security, privacy, and compliance properties as first class citizens.

Consequently, the demand for an integrating means for specifying security and compliance requirements into languages that fulfil the need of business experts, system experts, and security experts, is increasing. Fulfilling the needs of business experts *and* system experts at the same time is already challenging—bringing the security experts to the same table, makes it even more challenging.

To meet this challenge, we developed SecureBPMN [8]: a security modelling language for expressing high-level security and compliance requirements such as role-based access control (RBAC), break-glass, separation-of-duty (SoD), delegation, or variants of the need-to-know principle. SecureBPMN is defined using a metamodel which makes it particularly suitable for integration into business process modelling languages that are themselves defined by a metamodel.

In this paper, we present SecureBPMN and its integration into BPMN. As BPMN is used in Aniketos for specifying service composition plans, this integration provides a language that allows for specifying, analysing security properties on the level of service compositions plans. Thus, SecureBPMN provides the foundation for the secure and compliant execution of service compositions.

2   Using BPMN for Modelling Service Orchestrations

The modelling in BPMN is done by expressing business processes through business models. A BPMN model is an executable specification of the workflow, i.e., a flowchart based diagram that captures the basic structure and flow of activities and data within a business process. From a high-level perspective, the development of a system using BPMN is divided into two major phases:

1. During the *design phase*, a service developer—together with domain or business experts—designs the process model, i.e., the *service composition plan*. This process model comprises both automatic services and human interactions with these services.
2. During the *deployment phase*, the process model is deployed in a business process execution engine, which can act as a service orchestrator.

This high-level view does not include several other tasks involved in system development such as the implementation of actual services and the design of the user interface.

Figure 1 shows a BPMN diagram modelling a service composition that provides a travel booking service to customers. First, customers enter their flight and hotel preferences into the system (such kind of user interactions are modelled by user tasks in BPMN). Next, two web services (modelled as service tasks) are executed and connected via parallel gateways. These web services can be operated by different service providers and, in our example, provide functionalities

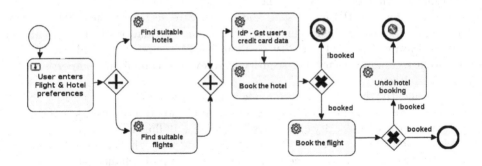

Fig. 1. A composed service for booking flights and hotels

for finding suitable hotel and flight information respectively. Here the parallel gateways ensure that the service which queries customer's credit card data will only be executed if both the Find suitable hotels and Find suitable flights tasks are terminated successfully. By using exclusive gateways the service developer is able to indicate that the Book the hotel task might fail. In case the booking is failed (!booked), an error boundary event will be reached.

3   Security in Service Orchestrations

Our motivating example, represented in Figure 1, requires already a surprisingly large number of security and compliance requirements; for example:

- While all users should be able to search for hotels and flights, certain offers should only be available to premium customers. Moreover, travel arrangements that are above a certain limit (e. g., cost more than 5 000 Euro) might require additional approval steps to avoid credit card fraud. Thus, already this simple scenario requires a *fine-grained access control* that cannot be modelled using a simple role-based access control model. Moreover, we want to ensure that the person booking the travel and the credit card holder are the same (*binding of duty*).
- To avoid fraud or price-fixing agreements, we demand that the services for finding hotels (flights) and the booking service, are from different service providers. Of course, such a strict application of the *separation of duty* principle may hinder some travel agencies and we might want to relax this requirement such that it only holds for travels that costs more than 1000 Euro. Thus, separation of duty (as well as complementary binding of duty) should restrict individual permissions to execute an action on a task and not whole tasks (actions).
- The credit card company needs to know the price for the flight and hotel but it needs to know neither the travel destination nor the exact travel dates. Applying the principle of *need to know* or *least privilege*, can ensure such confidentiality requirements.

- Applying the discussed security and compliance requirements strictly may harm the business, e. g., if travel requests are done by an assistant to the holder of the credit card. Thus, a controlled way for transferring rights such as through *delegation*, is essential. To ensure that a delegation of tasks does not violate more important compliance rules, we also need to be able to specify restrictions on delegations (e. g., certain tasks might not be delegable at all or only delegable to persons that already possesses the necessary access rights).

Even this simple scenario shows that describing the non-functional security and compliance requirements is a significant part of the overall business process design. In real-world scenarios, the effort for specifying and implementing the non-functional requirements can easily outgrow the effort for specifying and implementing the functional requirements.

4   SecureBPMN

Security and compliance should be modelled together with the service orchestration this is while building the service composition, instead of addressing them as an after-thought. To address this need, we used a metamodel-based (Brucker and Doser [9] discuss the details of metamodel-based language extensions) approach for defining SecureBPMN. Overall, SecureBPMN is a security language that easily can be integrated into business process modelling languages or work flow modelling languages. Figure 2 shows the (slightly simplified) metamodel of SecureBPMN and its integration into BPMN. SecureBPMN allows for describing the following security and compliance requirements:

- *Access Control:* the core of SecureBPMN is a hierarchical role-based access control (RBAC) [3] language supporting constraints (AuthorizationConstraint) on the permissions. The constraints can be used to express requirements like "a credit card payment shall be approved only if it is requested by the card holder." A Subject in SecureBPMN can be an individual User or a Group of subjects. Subjects are mapped to a Role hierarchy. SecureBPMN allows to permit (Permission) the actions (Action) on resources (Resource). In case of BPMN, resources are instances of the BPMN meta-classes Process, Activity, or ItemAwareElement. This part of SecureBPMN is, conceptually, very close to SecureUML [7].
- *Delegation:* SecureBPMN supports delegation with (TransferDelegation) and without (SimpleDelegation) transferring *all* (including access to data or back-end systems) access rights that are necessary to execute a task. The former only allows to delegate tasks to subjects that already possess the necessary rights. The latter allows to delegate tasks to arbitrary subjects that, then, can act on behalf of the original subject (Delegator). The number of delegations can be restricted by maxDepth: a maxDepth of 'zero' forbids any delegation explicitly, and value of 'one' forbids a delegatee to delegate a task further. A delegation can be negotiable, i. e., the delegatee can refuse to do

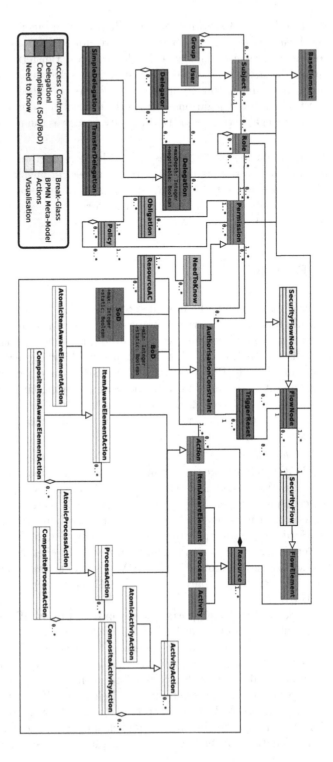

Fig. 2. The SecureBPMN metamodel (simplified) and its connection to the BPMN metamodel

a delegated task. If a delegation is not negotiable, it is an order and the delegatee has to do this task.

- *Permission-Level Separation and Binding of Duty:* SecureBPMN models separation of duty (SoD) and binding of duty (BoD) as a sub-type of AuthorizationConstraint. In contrast to existing works such as[18], which constrain all actions on a task or service, our approach results in a fine-grained notion of these properties on the level of single permissions. Moreover, SecureBPMN generalises the usually binary SoD and BoD constraints to n-ary constraints: an SoD constraints models, that a Subject is not allowed to "use" more than max permissions out of n (max $< n$); BoD is generalised similarly. If a SoD (BoD) constraint is already guaranteed by the RBAC configuration, it is called static SoD (BoD). Additionally, SecureBPMN supports history-resets (TriggerReset) for SoD (BoD) for processes with loops (similar to the work of Basin et al. [6]). Such resets allow to model that a SoD (BoD) constraint only needs to hold for the last (successful) execution of a loop and, thus, avoid the risk of successively "consuming" all subjects and, eventually, resulting in a dead lock.

- *Need-to-Know:* a strict application of the need-to-know principle (NeedTo Know) is another important security property. In the context of business process-driven systems, this mainly refers to restricting the access to process variables or data objects (instances of the BPMN meta-class ItemAwareElement) and, thus, the process model internal data-flow. To allow the fine-grained access to certain resources (e. g., access to the travel details is not allowed, if the travel takes longer than 14 days), we model the need to know principle as a specialised Permission that is associated with a specific authorisation constraint (ResourceAC).

- *Exceptional Access Control:* The strict enforcement of security and compliance requirements always bears the risk of hindering legitimate business transactions. Thus, an increasing number of enterprises implement break-glass or exceptional access control mechanisms that allow regular users to override access control decisions in a controlled manner, e. g., adhering to certain obligations (Obligation) that are either defined on the permission or policy level. SecureBPMN supports such a mechanism using a hierarchy of security policies (defined by the meta-class Policy) implementing the approach presented in [11].

Conceptually, the integration of the SecureBPMN metamodel into the metamodel of BPMN is straight forward: BPMN defines the resources and actions that are constrained by the SecureBPMN language. On a technical level, the need for diagrammatical representations of parts of the language as well as the fact that we can extend a metamodel only by subclassing (and not by introducing new superclasses) creates additional complexity:

- The SecureBPMN metamodel contains classes (SecurityFlowNode and SecurityFlow) that are not necessary for modelling security and compliance requirements. Their sole purpose is to provide a diagrammatic specification of certain requirements, e. g., SoD.

– Conceptually we would only like to specify a common hierarchy of actions, but technically this is impossible. To integrate SecureBPMN into BPMN, we need to define this hierarchy for each resource in BPMN (e. g., Activity) separately.

These parts of the metamodel (see Figure 2) are specific to BPMN and not part of the core of SecureBPMN.

5   Discussion and Future Work

We report a number of challenges and suggestions for future work that have emerged from discussions with product groups of SAP SE and our own experience in applying SecureBPMN in several case studies in the domains air traffic management (see Chapter 14) and e-government (see Chapter 15).

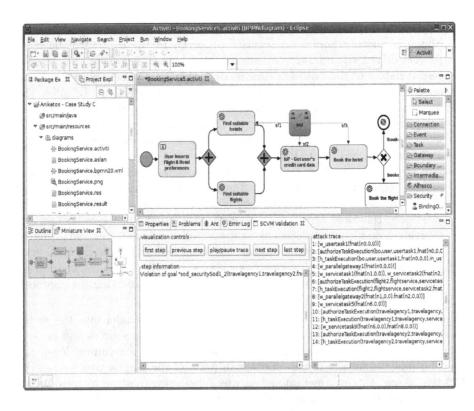

Fig. 3. Specifying security requirements diagrammatically with SecureBPMN as well as using specialised user interfaces

5.1   Security and Compliance Properties

The selection of security and compliance properties supported by SecureBPMN is based on discussion with various experts at SAP SE as well as our own applications to case studies (e. g., see Chapter 14 and Chapter 15). In our experience, these properties cover the most important needs of business experts and, moreover, they can be expressed on the process level. Of course, there is a plethora of equally important security requirements and mechanisms (e. g., encryption as one means for realising confidentially) that need to be considered as well. In particular the security mechanisms are usually on a technical level and, thus, need to be defined during the implementation of a secure service composition. Nevertheless, the integration of technical properties into compositions plans (or business process descriptions) is an interesting line of future work.

5.2   Visualising Security Properties

One important property of BPMN is its support for describing business processes in a diagrammatic way that supports both the business experts and the system experts. Consequently, when extending such a language with a domain specific language for modelling security and compliance properties, it is tempting to provide visual representations for those properties as well. Figure 3 shows the user interface of our SecureBPMN modelling environment (which is based on Activiti BPMN Platform) in which we implemented a visual notation for SoD and BoD constraints (centre of the window). Applying this to larger case studies resulted quickly in over-populated diagrams that neither helped the business expert nor the security expert. Thus, we refrained from this approach and implemented dedicated property panes (lower part of the window). While such dedicated user interfaces provide the necessary tools for power users (i. e., security experts), they are not the best choices for increasing the awareness of business experts for security and compliance requirements. Thus, we still consider the question of finding a good (visual) representation of security and compliance requirements that can be easily understood by business experts, system experts, and security experts to be open.

5.3   Diagrams vs. Models

Many users of diagrammatic modelling languages identify the models with their visual representation, e. g., the business process diagram. This misconception is, sadly, also perceptible in most business process modelling tools: these tools present the process diagram in the centre of their user interface (see Figure 3 for an example) and provide no access to the underlying model. We argue, that a model is something much more fundamental than a diagram, i. e., a diagram is only a selected view on the model. Thus, often several diagrams, each of them visualising different aspects of a model, are necessary to capture the actual model. While this need for different views (including, e. g., an abstract, tree-like view of all model elements and their properties) is already prevalent for modelling the functional aspects of a business process, it becomes inevitable when non-functional aspects such as security, compliance, or performance are added. Moreover, separating the model from its (visual) representation should also avoid the need for adding meta-classes purely for providing a visualisation (e. g., SecurityFlowNode and SecurityFlow in Figure 2).

5.4   Runtime Enforcement

While not the main scope of this chapter, we want to mention that modelling security and compliance requirements is only the beginning: these requirements need to be fulfilled at runtime, i. e., while executing the business processes in a business process execution engine. For example, in our prototype [13] we generate XACML [19] policies from the SecureBPMN models. An extended version of the Activiti BPMN runtime uses the generated XACML policies to enforce the access control, SoD/BoD, and the delegation requirements at runtime.

Within the Aniketos platform, we monitor compliance with various security and trustworthiness requirements using ConSpec [1], see Chapter 14 for details.

6   Conclusion and Related Work

We presented SecureBPMN, a security and compliance modelling language and its integration into BPMN. The integration of SecureBPMN, as a domain-specific language, into BPMN results in a modelling language that supports both security and compliance requirements as well as functional business requirements. Within the Aniketos platform, the security requirements are elicited using the socio-technical modelling language and tool (see Chapter 5, Chapter 6, and Chapter 7).

SecureBPMN is supported by a BPMN modelling and execution framework [10, 13] that builds the back-bone of the Aniketos Secure Composition Framework (see Chapter 9). This Framework, in addition to the modelling and secure execution of service composition plans, supports the analysis of the consistency and correctness of the implementation of security and compliance properties.

There is a large body of literature extending graphical modelling languages with means for specifying security or privacy requirements. One of the first approaches is SecureUML [17], which is conceptually very close to the access control part of our BPMN extension. SecureUML is a metamodel based extension of UML that allows for specifying RBAC-requirements for UML class models and state charts. There are also various techniques for analysing SecureUML models, e. g., Basin et al. [5] or Brucker et al. [12]. While based on the same motivation, UMLsec [16] is not defined using a metamodel. Instead, the security specifications are written, in an ad-hoc manner, in UML profiles. In contrast, integrating security properties into business processes is a quite recent development, e. g., motivated by the work of Wolter and Schaad [24]. In the same year, Rodríguez et al. [22] presented a metamodel based approach introduction a secure business process type supporting global security goals. In contrast, our approach allows the fine-grained specification of security requirements for single tasks or data objects. Similar to UMLsec, Mülle et al. [18] present an attribute-based approach (i. e., the conceptual equivalent of UML profiles) of specifying security constraints in BPMN models without actually extending BPMN. Similarly, Salnitri et al. [23] extend BPMN with means for specifying the security properties of RMIAS [14].

Besides the modelling of (rather technical) security and compliance requirements, integrating risk and attack models into business processes is an important line of research. For example, Altuhhova et al. [2] present an integration of the information security risk management model into BPMN. In what sense, such risk modelling and security requirement approaches can be combined, is still an open question. For example, one could try to use SecureBPMN for describing countermeasures for the risks and threats expressed in the information security risk management model.

References

[1] Aktug, I., Naliuka, K.: Conspec - a formal language for policy specification. Sci. Comput. Program. 74(1-2), 2–12 (2008), doi:10.1016/j.scico.2008.09.004

[2] Altuhhova, O., Matulevicius, R., Ahmed, N.: Towards definition of secure business processes. In: Bajec, M., Eder, J. (eds.) CAiSE Workshops. LNBIP, vol. 112, pp. 1–15. Springer, Heidelberg (2012)

[3] American National Standard for Information Technology – Role Based Access Control. ANSI, New York (February 2004) ANSI INCITS 359-2004

[4] Basel Committee on Banking Supervision. Basel III: A global regulatory framework for more resilient banks and banking systems. Technical report, Bank for International Settlements, Basel, Switzerland (2010)

[5] Basin, D., Clavel, M., Doser, J., Egea, M.: Automated analysis of security-design models. Information and Software Technology 51(5), 815–831 (2009), Special Issue on Model-Driven Development for Secure Information Systems, doi:10.1016/j.infsof.2008.05.011, ISSN 0950-5849

[6] Basin, D., Burri, S.J., Karjoth, G.: Separation of duties as a service. In: Proceedings of the 6th ACM Symposium on Information, Computer and Communications Security, ASIACCS 2011, pp. 423–429. ACM Press (2011), doi:10.1145/1966913.1966972, ISBN 978-1-4503-0564-8

[7] Basin, D.A., Doser, J., Lodderstedt, T.: Model driven security: From UML models to access control infrastructures. ACM Transactions on Software Engineering and Methodology 15(1), 39–91 (2006), doi:10.1145/1125808.1125810, ISSN 1049-331X.

[8] Brucker, A.D.: Integrating security aspects into business process models. it - Information Technology 55(6), 239–246 (2013), doi:10.1524/itit.2013.2004, ISSN 2196-7032

[9] Brucker, A.D., Doser, J.: Metamodel-based UML notations for domain-specific languages. In: Favre, J.M., Gasevic, D., Lämmel, R., Winter, A. (eds.) 4th International Workshop on Software Language Engineering, ATEM 2007 (October 2007)

[10] Brucker, A.D., Hang, I.: Secure and compliant implementation of business process-driven systems. In: Rosa, M.L., Soffer, P. (eds.) Data Base Design Techniques 1978. LNBIP, vol. 132, pp. 662–674. Springer, Heidelberg (1982)

[11] Brucker, A.D., Petritsch, H.: Extending access control models with break-glass. In: Carminati, B., Joshi, J. (eds.) ACM SACMAT, pp. 197–206. ACM Press (2009), doi:10.1145/1542207.1542239, ISBN 978-1-60558-537-6

[12] Brucker, A.D., Doser, J., Wolff, B.: A model transformation semantics and analysis methodology for secureUML. In: Wang, J., Whittle, J., Harel, D., Reggio, G. (eds.) MoDELS 2006. LNCS, vol. 4199, pp. 306–320. Springer, Heidelberg (2006), An extended version of this paper is available as ETH Technical Report, no. 524

[13] Brucker, A.D., Hang, I., Lückemeyer, G., Ruparel, R.: SecureBPMN: Modeling and enforcing access control requirements in business processes. In: ACM SACMAT, pp. 123–126. ACM Press (2012), doi:10.1145/2295136.2295160, ISBN 978-1-4503-1295-0

[14] Cherdantseva, Y., Hilton, J.: A reference model of information assurance amp;amp; security. In: 2013 Eighth International Conference on Availability, Reliability and Security (ARES), pp. 546–555 (September 2013), doi:10.1109/ARES.2013.72

[15] HIPAA. Health Insurance Portability and Accountability Act of 1996 (1996), http://www.cms.hhs.gov/HIPAAGenInfo/

[16] Jürjens, J., Rumm, R.: Model-based security analysis of the german health card architecture. Methods Inf. Med. 47(5), 26–1270 (2008) ISSN 0026-1270

[17] Lodderstedt, T., Basin, D., Doser, J.: SecureUML: A UML-based modeling language for model-driven security. In: Jézéquel, J.-M., Hussmann, H., Cook, S. (eds.) UML 2002. LNCS, vol. 2460, pp. 426–540. Springer, Heidelberg (2002)

[18] Mülle, J., von Stackelberg, S., Böhm, K.: A security language for BPMN process models. Technical report, University Karlsruhe, KIT (2011), http://digbib.ubka.uni-karlsruhe.de/volltexte/1000023041

[19] OASIS. eXtensible Access Control Markup Language (XACML), version 2.0 (2005a), http://docs.oasis-open.org/xacml/2.0/XACML-2.0-OS-NORMATIVE.zip

[20] OASIS. Web services business process execution language (BPEL), version 2.0 (April 2007), urlhttp://docs.oasis-open.org/wsbpel/2.0/wsbpel-v2.0.pdf.

[21] Object Management Group. Business process model and notation (BPMN), version 2.0 (January 2011), Available as OMG document formal/2011-01-03

[22] Rodríguez, A., Fernández-Medina, E., Piattini, M.: A BPMN extension for the modeling of security requirements in business processes. IEICE - Trans. Inf. Syst. E90-D, 745–752 (2007), doi:10.1093/ietisy/e90-d.4.745, ISSN 0916-8532

[23] Salnitri, M., Dalpiaz, F., Giorgini, P.: Modeling and verifying security policies in business processes. In: Bider, I., Gaaloul, K., Krogstie, J., Nurcan, S., Proper, H.A., Schmidt, R., Soffer, P. (eds.) BMMDS/EMMSAD. LNBIP, vol. 175, pp. 200–214. Springer, Heidelberg (2014)

[24] Wolter, C., Schaad, A.: Modeling of task-based authorization constraints in BPMN. In: Alonso, G., Dadam, P., Rosemann, M. (eds.) BPM 2007. LNCS, vol. 4714, pp. 64–79. Springer, Heidelberg (2007)

The Aniketos Service Composition Framework
Analysing and Ranking of Secure Services

Achim D. Brucker[1], Francesco Malmignati[2], Madjid Merabti[3], Qi Shi[3],
and Bo Zhou[3]

[1] SAP SE, Vincenz-Priessnitz-Str. 1, 76131 Karlsruhe, Germany
achim.brucker@sap.com
[2] Selex ES S.p.A, A Finmeccanica Company, Italy
francesco.malmignati@guests.selex-es.com
[3] Liverpool John Moores University, Liverpool, United Kingdom
{m.merabti,q.shi,b.zhou}@ljmu.ac.uk

Abstract. Modern applications are inherently heterogeneous: they are
built by composing loosely coupled services that are, usually, offered and
operated by different service providers. While this approach increases the
flexibility of the composed applications, it makes the implementation of
security and trustworthiness requirements much more difficult. Therefore
there is a need for new approaches that integrate security requirements
right from the beginning while composing service-based applications, in
order to ensure security and trustworthiness.

In this chapter, we present a framework for secure service composition using a model-based approach for specifying, building, and executing
composed services. As a unique feature, this framework integrates security requirements as a first class citizen and, thus, avoids the "security
as an afterthought" paradigm.

Keywords: secure service composition, BPMN, service modelling, service availability.

1 Introduction

A service-oriented architecture (SOA) provides a platform for services developed by different providers to work together [23]. Facilitated by standardised
inter-operation and description languages, such as WSDL [10], services can be
composed to form a larger application based on users' requirements.

The focus of research in SOA was traditionally on the realisation of service
composition in terms of how to construct the services so that they can work
together seamlessly. With the continuous development of SOA, it has been realised lately that the security issue has become a barrier that hinders wider
application of SOA. Apart from the conventional security problems faced by
other systems, e. g., confidentiality, integrity, privacy and so on, the situation in
SOA is more complicated given the fact that the services are developed by different providers. Concerns over inconsistent security policies and configurations
must be addressed as top priority.

A.D. Brucker et al. (Eds.): Secure Service Composition, LNCS 8900, pp. 121–135, 2014.

We propose a *secure* and *trustworthy* service composition framework that supports the service developer with the capability of composing services with security requirements in mind. The services are modelled and composed using a toolchain supporting the Business Process Model and Notation (BPMN) [19]. A service developer first constructs a BPMN service composition plan based on his/her functional requirements. It specifies what are the tasks needed and how these tasks interact with each other. We extend the BPMN notations so that certain security requirements can be specified within the BPMN composition plan as well. After searching for suitable services in an open marketplace, the abstract BPMN composition plan will be associated with concrete services for each task in the plan. The service composition is verified and guaranteed to comply with the service developer's security requirements before deployment.

Unlike other SOA solutions, our framework takes the security requirements into account during the service composition process. A service developer can specify his/her security needs directly in the extended BPMN composition plan so only those services that satisfy the security requirements will be selected. In addition, the service developer is given the flexibility to set priorities that will be used to quantify and compare service compositions, from all three aspects of security, quality of service, and cost. This is particularly useful when the service developer faces a wide range of choices.

2   The Aniketos Secure Service Composition Framework

Building secure and trustworthy composite services on top of a SOA is a challenging task. At *design-time* the service developer needs to select the optimal set of services that satisfies both the functional and security requirements put by the end user. At *runtime*, a service may become unavailable due to various reasons and has to be replaced automatically with alternative services that, at least, offer the same security and trust guarantees. In addition, the service developer also needs to decide if a given security property should be enforced statically or dynamically. One the one hand, a static enforcement creates less overhead at runtime, it reduces the flexibility of service substitution or re-composition. On the other hand, a dynamic enforcement is usually more flexible but requires more system resources at runtime. Thus, a service designer needs to balance the system resources while fulfilling the security and compliance requirements.

To support the service developer in building flexible, secure, and trustworthy services through composition, we propose a *secure service composition framework* that addresses both the design-time and runtime service compositions. In this chapter we focus only on the technical parts of the design-time process, i.e., we exclude the requirements elicitation, as well as the service deployment and runtime adaptation parts.

Figure 1 gives an high-level overview of the *Aniketos Service Composition Framework* which is the design-time modelling and analysis part of the Aniketos platform [4]. At the beginning, domain experts together with requirement engineers specify the high-level business process as well as the security and trust

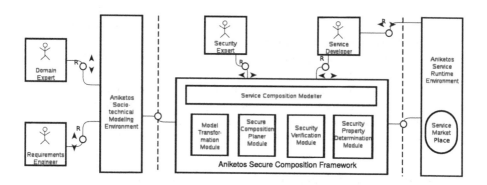

Fig. 1. The Aniketos Service Composition Framework

requirements by using the *Aniketos Socio-technical Modelling Tool* [20]. It provides the opportunity to express security needs not just from technical, but also from social aspects. From these semi-formal descriptions, the *model transformation module* helps to generate composition plans, which are presented in BPMN format. These composition plans are coarse-grained. Thus, before these composition plans can be deployed in the *Aniketos Service Runtime Environment*, they will be refined by a service developer using the *Aniketos Secure Composition Framework*.

The *Aniketos Service Composition Framework* provides an Eclipse-based environment (the *Service Composition Modeller*) to the service developer for refining the composition plans as well as checking their security and trust properties. Specifically, the service developer can use the following component modules:

– *Model Transformation Module:* As described above, this module helps to generate the basic elements of the composition plan from the requirement document that expressed in the Aniketos Socio-technical Modelling Language [20] (see Chapter 5, Chapter 6, and Chapter 7).
– *Secure Composition Planer Module:* This module allows the service developer semi-automatically select the secure services for a given composition plan (see Section 4 for more details). To check the compositions comply with the security requirements, this module uses the Security Verification Module as well as the Security Property Determination Module.
– *Security Verification Module:* This module provides formal validation and verification solutions for composed services (and, not discussed in this chapter, atomic services [9]). For example, role-based access control and separation of duty properties (see Section 3 for details) are verified by the Security Verification Module (see Chapter 8 and Chapter 10).
– *Security Property Determination Module:* This module provides an uniform interface for accessing security properties of services. Moreover, this module stores the verification status of security properties to avoid an unnecessary (expensive) re-verification.

- *Service Marketplace:* This component registers and stores the services for open access. Secure Composition Planner Module selects services from the Service Marketplace (see Chapter 4).

The *Aniketos Service Composition Framework* supports composition of services, as well as the transformation from social to technical modelling of security requirements. It provides formal verification of these security requirements and helps the end user to choose the most suitable services. In the next two sections, we will focus on the two key research challenges: 1) Analysing the consistency of security properties and 2) quantifying and ranking service compositions.

3   Modelling and Verifying Security Properties

In this section, we present a validation approach for fine-grained separation-of-duty and binding-of-duty constraints. This work is implemented as core technique for the security verification module mentioned in Section 2 and assumes composition plans as discussed in Chapter 8.

3.1   Analysing SecureBPMN Models

Modelling non-functional requirements, right from the beginning, is important but it can only be the first step in building secure and trustworthy service-oriented systems, which requires various analysis techniques, e.g., for

1. checking the *internal consistency* of the security specification, for example ensure the access control requirements and need-to-know requirements do not contradict each other.
2. checking the *information (data) flow* on the process level to examine information flow requirements as well as high-level need-to-know requirements.
3. checking that process-level security requirements are fulfilled on the *implementation and configuration level.* This is particular important for implementation and configuration artifacts that are not generated in a model-driven approach.
4. checking that the service compositions (business processes) are *executable* if the security requirements are enforced, i.e., there exists a valid execution trace from a start to an end event.
5. analysing and *comparing* different techniques (e.g., resulting in different costs or runtime resource requirements) for implementing security requirements.

In this section, we discuss, as an example, an analysis method for checking the consistency between role-based access control (RBAC) and separation of duty (SoD)/binding of duty (BoD) specifications (see Chapter 10). This analysis method contributes to both the item 1 and item 5 mentioned above. Our modular architecture allows to integrate other analysis approaches easily and our prototypes already support other analysis as well. For example, [9] presents an analysis that contributes to the item 3.

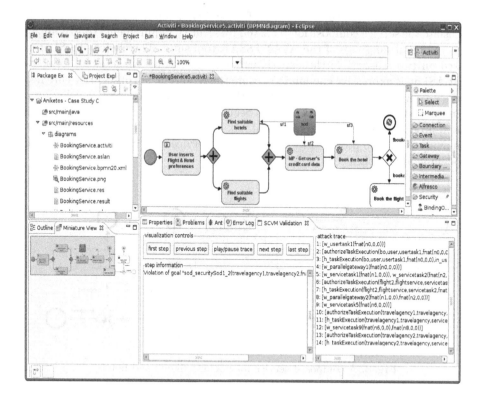

Fig. 2. Security Validation within the Activiti BPMN Editor

Adding constraints such as SoD or BoD to a system that is already restricted by RBAC results in questions like the following: "Is the SoD constraint already guaranteed by the RBAC configuration?" If an RBAC configuration ensures a SoD constraint, e.g., as two tasks are only executable by different roles r_1, r_2 and there is no user u_i that is assigned to both roles r_1 and r_2, we call this a *static separation of duty*. Otherwise, we call it a *dynamic separation of duty*.

While static separation of duty constraint do not need to be enforced at runtime and, thus, reduce the runtime costs, it requires to re-check the SoD constraint after each and every modification of the RBAC configuration (e.g., adding new roles, changing the role assignment of subjects). In contrast, dynamic separation of duty constraint requires a runtime check for each access to a resource that is constrained by the separation of duty. Although dynamic SoD is more flexible, it requires additional resources and, thus, costs, at runtime. Moreover, additional security checks might result in delays for users and, thus, might reduce the overall usability of the system.

To address these issues, we use an analysis method inspired by the work of Arsac et al. [5]. We extended their work significantly to support n-ary SoD (BoD) constraints as well as constraints on the level of constrained permission (instead the task-level). As Arsac et al. [5], we use the AVANTSSAR tool suite (www.avantssar.eu) as back-end for our formal analysis. Consequently, we translate the service composition plan and its security requirements to ASLan [5], i. e., the input language of the AVANTSSAR tool suite. The choice of ASLan is based on two reasons: 1) the experiments carried out by Arsac et al. [5] show that ASLan is expressive enough to capture the requirements of security enriched service compositions and 2) the use of the same tools allows for developing a common verification back-end for our SecureBPMN-based approach as well as the approach developed by Arsac et al. [5]. In fact, we could demonstrate that the analysis can be provided as a cloud-based service that can be used by both modelling approaches [11].

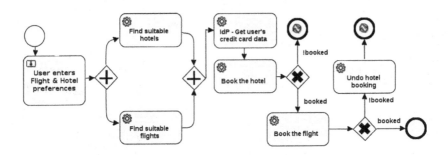

Fig. 3. A composed service for booking flights and hotels

Assume, in our example from Chapter 8 (see Figure 3), we want to counterfeit fraud or price-fixing agreements. Therefore, we require that the services Find suitable flights and Book the flight are operated by different provides (and similarly, for the hotel booking). The actual RBAC configuration is inferred automatically from the information available in the service marketplace (i. e., the service-level agreements).

Our formal analysis translates the security configuration (here, RBAC and SoD/BoD) as well as the security properties that should be verified into the formal language ASLan [5]. In our example, the result of this translation (only an excerpt) for the security configuration looks like the following:

```
hc rbac_ac(Subject, Role, Task)
        := CanDoAction(Subject, Role, Task)
        :- user_to_role(Subject, Role), poto(Role, Task)
hc poto_T6 := poto(TravelAgency1, Find suitable flights)
hc poto_T7 := poto(TravelAgency1, Book the flight)
```

The security goal, in this case a SoD constraint between the services Find suitable flights and Book the flight looks as below:

```
attack_state sod_securitySod1_1(Subject0,Subject1,
                        Instance1,Instance2)
:= executed(Subject0,task(Find suitable flights,Instance1)).
    executed(Subject1,task(Book the flight;Instance2))
    &not(equal(Subject0,Subject1))
```

This configuration, obviously, violates the SoD constraint as the TravelAgency1 can do both searching for flights and booking them. In this case, a dishonest travel agency could prefer flights with a higher bonus for the travel agency that are not necessarily the cheapest for the traveller. This is detected by our formal analysis, e. g., the verification module returns the following "attack trace:"

```
1. [w_usertask1(fnat(n0,0,0))]
2. [authorizeTaskExecution(bo,user,usertask1,fnat(n0,0,0))]
3. [h_taskExecution(bo,user,usertask1,fnat(n0,0,0),
                            in_usertask1,out_usertask1)]
4. [w_parallelgateway1(fnat(n0,0,0))]
5. [w_servicetask1(fnat(n1,0,0)),
                    w_servicetask2(fnat(n2,0,0))]
6. [authorizeTaskExecution(flight1,flightservice,
                            servicetask2,fnat(n2,0,0)),
     authorizeTaskExecution(travelagency1,travelagency,
                            servicetask1,fnat(n1,0,0))]


                        . . .


15. h_taskExecution(travelagency1, travelagency,
                    servicetask9,fnat(n8,0,0),
                    in_servicetask9,out_servicetask9)
```

Of course, this textual representation is not well-suited to practitioners. Therefore, we developed a user-friendly visualisation of such an attack in terms of the high-level composition plan (i. e., on the level of the BPMN model). Figure 2 shows how our prototype visualises such a violation to the service developer. Here, the service developer is able to manually step through all necessary actions that a dishonest agency would execute to actually violate the SoD constraint.

After such an analysis, the service developer needs to decide how to mitigate this risk. In general, there are several options, among them

- re-design the composition plan, to avoid the need for a particular separation of duty constraint,
- instruct the service composition framework to ensure the selection of different service providers, or
- enforce a dynamic separation of duty at runtime. For this, our prototype can generate configurations for XACML [18] based access control infrastructures.

Certainly, the concrete mitigation plan depends on the actual use case.

4   Quantifying and Ranking Service Compositions

The security property modelling and verification techniques allow the service consumer specify certain security properties that the service composition has to comply with. In practice, the number of compositions that satisfy the security requirements could still be large. Therefore another dilemma always faced by the service consumer is to make a choice from the service composition pools.

In this section, we introduce the mechanism used in Aniketos platform for quantifying and ranking service compositions, i. e., we support the service consumer in choosing, based on an automated recommendation, the most suitable service composition. This recommendation should be made based on the property of the composition as a whole, rather than just based on individual sub-services in the composition. As a starting point, we try to solve this issue from three aspects, which are the three factors that mostly considered by service consumers: encryption (security), availability (QoS), and cost (business).

In most of the cases web services are made available together with a service-level agreement (SLA). SLA is a formal guarantee that has to be accepted by service consumers before the service being used. SLA normally specifies the properties of a service across different level. For example, on business level it describes what kind of functionality the service offers and how the users will be charged (cost); on technical level it may describe what kind of security protection is deployed (e. g., encryption) and the number of shutdowns the service might encounter each year (availability). We focus on these three properties in this section not only because they are normally included in the SLA, it is also because they are the properties that verifiable at runtime. For example, the availability of service can be easily recorded and calculated by examining the logs stored in the system.

This work is implemented as key part for the security composition planner module mentioned in Section 2.

4.1   Encryption – The Weakest Link

There are some cases when the weakest link principle is particularly applicable to service composition. It states that when services are composed together, the security capability of the composite service is equal to what the weakest service or link is offering. This security principle is applicable to many security properties and *encryption* is one of them. When encryption is applied to communications between services, the services may adopt different encryption algorithms or key lengths which give them different encryption strength. In order to communicate with each other, the service with advanced encryption algorithm may have to degrade its encryption strength during the composition. Thus the composite services literally use the weakest encryption strategy in part of their communications. For example, consider the case in Figure 4 where service A supports encryption algorithms of Blowfish and 3DES, service B supports Blowfish and AES, and service C supports 3DES and AES. To communicate with each other, the link between service A and B is encrypted with Blowfish and the link between B and C is encrypted with AES. Therefore the overall strength of the composition, in terms of keeping communications confidential, is the weaker one between Blowfish and AES.

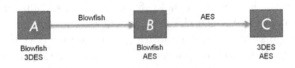

Fig. 4. Set Ranking Criteria

In Aniketos, the weakest link principle is used to determine the security capacity of the composite services. It should be noted however, that the weakest link principle is not universally applicable. There are cases where alterations to a service composition can be utilised to improve the security of a composite service to be greater than that of the weakest component. An example might be where a firewall service is used to shield an otherwise vulnerable service from outside attack. The use of the firewall mitigates the vulnerability exposed by the weaker service. And vice versa it may also apply in reverse: the introduction of a component may serve as an exacerbating factor that reduces the security of the overall composition to a degree beyond that posed by the service were it to act in isolation. This often results from interactions between incompatible security properties.

To simplify the issue, in this study we focus on the encryption. Therefore each link between services is checked, and the encryption strength of the composition is determined by the weakest link, i. e.,

$$E = \min_{i=1}^{n} E_i$$

where E is the encryption strength of the composition and E_i is the encryption strength for each link i in the composition. E_i is determined by the strongest algorithm, which supported by both services at each end of the link i.

The quantitative value (from 0.9 to 0 in our case), however is predetermined by expertise in advance based on Table 1. Please note that as claimed in [14], the quantitatively ranking of encryption algorithms is possible but heavily depends on the metrics and target scenario. Table 1 is just a guideline and rather used to demonstrate our ideas in this front.

Table 1. Quantitative Value of Encryption Algorithms

Algorithm Name	Quantitative Value
Serpent	0.9
AES (Rijndael)	0.8
3DES	0.7
CAST128/256	0.6
Twofish	0.5
Blowfish	0.4
MARSH	0.3
Other algorithms	0.2
Codings	0.1
Plain text	0

4.2 Availability

Availability is another aspect being used to compare services. It relates to the quality of services (QoS). Availability in this scenario means the available time ratio of a service. Unexpected shutdown of a service could cause severe damage to service consumers' business and service developer's reputation. Therefore seeking guarantee from service developer about the service availability is one of the top priories for service consumers, before they commit to use the service. The situation gets complicated in service composition because a composition's availability is decided by not only the technical specifications of the sub-services, but also by the structure of the composition.

Take the example of the travel agency in Figure 3 on page 126, most of the services are placed in sequential order. That means if one of the sub-service is not available, the entire composition will stop. Therefore the availability of sequential tasks is the product of all the sub-services' availability value in percentage. However, the services Find suitable hotels and Find suitable flights are executed in parallel. It means these two services can be carried out separately. Nonetheless they still have to be both finished before the next task Get user's credit card data can be executed. Therefore for parallel tasks the availability value is the minimum among them. For services that are exclusive to each other, the availability of the composition depends on which service has been eventually used.

Table 2 shows the rules that we used for calculating the availability of composite services. In this study we assume that the services are independent from each other. If in Figure 3 each service has the following availability value: Find suitable hotels: 0.99, Find suitable flights: 0.96, Get user's credit card data: 0.97, Book the hotel: 0.99, Book the flight: 0.98, and Undo hotel booking: 0.94. The *availability* value for a successful transaction will be calculated as:

$$A = \min(0.99, 0.96) \times 0.97 \times 0.99 \times 0.98 = 0.90$$

where A represents availability of the composition.

Table 2. Rules to Calculate Availability

	Description	Calculation
O—O	Sequence	$\prod_{i=1}^{n} A_i$
✦	Parallel	$\min(A_1, \ldots, A_n)$
✖	Exclusive	A_i

4.3 Cost

Finally the last factor that also plays important role in consumer's decision making is the *cost*. Higher security and quality of service normally means higher price, which must be within a consumer's budget. Comparing to *encryption* and *availability*, calculating the *cost* of a service composition is more straightforward. When discount is not considered, it is simply the sum of all the sub-services' costs, i. e.:

$$C = \sum_{i=1}^{n} C_i$$

where C is the cost for the composition and C_i is the cost for sub-service i.

4.4 Ranking Compositions

In Aniketos we implemented a simple user interface providing prioritising options so the service consumers can specify the criteria that they want to use to rank secure service compositions. As shown in Figure 5, the service consumer basically

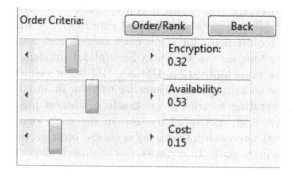

Fig. 5. Set Ranking Criteria

can choose how much weights he wants to put on each criterion of encryption, availability, and cost. Assume the consumer sets the weights to 0.32, 0.53 and 0.15 respectively for availability and cost, the overall value V for each service composition will be:

$$V = 0.32 \times E + 0.53 \times A + 0.15 \times \frac{B - C}{B}$$

where E represents the value of encryption strength, A represents the value of availability, C represents cost, and B represents the consumer's budget. Apparently higher value of E and A, and lower value of C will result in greater value of V. In this way the generated service compositions can not only be security-wise verified by our SecureBPMN extensions, but also ranked easily based on consumer's other priorities.

The Aniketos platform targets secure service composition at both design-time and runtime. Therefore the prioritising options set by consumer at design-time will be stored in the consumer's policy configurations and referred back at runtime. So the ranking mechanism will still work on behalf of the consumer at runtime, in case the service composition changes.

Please note that the ranking is for service compositions that already satisfy users' requirements, i. e., the service compositions ranked here should have acceptable values in E, A and C first. This can be easily enforced by put threshold values for each of the criteria.

5   Conclusion and Related Work

5.1   Related Work

We see three areas of related work: 1. modelling of security requirements for process models, 2. analysing security properties of process models, and 3. determining security of composite services.

There is a large body of literature extending graphical modelling languages with means for specifying security or privacy requirements. One of the first approaches is SecureUML [16], which is conceptually very close to our BPMN extension. SecureUML is a meta-model-based extension of UML that allows for specifying RBAC-requirements for UML class models and state charts. There are also various techniques for analysing SecureUML models, e. g., [6] or [8]. While based on the same motivation, UMLsec [15] is not defined using a meta-model. Instead, the security specifications are written, in an ad-hoc manner, in UML profiles. Integrating security properties into business processes is a quite recent development, e. g., motivated by [25]. In the same year, [21] presented a meta-model based approach introducing a secure business process type that supports global security goals. In contrast, our approach allows the fine-grained specification of security requirements for single tasks or data objects. Similar to UMLsec, [17] presented an attribute-based approach (i. e., the conceptual equivalent of UML profiles) of specifying security constraints in BPMN models without actually extending BPMN.

With respect to the validation of security requirements on the business process level, the closed related work is the work of [24] and [5] that both support the checking if an access control specification enforces binary static of duty and binding of duty constraints. Apart from security properties, there is also a strong need for checking the consistency of business process itself, e. g., the absence of deadlocks. There are several works that concentrate on this kind of process internal consistency validation, e. g., [12] and [2]. Moreover, there are several approaches for analysing access control constraints over UML models, e. g., [22], [8], and [15]. These approaches are limited to simple access control models, as the UML models are usually quite distant from business process descriptions that comprising high level security and compliance goals.

Last but not least, determining the properties of composite service based on its sub-services is another area that attracts attentions from research community. Most of the work related to security focus on determining trust due to its subjectiveness and openness. This undermines the need for solutions to determine other properties as well. [13] described how to present trustworthiness for composite services based on various factors such as reputations and qualities of the services. The method took the structure of the composition into account.

[28] proposed a classification method that abstracts and quantifies service compositions based on five key security aspects: confidentiality, integrity, availability, accountability and non-repudiation. There are also other works that focus on security properties of system-of-systems such as [27] and [26]. Comparing to these works, our approach concentrates on the most objective and justifiable properties in encryption, availability and cost, which represents security, QoS and business respectively. Our solution also gives the flexibility to the service consumers so they can decide how to rank the service compositions themselves.

5.2   Lessons Learned

We discussed our approach with various business process modelling experts at SAP SE. Overall, these experiences show that our approach is applicable to a wide range of applications domains.

Our evaluation showed that the discussed security and compliance requirements can be expressed at the business process level. Moreover, they are sufficient for most modelling needs. Still, in particular our telecommunication case study raised the need for various notions of confidentiality. As such, confidentiality is not (yet) supported by SecureBPMN; currently, SecureBPMN only supports a very specific form, the need-to-know-principle. Confidentiality, in terms of requiring encrypted communications between the different services (tasks) is another important requirement. The choice of the correct encryption technology (in fact, on a technical level, we need to ensure that data is only communicated over authenticated and secured channels) requires a multitude of technical decisions (e. g., encryption algorithms, length of cryptographic keys). As these are merely technical decisions, we can only record the high-level requirement on the process level and need to refine them interactively during the implementation of a secure service composition.

Moreover, our evaluation showed that in practice, most service compositions are rather small (e. g., less than 15 services or tasks). On these sizes of models, our formal analysis usually is able to validate security or compliance properties within less then 20 seconds. While this is fast enough for the (interactive) design of service compositions, it is too slow for automatic service re-compositions at runtime. Therefore, the efficient caching, which needs to ensure the authenticity and validity, of validation results is of outermost importance.

5.3   Conclusion and Future Work

In this chapter we presented an integrated framework for modelling, analysing, and ensuring secure service compositions. This framework, called *Aniketos Service Composition Framework* is part of a larger platform that supports the end-to-end (i. e., ranging from the requirements elicitation to the actual operation of the developed system) development of secure and trustworthy SOA and cloud-based systems. This end-to-end integration is a unique feature of our approach that not only enables traditional security and consistency analysis on the model and implementation level, it also supports certain types of economical analysis approaches that allow the service consumers to decide between different security solutions based on their encryption strengths, availabilities and costs.

There are several lines of future work. One of them is the development of support for system audits, e. g., by integrating analysis techniques such as [1] or [3]. In particular, process mining approaches appear to be particularly interesting: combining process mining with our business process animation, i. e., the visualisation of attack traces, allows interactive investigation of the deviations of the actual service composition execution with the intended one. Moreover, we are also interested in the integration analysis techniques that check the internal consistency of processes, e. g., [12], as well as their reconfiguration, e. g., [2]. Finally, we intend to integrate security testing approaches, e. g., [7], for validating the compliance of services and (legacy) back-end systems in a black-box scenario.

References

[1] van der Aalst, W., de Medeiros, A.: Process mining and security: Detecting anomalous process executions and checking process conformance. ENTCS 121, 3–21 (2005)

[2] van der Aalst, W.M.P., Dumas, M., Gottschalk, F., ter Hofstede, A.H.M., La Rosa, M., Mendling, J.: Correctness-preserving configuration of business process models. In: Fiadeiro, J.L., Inverardi, P. (eds.) FASE 2008. LNCS, vol. 4961, pp. 46–61. Springer, Heidelberg (2008)

[3] Accorsi, R., Wonnemann, C.: inDico: Information flow analysis of business processes for confidentiality requirements. In: Cuellar, J., Lopez, J., Barthe, G., Pretschner, A. (eds.) STM 2010. LNCS, vol. 6710, pp. 194–209. Springer, Heidelberg (2011)

[4] Aniketos: Deliverable 5.1: Aniketos platform design and platform basis implementation (2011)

[5] Arsac, W., Compagna, L., Pellegrino, G., Ponta, S.E.: Security validation of business processes via model-checking. In: Erlingsson, Ú., Wieringa, R., Zannone, N. (eds.) ESSoS 2011. LNCS, vol. 6542, pp. 29–42. Springer, Heidelberg (2011)

[6] Basin, D., Clavel, M., Doser, J., Egea, M.: Automated analysis of security-design models. Information and Software Technology 51(5), 815–831 (2009)

[7] Brucker, A.D., Brügger, L., Kearney, P., Wolff, B.: An approach to modular and testable security models of real-world health-care applications. In: SACMAT, pp. 133–142. ACM Press (2011)

[8] Brucker, A.D., Doser, J., Wolff, B.: A model transformation semantics and analysis methodology for secureUML. In: Wang, J., Whittle, J., Harel, D., Reggio, G. (eds.) MoDELS 2006. LNCS, vol. 4199, pp. 306–320. Springer, Heidelberg (2006)

[9] Brucker, A.D., Hang, I.: Secure and compliant implementation of business process-driven systems. In: Rosa, M.L., Soffer, P. (eds.) Joint Workshop on Security in Business Processes (SBP). LNBIP, vol. 132, pp. 662–674. Springer, Heidelberg (1982)

[10] Christensen, E., Curbera, F., Meredith, G., Weerawarana, S.: Web services description language (WSDL) 1.1. Tech. rep., W3C (2001)

[11] Compagna, L., Guilleminot, P., Brucker, A.D.: Business process compliance via security validation as a service. In: Oriol, M., Penix, J. (eds.) Testing Tools Track of ICST. IEEE Computer Society (2013)

[12] Dijkman, R.M., Dumas, M., Ouyang, C.: Semantics and analysis of business process models in BPMN. Information & Software Technology 50(12), 1281–1294 (2008)

[13] Elshaafi, H., McGibney, J., Botvich, D.: Trustworthiness monitoring and prediction of composite services. In: ISCC, pp. 580–587 (2012)

[14] Jorstad, N., Landgrave, T.S.: Cryptographic algorithm metrics. In: 20th National Information Systems Security Conference (1997)

[15] Jürjens, J., Rumm, R.: Model-based security analysis of the german health card architecture. Methods Inf Med 47(5), 409–416 (2008)

[16] Lodderstedt, T., Basin, D., Doser, J.: SecureUML: A UML-based modeling language for model-driven security. In: Jézéquel, J.-M., Hussmann, H., Cook, S. (eds.) UML 2002. LNCS, vol. 2460, pp. 426–441. Springer, Heidelberg (2002)

[17] Mülle, J., von Stackelberg, S., Böhm, K.: A security language for BPMN process models. Tech. rep., University Karlsruhe, KIT (2011)

[18] OASIS: eXtensible Access Control Markup Language (XACML), version 2.0 (2005), http://docs.oasis-open.org/xacml/2.0/XACML-2.0-OS-NORMATIVE.zip

[19] Object Management Group: Business process model and notation BPMN, version 2.0 (2011), Available as OMG document formal/2011-01-03

[20] Paja, E., Dalpiaz, F., Poggianella, M., Roberti, P., Giorgini, P.: Modelling security requirements in socio-technical systems with sts-tool. In: Kirikova, M., Stirna, J. (eds.) CAiSE Forum, vol. 855, pp. 155–162 (2012)

[21] Rodríguez, A., Fernández-Medina, E., Piattini, M.: A BPMN extension for the modeling of security requirements in business processes. IEICE - Trans. Inf. Syst. E90-D, 745–752 (2007)

[22] Sohr, K., Ahn, G.-J., Gogolla, M., Migge, L.: Specification and validation of authorisation constraints using UML and OCL. In: di Vimercati, S.d.C., Syverson, P.F., Gollmann, D. (eds.) ESORICS 2005. LNCS, vol. 3679, pp. 64–79. Springer, Heidelberg (2005)

[23] Welke, R., Hirschheim, R., Schwarz, A.: Service-oriented architecture maturity. Computer 15(1), 662–674 (2011)

[24] Wolter, C., Meinel, C.: An approach to capture authorisation requirements in business processes. Requir. Eng. 15(4), 359–373 (2010)

[25] Wolter, C., Schaad, A.: Modeling of task-based authorization constraints in BPMN. In: Alonso, G., Dadam, P., Rosemann, M. (eds.) BPM 2007. LNCS, vol. 4714, pp. 64–79. Springer, Heidelberg (2007)

[26] Zhou, B., Arabo, A., Drew, O., Llewellyn-Jones, D., Merabti, M., Shi, Q., Waller, A., Craddock, R., Jones, G., Arnold, K.L.Y.: Data flow security analysis for system-of-systems in a public security incident. In: ACSF, pp. 8–14 (2008)

[27] Zhou, B., Drew, O., Arabo, A., Llewellyn-Jones, D., Kifayat, K., Merabti, M., Shi, Q., Craddock, R., Waller, A., Jones, G.: System-of-systems boundary check in a public event scenario. In: SoSE (2010)

[28] Zhou, B., Llewellyn-Jones, D., Shi, Q., Asim, M., Merabti, M., Lamb, D.: Secure service composition adaptation based on simulated annealing. In: ACSAC, pp. 49–55 (2012)

Compliance Validation
of Secure Service Compositions

Achim D. Brucker[1], Luca Compagna[2], and Pierre Guilleminot[2]

[1] SAP SE, Vincenz-Priessnitz-Str. 1, 76131 Karlsruhe, Germany
achim.brucker@sap.com
[2] SAP SE, Sophia-Antipolis, Mougins, France
luca.compagna@sap.com

Abstract. The Aniketos Secure Composition Framework supports the specification of secure and trustworthy composition plans in term of BPMN. The diversity of security and trust properties that is supported by the Aniketos framework allows, on the one hand, for expressing a large number of security and compliance requirements. On the other hand, the resulting expressiveness results in the risk that high-level compliance requirements (e. g., separation of duty) are not implemented by low-level security means (e. g., role-based access control configurations).

In this chapter, we present the Composition Security Validation Module (CSVM). The CSVM provides a service for checking the compliance of secure and trustworthy composition plans to the service designer. As proof-of-concept we created a prototype in which the CSVM module is deployed on the SAP NetWeaver Cloud and two CSVM Connectors are built supporting two well-known BPMN tools: SAP NetWeaver BPM and Activiti Designer.

Keywords: Validation, Security, BPMN, SecureBPMN, Compliance.

1 Introduction

The Aniketos Secure Composition Framework (see Chapter 4 and Chapter 9) supports the specification of secure and trustworthy composition plans in term of BPMN (see Chapter 8). The diversity of security and trust properties that is supported by the Aniketos Secure Composition Framework allows, on the one hand, for expressing a large number of security and compliance requirements. On the other hand, the resulting expressiveness results in the risk that high-level compliance requirements (e. g., separation of duty) are not implemented by low-level security controls (e. g., role-based access control configurations).

To ensure the compliance of service composition to the specified security requirements, we are integrating a model-checking based validation approach (see [3, 4, 8] for details) into the Aniketos platform. This integration into the Aniketos Secure Composition Framework [7] consists out of a server component (the Composition Security Validation Module) and an integration into the Activiti Designer which is also used as front-end the Aniketos Secure Composition Framework. Moreover, we provide an alternative integration into SAP

A.D. Brucker et al. (Eds.): Secure Service Composition, LNCS 8900, pp. 136–149, 2014.

NetWeaver BPM. Both modelling tools provide a provides accessible user interfaces that support the modelling of security requirements as well as the graphical rendering of the validation results.

2 The Composition Security Validation Module (CSVM)

Figure 1 provides a high-level overview of the architecture of the Composition Security Validation Module (CSVM). The overall architecture comprises two main elements: the CSVM itself and the CSVM Connector. The service designer uses a CSVM-enabled BPM client to validate the compliance of her business processes. The CSVM-enabled BPM client is a BPM client for which a CSVM connector has been developed and integrated.

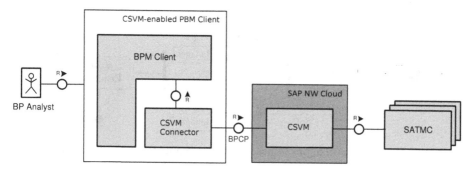

Fig. 1. High-level View of the CSVM Architecture

The security validation activity is triggered by the service designer. The CSVM connector retrieves all the security-relevant information necessary for the validation and creates an instance of the Business Process Compliance Problem (BPCP). The BPCP is send to the CSVM for validation. The BPCP is an XML specification that we devised to make our approach as much as possible independent from the targeted BPM client. It relies on the established BPMN2 standard [11] and extends it with a BPMN2-SEC schema that we defined to capture the security-relevant aspects of business processes.

The validation itself is handled by the CSVM that transforms the BPCP resource into a formal specification suitable for SATMC [2], a SAT-based model checker. As soon as the model checker completes its formal analysis the raw result is provided back to the CSVM that converts it into an XML format. The CSVM connector can now access and render the validation result. Alternatively the results can be consulted on the cloud, e. g., using a Web application.

2.1 Business Process Compliance Problem (BPCP)

The Business Process Compliance Problem (BPCP) is a client-independent data format that bundles the property that should be validated together with all information necessary for its validation. As such, the CSVM only needs the BPCP to validate the compliance of a given business process. In more detail, the BPCP is an XML specification that contains two elements:

- the composition plan (business process model) in standard BPMN2 format, optionally augmented details on Data Objects and their task input/output,
- the security-relevant aspects of the business process and corresponding validation results both specified in BPMN2-SEC.

In this section, we will base our examples on a simple business process for requesting travel approvals (see Figure 2). The security relevant aspects of the BPCP are described in BPMN2-SEC to ensure independent form a specific BPM client. For example both SecureBPMN (see Chapter 8), as used by the Aniketos platform, as well as the proprietary format used by SAP Netweaver BPM can easily be mapped to BPMN2-SEC.

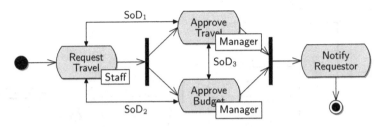

Fig. 2. A simple travel approval process with annotated security requirements

The BPMN2-SEC language (see Figure 3) allows mainly to express three aspects: 1. the *policy* underlying the targeted business process, 2. the *security properties* the business process is supposed to satisfy, and 3. the validation *result* (if any already obtained).

The Policy. The `Policy` element comprises both the role-based access control (RBAC) [14] relevant for the business process and the delegation policy the BPM client is subject to. The RBAC element allows for specifying the roles and users involved in the business process, the permissions, and the assignment of these permissions to users and roles. Listing 1.1 shows a simplified example of an RBAC section within a BPCP specification.

- `manager`, `staff`, and `reception` are roles (lines 2–7)
- `mickael` is a user (lines 8–11)
- the role `manager` is assigned to the user `mickael` (line 12)
- Two permissions are defined: one allows for executing the Approve Travel (`approvetravel`) activity (lines 15–20) and the other one prohibits, via the `negate` construct, the execution of the Request Travel (`requesttravel`) activity (lines 21–25)
- The permission to execute the Approve Travel activity is assigned to role `manager` (lines 29–30) while the prohibition is assigned to role `reception` (lines 31-32)

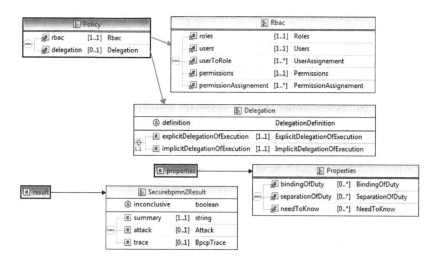

Fig. 3. The meta-model of BPMN2-SEC

```
    <rbac>
        <roles>
            <role id="manager"><name>Manager</name></role>
            <role id="staff"><name>Staff</name></role>
5           <role id="reception"><name>Reception</name></role>
            ...
        </roles>
        <users>
            <user id="mickael"><name>Mickael</name></user>
10          ...
        </users>
        <userToRole roleRef="manager" userRef="mickael" />
        ...
        <permissions>
15          <permission id="exe_approveTravel">
                <action>execute</action>
                <resource>bpmn2:main#approvetravel</resource>
            </permission>
            <permission id="noexe_requestTravel" negate="true">
20              <action>execute</action>
                <resource>bpmn2:main#requesttravel</resource>
            </permission>
            ...
        </permissions>
25      <permissionAssignement principalRef="manager"
            permissionRef="exe_approveTravel" />
        <permissionAssignement principalRef="reception"
            permissionRef="noexe_requestTravel"/>
        ...
30  </rbac>
```

Listing 1.1. BPMN2-SEC: RBAC example (simplified)

Moreover, BPMN2-SEC supports the specification of delegation (see [8] for details): the **delegation** element allows for specifying the intended delegation policy employed by the BPM client during the execution of the service composition. Basically the delegation policy defines under which conditions (if any) a user involved in a certain task of the business process can delegate to a colleague such a task.

Security Properties. The `Properties` element lists the security properties that the business process is required to achieve. These are the properties that our security validation approach will evaluate. Properties can be created on top of an enumeration of security property templates. Our approach can be easily extended to support other property templates provided they can be recast as an LTL (Linear Temporal Logic) formula which is a quite powerful and expressive logic. The properties currently defined and supported by CSVM are

Data Confidentiality: The access to sensitive data should be restricted to certain users.

Separation of Duty (SoD): Separation of duty aims to mitigate the risk of fraud by dividing the responsibility in executing critical parts of business processes.

Binding of Duty: In some cases, it is necessary for a group of business process activities to be performed by only one user so as to ensure the integrity of the data.

Need-to-Know (NtK): Users shall only be able to access only the information that is strictly necessary to accomplish their tasks, i. e., the tasks should be performed in an objective manner. For a critical task, data can be defined that should not be known by the principal executing the task.

Access Control Over Automated Tasks: Automated tasks are usually implemented by calling a service. Such services are often provided by external organisations should adhere to the access restrictions required by the service providers.

Listing 1.2 presents two simple example properties, namely SoD and Ntk, for a travel approval process: the first one captures a SoD between travel request and travel approval (lines 2-6) and the second one model a NtK stating that the manager that will execute the travel budget approval does not need to know the trip business reason (lines 7-11).

```
   <properties>
     <separationOfDuty id="sod1" maxUserActions="1" minUsers="2">
        <activityRef>bpmn2:main#requesttravel</activityRef>
        <activityRef>bpmn2:main#approvetravel</activityRef>
5    </separationOfDuty>
     <needToKnow id="needtoknow1">
        <activityRef>bpmn2:main#approvetravel</activityRef>
        <dataObjectRef>bpmn2:main#traveldata</dataObjectRef>
        <privatefield>reason</privatefield>
10   </needToKnow>
        ...
   </properties>
```

Listing 1.2. BPMN2-SEC: property example

Results. The `Result` element describes the validation result. Listing 1.3 shows an example validation result of our simple travel approval process. The validation result is not inconclusive (line 1) meaning that the model checker was able to determine whether there is an attack (i. e., a possible system trace that results in a system state violating the compliance or security requirements) or not (this is normally the case when the business process does not feature complex loops).

```
     <securebpmn2:result inconclusive="false">
         <securebpmn2:summary>
             Separation of Duty between Request Travel and
             Approve Travel
 5       </securebpmn2:summary>
         <securebpmn2:attacks>
             <securebpmn2:attack name="Separation Of Duty"
                     propertyRef="securebpmn2:main#sod1" type="SoD">
                 <securebpmn2:par>karl</securebpmn2:par>
10               <securebpmn2:par>requesttravel</securebpmn2:par>
                 <securebpmn2:par>approvetravel</securebpmn2:par>
             </securebpmn2:attack>
         </securebpmn2:attacks>
         <securebpmn2:trace>
15           <securebpmn2:step
                 flowElementRef="bpmn2:main#requesttravel"
                 name="Request Travel">
                 <securebpmn2:subStep type="claimed">
                     <securebpmn2:par>staff</securebpmn2:par>
20                   <securebpmn2:par>karl</securebpmn2:par>
                     <securebpmn2:par>requesttravel</securebpmn2:par>
                 </securebpmn2:subStep>
                 <securebpmn2:subStep type="executed">
                     <securebpmn2:par>staff</securebpmn2:par>
25                   <securebpmn2:par>karl</securebpmn2:par>
                     <securebpmn2:par>requesttravel</securebpmn2:par>
                 </securebpmn2:subStep>
             </securebpmn2:step>
             ...
30           <securebpmn2:step flowElementRef="bpmn2:main#approvetravel"
                 name="Approve Travel">
                 <securebpmn2:subStep type="delegationOfpermission">
                     <securebpmn2:par>mickael</securebpmn2:par>
                     <securebpmn2:par>manager</securebpmn2:par>
35                   <securebpmn2:par>karl</securebpmn2:par>
                     <securebpmn2:par>approvetravel</securebpmn2:par>
                 </securebpmn2:subStep>
             </securebpmn2:step>
             ...
40           <securebpmn2:step flowElementRef="bpmn2:main#approvetravel"
                 name="Approve Travel">
                 <securebpmn2:subStep type="claimed">
                     <securebpmn2:par>manager</securebpmn2:par>
                     <securebpmn2:par>karl</securebpmn2:par>
45                   <securebpmn2:par>approvetravel</securebpmn2:par>
                 </securebpmn2:subStep>
                 <securebpmn2:subStep type="executed">
                     <securebpmn2:par>manager</securebpmn2:par>
                     <securebpmn2:par>karl</securebpmn2:par>
50                   <securebpmn2:par>approvetravel</securebpmn2:par>
                 </securebpmn2:subStep>
             </securebpmn2:step>
         </securebpmn2:trace>
     </securebpmn2:result>
```

Listing 1.3. BPMN2-SEC: Validation results

More specifically, an attack has been found on one of the SoD properties (see lines 6-13). The counter-example trace is also reported (lines 14-55). In there, Karl claims and executes a Travel Request for himself (lines 15-28). Sometime in the future Karl got delegated by the manager Mickael to handle Mickael' managerial activities (delegation of permission, lines 30-39). We could imagine that Mickael got suddenly sick. Karl has now all the permissions associated with the manager role and, among other things, can claim and execute the approval of his own travel request (lines 41-54) violating the SoD requirement.

2.2   The CSVM Architecture

Figure 4 provides a detailed overview of the CSVM architecture. The CSVM Connector includes a loader component to load from the BPM client all data necessary to create the BPCP resource. It is often the case that not all the data that is necessary for a complete definition of a BPCP can be loaded from the BPM client (e. g., the security properties to be validated). The UI component provides graphical controls to collect the missing data, to configure the CSVM connector, to trigger the security validation process overall, to render the validation results, etc. The REST client takes care of preparing and sending the REST requests to the REST API of the CSVM. The controller component coordinates the interaction among all the components of the CSVM connector. The persistency component can be optionally implemented to enrich the CSVM connector in keeping track of all the validations that were carried out by business analysts within this specific CSVM connector.

The CSVM Server exposes a REST API whose incoming requests are handled by the Request handler component. BPCPs are REST resources that are stored with their validation status into the persistency layer (Persistency manager component). The BPC broker queues the pending BPCPs that are then pulled by BPC workers in order to be validated. The BPC worker first translates the BPCP into its formal representation in ASLan (see Chapter 9) that is fed in input to one external SATMC instance. The model checking task can be quite costly in terms of time and resource consumption. For the sake of performances one SATMC process should run on one virtual machine with 100% CPU and reasonable RAM allocation. The BPC workers manager component starts on-the-fly a new BPC worker thread and a corresponding external virtual machine with a new SATMC instance as soon as certain work-load customer-dependent criteria are reached. As soon as the model checker finishes the analysis, the BPC worker translates this outcome into the proper XML structure that is filled into the result element of the BPCP. The validation result is now ready to be consulted. The CSVM Portal provide a single web-based entry-point for the end-users that could for instance monitor the status of all their BPCP resources. The CSVM Portal also offers a full-fledged security validation environment available for those BPM Clients that wants to opt for a light integration with CSVM. Indeed, even customers employing BPM Clients that are not augmented with CSVM Connectors could get advantage of CSVM by just accessing the CSVM Portal and managing the entire security validation life-cycle there. Of course the level of interactivity

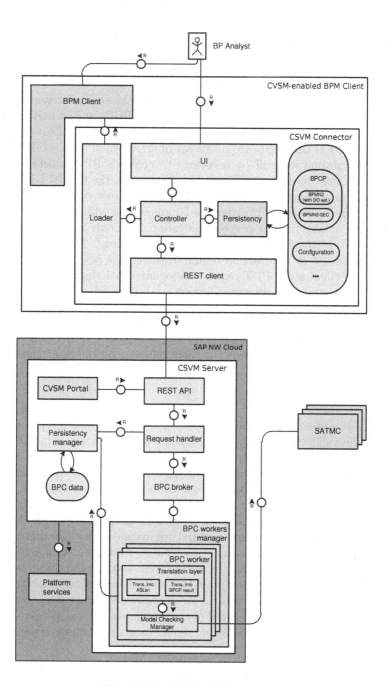

Fig. 4. The CSVM Architecture

and usability would definitely be not comparable to those BPM Clients featuring customized CSVM Connectors. This is why we consider more promising those business scenarios in which BPM Clients are enriched with CSVM Connectors.

2.3   The REST-Based Interaction Protocol

As mentioned the CSVM Connectors and the CSVM Server interact through a REST API that features methods for managing BPCPs and in particular their creation and reading of the validation results. In order to instantiate a new BPCP, the CSVM Connector exports a set of information from its BPM Client. This set of information will be necessary to create a BPCP meta-model. To allow BPM Client to export different files in parallel, the CSVM REST API is defined as a multiple-step resource creation. First, a new resource associated to the validation is created. This resource is unique and will remain accessible to the end-user at any time at a specific location. The only action required is to send a POST at the CSVM Server URI /validation/. After this, the client can export the set of information required to feed the newly created resource. To do so, the client sends PUT requests associated with data, on specific nested elements of its validation resource location.

After the creation of the validation resource, the client can start the validation process by asking for the result of a specific BPCP resource with a GET. As mentioned the security validation process may take some time and this is why it is treated asynchronously. Therefore the client may not get the result immediately.

3   Lessons Learned

In [3] and [5] we presented validation approaches for secure business processes that integrate the validation into the BPM Client. Our discussion with the product groups within SAP revealed that this approach has, in particular in an industrial environment, certain limitations ranging from technical issues like scalability to licensing and maintenance issues. For instance, some customers use both on-demand and on-premise BPM Clients while designing their business processes.

While both the on-demand and the on-premise BPM Clients could have been augmented with an implementation of the original security validation approach, the required effort for this was a clear obstacle. Additional commercialisation obstacles were also perceived on the BPM Client software producer side: while the Security Validation approach provides a nice-to-have differentiating feature, the long-term maintenance contracts for enterprise software does not go very well with the idea of a research proof-of-concept depending on (academic) third-party modules. All in all, the following requirements motivated us to switch for a cloud-based solution:

- CSVM shall be flexible enough to match the heterogeneous BPM customer landscapes including those in which multiple instances of different (on-demand or on-premise) BPM Clients are operated by multiple business analysts;
- CSVM shall be scalable with respect to multiple customer landscapes;

- CSVM shall be flexible enough to offer various degrees of integration within BPM Clients ranging from the most customisable one up to the lightest/simplest one:
  a) the BPM Client is augmented with its own customised CSVM UIs for e. g., specifying the security requirements of the business process under-design, rendering the results of the validation, etc;
  a) the BPM Client is just augmented with a button that outsources the overall security validation activity on the Cloud including e. g., security requirement specification, result rendering, etc;
- CSVM shall be expressive and flexible enough to be consumable by most of the commercial, state-of-the-art BPM Clients despite of their peculiarities and differences;
- CSVM shall be extensible enough to easily integrate new security properties within the validation life-cycle;
- CSVM shall be extensible enough to integrate novel, efficient techniques for validating BPCP; e. g., it shall be possible to add a novel model checker or different automated reasoning tool;

In our CSVM solution we decouple the security validation business logic from the rest of the approach and we take advantage of the Cloud paradigm as a vehicle to overcome some of the challenges that the original security valida-tion approach faced, especially with respect to commercialization. To assess and demonstrate our overall CSVM approach we focused on the proof-of-concept shown in Figure 5 in which the CSVM Server is deployed on the SAP NetWeaver

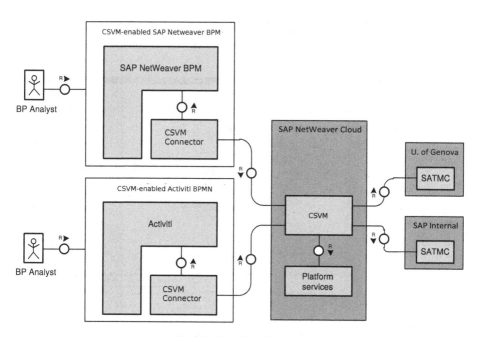

Fig. 5. Proof-of-Concept

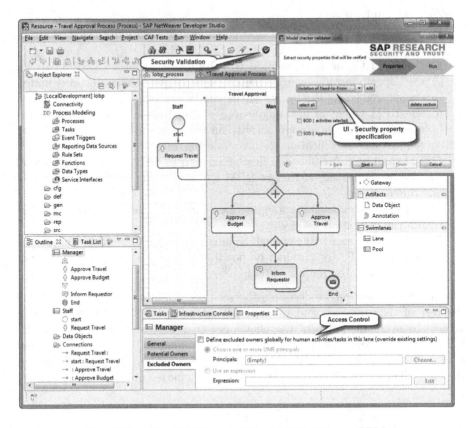

Fig. 6. Security Validation within SAP NetWeaver BPM

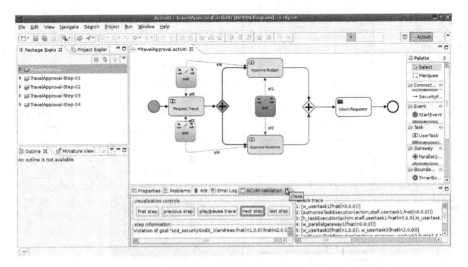

Fig. 7. Security Validation within the Activiti BPMN Editor

Cloud and its REST API is consumed by two BPM clients, SAP NetWeaver BPM (see Figure 6) and Activiti (see Figure 7). Both these BPM Clients use an Eclipse-based business process design environment. This is why we first developed a generic CSVM Connector for the Eclipse environment and then we customised it for our BPM clients.

The performance of the security validation activity, below 1 second, improved with respect to the experiments run and described in [3]. This is simply due to more powerful machines hosting the SATMC model checker. More interestingly, the CSVM architecture allows to efficiently handle parallel requests for security validation. In our proof-of-concept we only considered two machines hosting SATMC and still we were able to smoothly serve two business analysts designing medium-size business processes (around 50 tasks, 5 users and roles involved, and 5 data objects) and requesting for a security validation every 15 minutes. These are promising preliminary results that we aim to extend by setting up pilots with customers so to run more intensive experiments in real landscapes.

4 Conclusion and Related Work

4.1 Related Work

While there is a large body of literature extending business process modelling languages with means for expressing security and regulatory compliance properties, e. g., [6, 10, 12, 13, 16] only a few approaches support validation or testing of the specified properties. The closest related works are [15] and [13]. Wolter and Meinel [15] use SPIN for checking that if an access control specification enforces binary static separation of duty and binding of duty constraints. Salnitri et al. [13] use specialised algorithms implemented in a query engine for validating generic compliance requirements. Additionally, [5] presents an approach that allows to statically check that service implementations, e. g., in Java, conform to the process-level security and regulatory compliance specification.

Besides security properties, there is also strong need for checking the consistency of business processes itself, e. g., the absence of deadlocks. There are several works, e. g., [1, 9] that integrate these kind of process internal consistency validation checks locally into the business process modelling environment.

4.2 Conclusion and Further Work

In this paper we presented CSVM, a promising approach and research prototype to test business process compliance. CSVM takes advantage of the Cloud paradigm to provide on-demand security validation services to BPM systems. Once properly interfaced via a CSVM Connector, the BPM Client is enabled to consume CSVM services, allowing its business analysts to determine, in a push-button fashion, whether the business processes under-design are respectful of critical compliance and security properties. Moreover, the CSVM architecture meets core business requirements collected during internal projects run at SAP with the ultimate goal of increasing its chances to reach industrial commercialisation. We developed and deployed a proof-of-concept on top of our CSVM approach and demonstrated through preliminary results that it can serve multiple business analysts using heterogeneous BPM Clients even belonging to the same customer landscape.

Potential further steps include piloting with real customers, more intensive testing and assessment of CSVM scalability (e. g., using the elastic Amazon Cloud as hosting platform for SATMC instances to benchmark the BPC worker manager component), and integration of the implementation validation discussed in [5]. Last, but not least, we would like to explore if the availability of a common security validation technique like CSVM could pave the way for 1. establishment of domain-specific repositories of compliance requirements accessible for any BPM system, and 2. a systematic certification of business processes under-design that could be then compared in this regards and, e. g., sold at different prices depending also on the security and compliance they offer.

References

[1] van der Aalst, W.M.P., Dumas, M., Gottschalk, F., ter Hofstede, A.H.M., La Rosa, M., Mendling, J.: Correctness-preserving configuration of business process models. In: Fiadeiro, J.L., Inverardi, P. (eds.) FASE 2008. LNCS, vol. 4961, pp. 46–61. Springer, Heidelberg (2008)

[2] Armando, A., Carbone, R., Compagna, L.: LTL Model Checking for Security Protocols. Journal of Applied Non-Classical Logics 19(4), 403–429 (2009)

[3] Arsac, W., Compagna, L., Kaluvuri, S.P., Ponta, S.E.: Security validation tool for business processes. In: Breu, R., Crampton, J., Lobo, J. (eds.) SACMAT, pp. 143–144. ACM (2011a)

[4] Arsac, W., Compagna, L., Pellegrino, G., Ponta, S.E.: Security Validation of Business Processes via Model-Checking. In: Erlingsson, Ú., Wieringa, R., Zannone, N. (eds.) ESSoS 2011. LNCS, vol. 6542, pp. 29–42. Springer, Heidelberg (2011)

[5] Brucker, A.D., Hang, I.: Secure and compliant implementation of business process-driven systems. In: La Rosa, M., Soffer, P. (eds.) PM 2012 Workshops. LNBIP, vol. 132, pp. 662–674. Springer, Heidelberg (2012)

[6] Brucker, A.D., Hang, I., Lückemeyer, G., Ruparel, R.: SecureBPMN: Modeling and enforcing access control requirements in business processes. In: ACM Symposium on Access Control Models and Technologies (SACMAT), pp. 123–126. ACM Press (2012), doi: 10.1145/2295136.2295160

[7] Brucker, A.D., Malmignati, F., Merabti, M., Shi, Q., Zhou, B.: A framework for secure service composition. In: International Conference on Information Privacy, Security, Risk and Trust (PASSAT), pp. 647–652. IEEE Computer Society (2013), doi:10.1109/SocialCom.2013.97

[8] Compagna, L., Guilleminot, P., Brucker, A.D.: Business process compliance via security validation as a service. In: Oriol, M., Penix, J. (eds.) IEEE Sixth International Conference on Software Testing, Verification and Validation (ICST), pp. 455–462. IEEE Computer Society (2013) doi: 978-1-4673-5961-0

[9] Dijkman, R.M., Dumas, M., Ouyang, C.: Semantics and analysis of business process models in BPMN. Information & Software Technology 50(12), 1281–1294 (2008), doi:10.1016/j.infsof.2008.02.006

[10] Mülle, J., von Stackelberg, S., Böhm, K.: A security language for BPMN process models. Tech. rep., University Karlsruhe, KIT (2011)

[11] OMG: Business Process Modeling Notation, BPMN (2011), http://www.omg.org/spec/BPMN/2.0

[12] Rodríguez, A., Fernández-Medina, E., Piattini, M.: A BPMN extension for the modeling of security requirements in business processes. IEICE - Trans. Inf. Syst. E90-D, 745–752 (2007), doi:10.1093/ietisy/e90-d.4.745

[13] Salnitri, M., Dalpiaz, F., Giorgini, P.: Modeling and verifying security policies in business processes. In: Bider, I., Gaaloul, K., Krogstie, J., Nurcan, S., Proper, H.A., Schmidt, R., Soffer, P. (eds.) BPMDS 2014 and EMMSAD 2014. LNBIP, vol. 175, pp. 200–214. Springer, Heidelberg (2014)

[14] Sandhu, R.S., Coyne, E.J., Feinstein, H.L., Youman, C.E.: Role-based access control models. Computer 29(2), 38–47 (1996)

[15] Wolter, C., Meinel, C.: An approach to capture authorisation requirements in business processes. Requir. Eng. 15(4), 359–373 (2010), doi:10.1007/s00766-010-0103-y

[16] Wolter, C., Schaad, A.: Modeling of task-based authorization constraints in BPMN. In: Alonso, G., Dadam, P., Rosemann, M. (eds.) BPM 2007. LNCS, vol. 4714, pp. 64–79. Springer, Heidelberg (2007)

Aggregation and Optimisation
of Trustworthiness of Composite Services

Hisain Elshaafi, Jimmy McGibney, and Dmitri Botvich

Telecommunications Software and Systems Group
Waterford Institute of Technology, Waterford, Ireland
{helshaafi,jmcgibney,dbotvich}@tssg.org

Abstract. The chapter presents the Aniketos approach to aggregating and predicting the trustworthiness of services that are assembled from component services. Some of the important characteristics of service environments are that they are dynamic, distributed and loosely coupled. These characteristics result in the existence of different levels of functional and non-functional attributes of the services operating in such environments. Consequently, it creates challenges for interacting service consumers that require to only deal with services that are trustworthy. In service compositions, the component services may be mandatory or optional and vary in their contribution to the trustworthiness of the composite service. Composition techniques must be able to select trustworthy components and to dynamically adapt to subsequent changes in the services and the environment. The availability of multiple services providing the same or similar functionality but with different trustworthiness levels helps composite service providers to establish and maintain trustworthy compositions.

1 Introduction

The chapter presents the Aniketos approach to the monitoring, aggregation and prediction of trustworthiness of services that are assembled from lower level component services. The chapter discusses the aggregation of the trustworthiness attributes for composite and component services into a common trustworthiness level. The techniques consider a number of criteria during the aggregation. One of such criteria is that component services in a composition may vary in their importance to the composite service as a whole. For example, in a travel service a user may not appreciate all component services to the same extent such as car rental, medical insurance, flight booking, etc. Therefore, it is more useful to see a composite service as a unit that is composed of unequal subunits in terms of their contribution to the trustworthiness of the service. The components may differ also in the probability of their execution in their composite service due to reasons such as limitations in their resource capacity.

The chapter is organised as follows. Background and related work are discussed in Section 2. Section 3 explains techniques for the aggregation and calculation of the trustworthiness of a composite service based on the service's composition plan. It also includes calculation of service costs. Section 4 discusses

A.D. Brucker et al. (Eds.): Secure Service Composition, LNCS 8900, pp. 150–172, 2014.

the aggregation of trustworthiness attributes in order to collectively evaluate candidate services and constructs. The section also discusses the function and architecture of the Aniketos trustworthiness monitoring and prediction module and optimisation of service compositions. Section 5 describes experiments using simulations of the trustworthiness based service selection and composition trustworthiness computation. A summary is described in Section 6.

2   Background and Related Work

2.1   Trust and Reputation Systems and Models

Several systems and models have been developed for trust and reputation and their management in a variety of distributed environments. Common examples include *REGRET* [1] and *FIRE* [2] models. REGRET relies on direct experience, witness, and social information to decide on the trustworthiness (reputation) of an interacting agent in a multi-agent system while also taking context into consideration. FIRE model combines multiple trust sources namely, direct experience, witness information, role-based rules, and references. References can be produced by agents that have previously interacted with the target agent certifying its behaviour.

Noorian and Ulieru [3] illustrate and describe a framework for classifying and comparing trust and reputation systems. Similar frameworks were proposed by Khalid et al. [4] and Hoffman et al. [5]. Khalid et al. [4] discuss the components that are required to build trust and reputation models and describe phases of the trust computation process. Hoffman et al. [5] describe design elements of trust and reputation systems with more focus on attacks against those systems.

2.2   Trustworthiness of Services and Components

Web services standards, such as WS-Trust [6], refer to *trust* only within the context of trusting the identity of a service as noted by Singhal et al. [7]. However, establishing a service identity does not necessarily mean that the service itself is trustworthy. For instance, the service can be temporarily unreliable or unavailable. Therefore, we consider trust a multidimensional concept.

Malik and Bouguettaya [8] discuss a framework for establishing trust in service oriented environments named *RATEWeb*. The framework operates by aggregating reputation ratings from consumers in a P2P fashion. RATEWeb provides a collaborative model in which Web services share their experiences of the service providers with their peers through consumer feedback ratings. The authors don't provide enough details of the reputation mechanisms that support service composition e.g. aggregation of component service reputations.

Takabi et al. [9] discuss some existing research problems that justify our approach in optimising the trustworthiness of services and the collaboration between composite services. They describe the barriers and possible approaches to solutions in providing trustworthy services. They state that a trust framework is needed to allow capturing parameters required for establishing trust and to manage evolving trust requirements.

Other examples of research in the area of trust in service compositions and selection are the works by Paradesi et al. [10] and Hang and Singh [11]. Both study issues related to deriving the trustworthiness of compositions from that of atomic services and the selection of the most trustworthy components. Although their approaches are useful in solving certain aspects of research problems in composition trustworthiness, the determination and evaluation of component trustworthiness attributes are not investigated.

2.3   Threats against Determination of Component Trustworthiness

Any usable approach for determining the trustworthiness of component services based on their composite services has to strive to meet certain requirements. Examples of such requirements are fairness and protection from threats. Our approach needs to be robust and aware of threats that exist as a result of vulnerabilities in the trustworthiness determination mechanisms especially when monitoring the behaviour of individual components is not possible. See Chapter 2 for details on threats and countermeasures for trustworthiness systems.

2.4   Trustworthiness Attributes of Services

Several research studies exist on relating consumer satisfaction, QoE (Quality of Experience), service quality and quality dimensions. Lee and Lin [12] identify a set of service quality attributes and relate them to consumer satisfaction. Their survey indicates the main quality dimensions that affect consumer satisfaction are reliability, security and responsiveness. Li and Suomi [13] propose an eight-dimension scale to measure service quality based on the commonly used SERVQUAL scale [14]. Udo et al. [15] examine the impact of service quality on perceived satisfaction and other consumer behaviours. Ciszkowski et al. [16] propose a framework that enables providers to facilitate composite service adaptation according to consumer expectations and maintain QoE at a satisfactory level. Adaptation techniques are also described by other researchers e.g. [11, 17].

2.5   Aggregation of Attributes

Techniques for the aggregation of QoS (Quality of Service) including reputation, reliability and response time in some BPEL and OWL-S supported workflow constructs are described by Hwang et al. [18]. However, the reputation of a workflow is regarded as sum of component reputations which as described earlier can cause inaccurate results because the dependency between components means the reputations of components affect each other. Additionally, no consideration is given to the variation in the importance of components. Grassi and Patella [19] propose mechanisms to recursively aggregate the reliability of a composite service based on the reliabilities of its components.

The work described in this chapter is a reviewed and extended version of the authors' previous work [20, 21].

3   Trustworthiness Attributes and Aggregation

In this work, the trustworthiness level T_{cs} of a composite service is modelled in general as a function g of the trustworthiness of its components:

$$T_{cs} = g\left(\{T_1, T_2, ..., T_m\}\right) \tag{1}$$

However, the calculation of the trustworthiness level depends on the trustworthiness attributes and the structure of the business process. The selection of component services statically during design time or dynamically is based on the predicted trustworthiness level of the composite service. Trustworthiness attributes include a set of attributes that are used to determine the overall trustworthiness level as discussed in Subsection 3.1.

Selected services are executed in a business process. The process is viewed externally as a Web service. The calculation of the trustworthiness of the composite service depends on the way the abstract service is constructed. It also depends on the probability of execution and the importance of the component services in the composition. Component services in a composition may vary in their importance to the composite service as a whole.

3.1   Trustworthiness Attributes

The identification of a set of attributes suitable for a particular business activity or for a service environment depends on context, requirements and possibly other factors. In this chapter, we consider a set of common trustworthiness attributes that can affect the overall trustworthiness of a CS.

- *Reliability* (r): the rate of successful executions of a service without full or partial failures per total number of executions ($0 \le r \le 1$).
- *Uptime* (a): the percentage of time of availability of a service for the admission of requests over the total measurement time ($0 \le a \le 1$). Uptime is used as a synonym for availability.
- *Reputation* (p): the data available about a service from consumer satisfaction ratings. We consider the reputation as a value p where $0 \le p \le 1$.
- *Security* ($\mathcal{S}$): includes a number of attributes such as encryption, confidentiality, non-repudiation and authentication. A security attribute σ_i for a service s_i is a boolean $\sigma_i \in \{0, 1\}$ with 1 representing the fulfilment of the attribute and 0 for non-fulfilment. For example in encryption the fulfilment means the messages are securely encrypted with at least a minimum allowed key length.
- *Response Time* (t): the response time of a service is used as a metric of performance. After aggregation of the component response times, the composite service response time is measured against required response time in the service contract.
- *Capacity* (y): the number of executions that can be performed simultaneously. The aggregation of the capacity may result in an overall composite service capacity that does not fulfil the requirements of the service contract.

– *Cost* (*c*): monetary cost of a service. Cost is often considered a trustworthiness attribute e.g. Bianco et al. [22]. However, we include cost in the aggregation techniques in any case as it is an important factor in service composition optimisation.

3.2   Service Composition Constructs

Component services are executed in a BPMN [23] business process which is viewed externally as a Web service. The prediction of composite service trustworthiness depends on the way the process is constructed. It also depends on the probability of execution and the importance of the components in the composition. For example, in a travel service a user may not appreciate all component services to the same extent such as car rental, medical insurance, flight booking, etc. The probability of execution of a component service may be based on the characteristics of the process or on limited supply of the component service. For example, in an emergency composite service a fire or ambulance service may be required in an estimated percentage of executions. An example of limited capacity is where a certain car rental service is most trustworthy but has limited supply. In that case more demand requires additional supply from other possibly less trustworthy car rental service providers.

A BPMN business process consists of one or more path constructs. Each construct contains one or more service activities. A component service is selected for each activity. The following are common constructs (illustrated in Table 1):

– *Sequence:* Services are invoked one after another.
– *Synchronized Parallel (AND split/AND join):* Two or more services are invoked in parallel and their outcome is synchronized. All services must be executed successfully for the next activity (service) to be executed.
– *Loop or Iteration:* A service is invoked in a loop until a condition is met. We assume that the number of iterations or their average is known.
– *Exclusive Choice (XOR Split/XOR join):* A service is invoked instead of others if a condition is met. We assume that the likelihood of each alternative service to be invoked is known.
– *Unsynchronized Parallel (AND split/OR join):* Two or more services are executed in parallel but no synchronization of the outcome of their execution. The next activity can commence as soon as one service is completed.
– *Multi-choice with Synchronized Merge (OR split/AND join):* Multiple services may be executed in parallel. Subsequent services can begin execution when all executing branches are completed. In BPMN, inclusive gateways are used to split and merge the process flow.
– *Unordered Sequence:* Multiple services are executed sequentially but arbitrarily.

We use θ to denote a service construct in a composition. In BPMN, AND join/split gateway is signified with '+', OR with 'O' and XOR with '×'. An empty gateway '◇' means it waits for one incoming branch before triggering the outgoing flow. We use the empty gateway in merging Unsynchronised Parallel paths. *Inclusive* gateways '◇' are used to split and merge the process flow in Multi-Choice with Synchronized Merge. Less common and more complex constructs and patterns are supported by modelling languages and products to varying degrees. The structure of business processes including BPMN-based business processes are described by researchers e.g. [24–26].

3.3   Aggregation of Attributes

Table 1 shows our functions for calculating the considered trustworthiness attributes per service construct. The following discussion details the approaches for their aggregation.

For the purpose of trustworthiness attribute aggregation, a CS is represented as a hierarchy of constructs. In order to aggregate the values of an attribute, the workflow undergoes a series of reductions until the highest level construct is reached. The innermost constructs are reduced first at each step. The type of the final construct depends on the outermost pair of component services or gateways (i.e. start and end services or gateways). Figure 1 illustrates the reduction of the workflow of a composite service containing a variety of construct types. The CS is reduced to a final sequence construct in step (3). A reduced construct is treated like a component service during attribute aggregation.

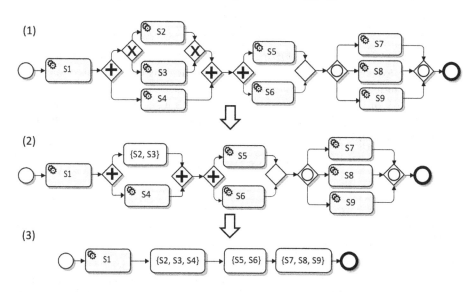

Fig. 1. Hierarchical Reduction of CS Constructs

Reliability and Uptime

Reliability and uptime aggregations are similar. For the sake of brevity, equations described for reliability in this section are also applicable to uptime.

(i) *Sequence, Synchronized Parallel* and *Unordered Sequence*: A failure of a component means failure of subsequent dependent components. This is unlike some other types of constructs (e.g. Unsynchronized Parallel) where subsequent components may be partially independent of the failure of the construct components and can be executed as long as a minimum set of components succeeds. Therefore, we calculate the reliability of the composite service as a product of that of its components. Similarly, the downtime of any mandatory component in these constructs results in the unavailability of the whole construct because of the dependency between their components.

$$r_\theta = \prod_{i=1}^{n} r_i \tag{2}$$

(ii) *Loop*: The reliability and uptime of a Loop containing n iterations of a service s_i is the same as a Sequence construct of n copies of s_i i.e. $r_\theta = r_i{}^n$.

(iii) *Exclusive Choice*: The reliability and uptime of this construct is the sum of that of the exclusive components multiplied by their probabilities of execution in the composite service.

(iv) *Unsynchronized Parallel*: Since an Unsynchronized Parallel construct only fails if all constituent services fail, its reliability (and similarly for uptime) is calculated as follows:

$$r_\theta = 1 - \prod_{i=1}^{n}(1 - r_i) \tag{3}$$

(v) *Multi-choice with Synchronized Merge*: In each subset of components that may be executed in parallel, all its components must be executed successfully. Therefore, we sum the probabilities of each subset multiplied by the reliability of that subset. In a construct θ with a set S of components and two or more probable subsets of components that may be executed in parallel, its reliability is calculated as follows:

$$r_\theta = \sum_{j \subset S} \left(\rho_j \cdot \prod_{i \in j} r_i \right) \tag{4}$$

Reputation

Importance Weight of Components

Each component s_i in a composition has a weight ω_i based on its importance to the reputation of the composition $\omega_i \in \{\omega_1, ..., \omega_l\}$ where $0 \le \omega_i \le l$, l is the number of component services excluding alternatives in exclusive choice constructs and $\sum_{i=1}^{l} \omega_i = l$. We consider components in an Exclusive Choice construct as a single unit in terms of their weight ω_θ and its calculation, where θ is the service construct. For example, consider the case where a requirement may be satisfied by only one of two services $\{s_1, s_2\}$ and the trustworthiness of s_1 is more than that of s_2 but its capacity is limited to a certain quantity. When

s_1 becomes fully in use, s_2 is invoked. Therefore, a common weighting value is used. For a composition with m components and x exclusive choice constructs:

$$l = m - (n_x - x)$$

where n_x is the total number of components in the x constructs.

The weighting of the components is used in the calculation of the composite service reputation, such as in the case of a Sequence with n components. Further details on aggregation of reputation is in next subsection.

$$p_\theta = \prod_{i=1}^{n} p_i^{\omega_i} \tag{5}$$

In order to differentiate between mandatory and optional components, a weight threshold Ω is set. A component service with $\omega_i < \Omega$ is considered optional and can be excluded from the composite service execution when necessary for instance due to the unavailability of the component. Optional components can be excluded also from the aggregation of other trustworthiness attributes such as capacity. The component weights are useful when the capacity of some components are in full usage or close to becoming so. In that case non-critical components can be excluded from the composite service execution. This is particularly useful if the request would otherwise be rejected or when low remaining component resources can be saved for prioritised requests.

Aggregation of Reputation per Construct

The aggregation of reputation of components follows a similar approach to that of reliability but with consideration of the weights of components in the construct with some differences in the aggregation formulas for some constructs. This approach is based on our assumption that the reputations of the components of a composite service are interdependent and that the reputation of a composite service is influenced by the importance of each component as well as its reputation.

(i) *Sequence, Synchronized Parallel* and *Unordered Sequence*: The reputation is calculated as a product of that of constituent services taking the service importance into consideration as in Equation (5).

(ii) *Loop*: The reputation of a Loop containing n iterations of a service s_i is the same as a Sequence of n copies of s_i i.e. $p_i^{n \cdot \omega_i}$.

(iii) *Exclusive Choice*: Each service s_i among the alternative services in an Exclusive Choice has a probability ρ that it will be executed and $\sum_{i=1}^{n} \rho_i = 1$. As described earlier an Exclusive Choice is considered one unit in the composite service component reputation weights. Therefore, we aggregate reputation of the construct as sum of component reputations multiplied by their probabilities of executions.

$$p_\theta = \left(\sum_{i=1}^{n} \rho_i \cdot p_i \right)^{\omega_\theta} \tag{6}$$

(iv) *Unsynchronized Parallel*: Since all component services are executed, the reputation takes all services into consideration as in Equation (5).

Table 1. Aggregation of Trustworthiness Attributes and Cost per Process Construct

Construct	Reliability (r_θ)	Reputation (p_θ)	Encryption (∂_θ)	Resp. Time (t_θ)	Capacity (y_θ)	Cost (c_θ)
Sequence	$\prod_{i=1}^{n} r_i$	$\prod_{i=1}^{n} p_i^{\omega_i}$	$\min_{i=1}^{n} \partial_i$	$\sum_{i=1}^{n} t_i$	$\min_{i=1}^{n} y_i$	$\sum_{i=1}^{n} c_i$
Synchronized Parallel	$\prod_{i=1}^{n} r_i$	$\prod_{i=1}^{n} p_i^{\omega_i}$	$\min_{i=1}^{n} \partial_i$	$\max_{i=1}^{n} t_i$	$\min_{i=1}^{n} y_i$	$\sum_{i=1}^{n} c_i$
Loop	r_i^n	$p_i^{n \cdot \omega_i}$	∂_i	$n \cdot t_i$	y_i	$n \cdot c_i$
Exclusive Choice	$\sum_{i=1}^{n} \rho_i \cdot r_i$	$\left(\sum_{i=1}^{n} \rho_i \cdot p_i\right)^{\omega_\theta}$	$\min_{i=1}^{n} \partial_i$	$\sum_{i=1}^{n} \rho_i \cdot t_i$	$\sum_{i=1}^{n} \rho_i \cdot y_i$	$\sum_{i=1}^{n} \rho_i \cdot c_i$
Unsynchronized Parallel	$1 - \prod_{i=1}^{n}(1 - r_i)$	$\prod_{i=1}^{n} p_i^{\omega_i}$	$\min_{i=1}^{n} \partial_i$	$\min_{i=1}^{n} t_i$	$\max_{i=1}^{n} y_i$	$\sum_{i=1}^{n} c_i$
Multi-choice with Synchronized Merge	$\sum_{j\subset CS}\left(\rho_j \cdot \prod_{i\in j} r_i\right)$	$\sum_{j\subset CS}\left(\rho_j \cdot \prod_{i\in j} p_i^{\omega_i}\right)$	$\min_{i=1}^{n} \partial_i$	$\sum_{j\subset CS}\left(\rho_j \cdot \max_{i\in j} t_i\right)$	$\sum_{j\subset CS}\left(\rho_j \cdot \min_{i\in j} y_i\right)$	$\sum_{j\subset CS}\left(\rho_j \cdot \sum_{i\in j} c_i\right)$
Unordered Sequence	$\prod_{i=1}^{n} r_i$	$\prod_{i=1}^{n} p_i^{\omega_i}$	$\min_{i=1}^{n} \partial_i$	$\sum_{i=1}^{n} t_i$	$\min_{i=1}^{n} y_i$	$\sum_{i=1}^{n} c_i$

n= no. of construct components, ρ_i= probability of execution of component s_i, ρ_j= probability of execution of subset j of construct components

(v) *Multi-choice with Synchronized Merge*: In this construct, the execution of each subset j of all possible subsets of the set S of construct services $(j \subset S)$ is associated with a probability ρ_j that it will be executed where

$$\sum_{j \subset S} \rho_j = 1$$

The construct reputation considers both the probability of execution and weighting of component services:

$$p_\theta = \sum_{j \subset S} \left(\rho_j \cdot \prod_{i \in j} p_i^{\omega_i} \right) \tag{7}$$

Security

For security attributes, the level of security for an attribute in a composition follows the weakest link principle for all the composite service components (see e.g. [27] on the weakest link principle). Table 1 illustrates the aggregation for encryption ∂_i as an example security attribute. Suppose an attribute $\sigma_{k,i}$ is one of z evaluated (i.e. verified compliant/noncompliant) security attributes of components of a composite service; for a component s_i the attribute $\sigma_{k,i} \in \{0,1\}$ and $\sigma_{k,i} \in \{\sigma_{1,i}, \sigma_{2,i}, ..., \sigma_{z,i}\}$. We calculate the score for an attribute $\sigma_{k,cs}$ for a composite service with m components $\sigma_{k,cs}$ as:

$$\sigma_{k,cs} = \min_{i=1}^{m} \sigma_{k,i} \tag{8}$$

To aggregate the values of all security attributes in a composition and calculate the overall level of security $(0 \le \mathcal{S}_{cs} \le 1)$ based on z attributes we first take the weighted sum $\hat{\sigma}_{cs}$ of the verified attributes:

$$\hat{\sigma}_{cs} = \sum_{k=1}^{z} \gamma_k \cdot \sigma_{k,cs} \tag{9}$$

where γ_k ($\gamma_k \ge 0$) is the weight for the attribute $\sigma_{k,cs}$. It sets the effect of the attribute on the security level and trustworthiness. The value depends on multiple factors including the number of security attributes considered, the priority of each attribute, potential resulting attack graphs in the composite service and the likelihood of the related vulnerabilities being exploited. We propose the following formula for the level of security:

$$\mathcal{S}_{cs} = 1 - e^{-\hat{\sigma}_{cs}} \tag{10}$$

The value of γ_k should meet the following requirements:

- when all the composite service security attributes are fulfilled (i.e. $\sum_{k=1}^{z} \sigma_{k,cs} = z$) Equation (10) should result in a security level $\mathcal{S}_{cs} \approx 1$, and
- when a attribute that cannot be compromised is not fulfilled in the composite service, $\mathcal{S}_{cs}$ should fall below a preset security threshold (e.g. 0.95).

Response Time

(i) *Sequence* and *Unordered Sequence*: In both of these constructs the response time is summed to provide the total time of the construct execution; $t_\theta = \sum_{i=1}^{n} t_i$.

(ii) *Synchronized Parallel*: The components are executed in parallel but the next construct cannot commence its execution until all parallel components are complete. Therefore, construct response time equals that of the longest of its components' response times i.e.

$$t_\theta = \max_{i=1}^{n} t_i \tag{11}$$

(iii) *Loop*: The response time of a loop is the number of executions by its component's response time.

(iv) *Exclusive Choice*: We use the execution probability-based weighted average of the components response times as the construct's average response time.

(v) *Unsynchronized Parallel*: The next construct starts execution once the first executing component in this construct completes. Therefore, the minimum of the components response times is the construct response time.

(vi) *Multi-choice with Synchronized Merge*: The response time for each subset j with execution probability ρ_j equals the longest of its components response times. Subsequently, as in the Exclusive Choice we take the weighted average of the subsets' response times.

$$t_\theta = \sum_{j \subset S} \left(\rho_j \cdot \max_{i \in j} t_i \right) \tag{12}$$

Capacity

(i) *Sequence, Synchronized Parallel* and *Unordered Sequence*: The capacity of each of these constructs equals the minimum capacity among its components when buffering is not taken into consideration.

$$y_\theta = \min_{i=1}^{n} y_i \tag{13}$$

(ii) *Loop*: Since the same component is executed sequentially, the construct's capacity is the same of that of the component i.e. $y_\theta = y_i$.

(iii) *Exclusive Choice*: The construct capacity is the execution probability-based weighted average of the capacities of exclusive components.

(iv) *Unsynchronized Parallel*: At least one component of this construct is required to be executed. Therefore, its capacity equals the maximum component's capacity.

$$y_\theta = \max_{i=1}^{n} y_i \tag{14}$$

(v) *Multi-choice with Synchronized Merge*: All components in each subset j of the construct components with probability of execution ρ_j must have the capacity to execute the composite service. Therefore, the minimum of their capacity provides the capacity of the subset. The capacity of the construct is the total of product of the subset capacities by their probabilities.

The capacity aggregation methods above do not describe how to consider buffering. Concisely, we set a threshold for the composite service execution queue size. The threshold value is based on constructs capacities, their response times and the total allowed composite service response time. The buffering maximises the usage of the components capacities and significantly increases the capacity of the composite service.

Cost

(i) *Sequence, Synchronized Parallel, Unsynchronized Parallel* and *Unordered Sequence*: Since all components in the constructs are executed, their cost is the sum of the cost of all components.

(ii) *Loop*: The cost of a loop construct of n iterations of a service s_i is the same as a Sequence construct of n copies of s_i i.e. $n \cdot c_i$.

(iii) *Exclusive Choice*: Since each service among the alternative services in the construct has a probability ρ that it will be executed and $\sum_{i=1}^{n} \rho_i = 1$, its cost is the probability-based weighted average of that of each component service.

(iv) *Multi-choice with Synchronized Merge*: The calculation of cost in this construct is the execution probability-based weighted average of the cost of execution of each subset of components.

$$c_\theta = \sum_{j \subset S} \left(\rho_j \cdot \sum_{i \in j} c_i \right) \tag{15}$$

3.4   Trustworthiness Update Procedure

An algorithm is proposed here to predict and update the trustworthiness attributes of a service. The algorithm is faster than those proposed for multiagent systems in REGRET [1] and FIRE [2] since there is no need to recursively run through all the ratings with each new rating received. In this algorithm, the reputation is determined using moving averages that are updated with every new rating. Older ratings reduce in value over time. The comparison with those algorithms is further discussed in the evaluation.

The reputation of a service s_i is determined by two values; the *reputation* p_i, $0 \leq p_i \leq 1$ and the *confidence* f_i in the score and $0 \leq f_i \leq 1$. Both of the two values (i.e. reputation and confidence score) are important in indicating the status of a composite and component services. Reduction of the reputation signifies receiving consistent bad ratings of the service while reduction in confidence indicates either low number of ratings received recently, significant fluctuations in the rating values or both. Those fluctuations may for example indicate that a service is not scalable enough to meet demands during peak times. The reputation p_i is calculated as a dynamically weighted moving average of the service's rating values. When a new rating is received the reputation is updated.

First, a value representing the *accumulated weight* w_i of all received ratings for a service is updated. This weight is based on the *recency* and the *category* of the ratings. Recency weight w_t indicates how recent are the ratings received for the service. The more recent the ratings the higher the weight because future ratings are more likely to be close to the latest ratings. Reputation ratings of a service can be classified into a set of categories or types with different weights depending on the way they are gathered. Examples of types of consumer ratings may include feedback on satisfaction, value, speed, etc. A service's customers might not value those categories equally and hence the customisable category weighting w_g.

Recency weight w_t decays exponentially and $0 \leq w_t \leq 1$, as follows:

$$w_t = e^{-\lambda \cdot \Delta t} \tag{16}$$

where λ is the decay constant; a customisable positive number that controls the rate of decay, and Δt in relation to a single rating is the age of that rating i.e. the difference between the current time and the time when the rating took place, while Δt for the reputation from the latest update is the age of the last update of the accumulated weight w_i.

The accumulated weight of the reputation w_i ($w_i > 0$) is updated when a new rating value a is received, as follows:

$$w_i \leftarrow w_i \cdot w_t + w_P \tag{17}$$

where w_P is the weight of the new rating value P which is calculated as follows:

$$w_P = \beta \cdot w_{t_P} \cdot w_{g_P} \tag{18}$$

where w_{t_P} and w_{g_P} are the recency weight and category weight for the rating P respectively. The value w_{t_P} is calculated as in Equation (16). The value β is the credibility value of the rater which is used to protect from malicious raters. The main approaches in dealing with the problem are through majority rule [8] and rating of consumers and data sources. Reputation ratings that are sent to the trustworthiness module (see Subsection 4.2) must include ConsumerID and TransactionID fields in order to protect from vulnerabilities such as *slandering*. Slandering refers to providing false reports to decrease the reputation of the victims (see also Subsection 2.3 on threats to trust and reputation systems).

For a rating that is generated at the time of calculation (i.e. $\Delta t = 0$ and $w_P = \beta \cdot w_{g_P}$), the new accumulated weight:

$$w_i \leftarrow \beta \cdot w_i \cdot w_t + w_{g_P} \tag{19}$$

To facilitate the recalculation of the trustworthiness level when new ratings are received, the values of w_i and p_i are stored after each update. The following is the formula for updating p_i after receiving a new rating.

$$p_i \leftarrow \frac{(w_i - w_P) \cdot p_i + w_P \cdot P}{w_i} \tag{20}$$

Since confidence reflects both the frequency of receiving new ratings and the stability of their values as described earlier, the confidence value of service s_i, f_i is calculated as:

$$f_i = f_\eta \cdot f_\delta \tag{21}$$

where f_η is called the *ratings' quantity confidence* indicating how frequent new ratings are received; and f_δ the *ratings' quality confidence* which indicates the stability of the ratings values. The more frequent and stable the ratings the more the confidence i.e. certainty in relation to the calculated reputation. The following formula calculates f_η:

$$f_\eta = 1 - e^{-\alpha \cdot w_i} \tag{22}$$

where α is a constant parameter that can be used to adjust the slope of the relationship between the sum of the ratings' weights and the quantity confidence. The higher the value of α the faster the full confidence (i.e. 1) is reached. It can be set to any positive value but for gradual increase in confidence it should typically be set to a value between 0 and 1. The confidence increases in proportion to the number of ratings and to the degree of their recency.

The quality confidence f_δ is calculated as follows:

$$f_\delta = 1 - d_i \tag{23}$$

where d_i is the deviation history of the ratings around the reputation, calculated as in Equation (24).

$$d_i \leftarrow \frac{(w_i - w_P) \cdot d_i + w_P \cdot |p_i - P|}{w_i} \tag{24}$$

To help update the reputation when new ratings are received, the value of d_i is stored after each update. The result from $|p_i - P|$ is the absolute difference between the overall reputation and individual rating value. The value of f_δ indicates the deviation of the ratings around the overall reputation and ranges between 0 (highest deviations) and 1 (lowest deviations).

4   Service Trustworthiness and Selection

4.1   Aggregated Trustworthiness

A trustworthy composite service may incorporate a set of components that are collectively trustworthy but their attribute values vary. Therefore, considering trustworthiness attributes individually and setting their threshold can exclude some more trustworthy components or constructs than those selected. A unified view of trustworthiness during selection can have advantages as it weighs all attributes together in the selection decision. However, multidimensional trustworthiness is a complex concept as it involves heterogeneous attributes where, for example, some can be affected by the dependency between components e.g. reliability, while others are not interdependent e.g. response time. Additionally, attributes are affected in different fashion by the types of paths in composite service processes. Therefore, any combination of those attributes into a common value or ranking system can only be an approximation.

Multi-Criteria Decision Making approaches have been suggested to rank services or constructs according to their attributes. Malik and Bouguettaya [8] suggest the use of *Simple Additive Weighting* citing that it provides results comparable to more sophisticated methods. Zia ur Rehman et al. [28] describe a method called *Exponential Weighted Difference* that restricts the effect of mutual cancellation between criteria (attribute values) exceeding and below requirements.

Each trustworthiness attribute has a computed or monitored value and a required value. The required value is based on consumer expectation and/or composite service provider requirements. In order to perform common mathematical operations on the attributes and rank services based on their collective trustworthiness, the attributes need to be normalised. Additionally, prioritisation of the attributes ensures that the more important attributes to service trustworthiness are given more weight in the decision.

Normalisation of attributes to obtain attribute values using the same measurement units, requires that we determine the maximum and minimum allowed values for each attribute. Attributes differ in their measurement units e.g. continuous vs. discrete value, and in their optimal values i.e. maximum vs. minimum. For example, for reliability the minimum value is 0 and the maximum is 1 (optimal). Defining maximum and minimum values may not be as straightforward for some attributes. For example, the minimum response time (optimal) can be set to approximately 0 while the maximum can be defined as the maximum acceptable response time before considering the execution as unsuccessful. Additionally, some attributes may be discrete or binary such as compliance attributes particularly those that are security related such as non-repudiation and integrity.

Equation (25) shows how to determine the normalised value $\tau_{h,norm}$ for an attribute τ_h of a service s_i with N attributes depending on their optimal value, $\tau_h \in \{\tau_1, ..., \tau_N\}$.

$$\tau_{h,norm} = \begin{cases} \frac{\tau_{h,max} - \tau_{h,val}}{\tau_{h,max} - \tau_{h,min}} & if \; \tau_{h,min} \; is \; optimal \\ \frac{\tau_{h,val} - \tau_{h,min}}{\tau_{h,max} - \tau_{h,min}} & if \; \tau_{h,max} \; is \; optimal \end{cases} \tag{25}$$

where $\tau_{h,val}$ is the actual attribute value, $\tau_{h,max}$ is the maximum, $\tau_{h,min}$ is the minimum value and $\tau_{h,max} \neq \tau_{h,min}$. The equation is applicable also when the type of the attribute values are binary or discrete.

Selection candidate services or constructs can then be ranked based on their scores. A score τ_θ for a construct θ is calculated using the weighted average of the difference between normalised attributes and their specified thresholds $\tau_{i,req}$.

$$\tau_\theta = \frac{1}{N} \sum_{h=1}^{N} \lambda_h (\tau_{h,norm} - \tau_{h,req}) \tag{26}$$

where λ_h is the weight of attribute τ_h, $\lambda_h \geq 0$ and $\sum_{h=1}^{N} \lambda_h = N$. The value τ_θ can be easily standardized to a value between 0 and 1 to represent the trustworthiness level. In case of attribute values above thresholds, the difference $(\tau_{h,norm} - \tau_{h,req})$ can be reset to 0 to prevent mutual cancellation.

4.2   Trustworthiness Module

A trustworthiness software module is developed for the runtime monitoring and prediction of composite service trustworthiness as part of Aniketos Platform based on a set of mechanisms and metrics to ensure contract compliance. Monitoring is the process of checking that service contracts are fulfilled over time, particularly if changes can occur to operational or business environments or to internal service quality, security or reputation. Monitoring is also used to detect vulnerabilities and discover attacks on a service, e.g. by making use of intrusion detection systems or dynamic testing tools available in the environment.

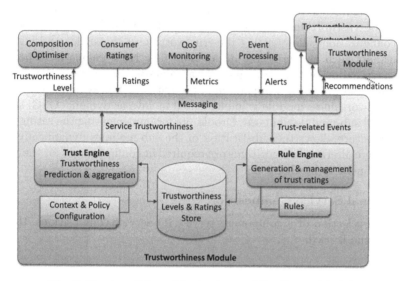

Fig. 2. Trustworthiness Monitoring and Prediction Module

A composite service provider is a service provider that is responsible for constructing service compositions and offering them to consumers. A composite service provider is notified of important changes in the trustworthiness of the composite service as a result of one of its components. A component service that is below the satisfactory trustworthiness level can be replaced with another component service offering the same functionality but with better trustworthiness. The monetary cost of a composite service as a result of its adaptation is also determined. The consideration of costs ensures that a balance is maintained between both trustworthiness and cost efficiency of the service.

Figure 2 shows the architecture of the trustworthiness module. The trust events refer to the notifications received by the module from external components such as event processing, QoS monitoring, consumer ratings, security testing tools and other components. Those events include metrics and alerts that indicate violations or adherence to the service contracts, threats or changes in the environment. In addition to the direct experience through those events, the trustworthiness module can exchange recommendations with other online modules in relation to service trustworthiness. Composition plans and existing composite services can be evaluated by the module and their trustworthiness levels are calculated based on received BPMN models of the planned or existing composite service in XML format.

Incoming events are evaluated by a rules engine to generate trustworthiness attribute ratings. The rules calculate the rating for the event and add other properties including the event timestamp and the concerned trustworthiness attribute. Trustworthiness ratings are then stored by the module and can be used for calculating and updating the overall trustworthiness value of each service and its composite services. The trustworthiness value can be used by other components to optimise or evaluate the trustworthiness of composite services. Context configurations allow customisation of the trust context by adjusting the weighting of trustworthiness attributes e.g. security and performance attributes. Policy configurations allow setting the trustworthiness thresholds and algorithmic constants such as the rating decay rate. The trust engine is responsible for the aggregation of trustworthiness of a composite service from that of its components and providing a prediction of the trustworthiness value of a service.

The trustworthiness module is implemented in Java as dynamic OSGi service platform [29] sub-modules and uses Drools [30] for implementing the rating rules. This architecture allows the substitution of the sub-modules dynamically as in the case where alternative algorithms are required or configurations for the policy and context need to be changed.

4.3   Optimal Service Composition

For optimal selection of a component service for service compositions, the following formula is used:

$$\max \left(\omega_T \cdot T_{cs} + \frac{\omega_c}{C_{cs}} \right) \tag{27}$$

where C_{cs} is the cost of the composite service and T_{cs} is a representation of the trustworthiness calculated from security, reliability and reputation based on Equation (26). Values ω_T and ω_c are constants used to normalise the values of trustworthiness and cost respectively and to customise their priority.

In order to optimise service selection allowing to choose among the best component services as per the computation techniques described in this chapter, an optimisation solution is needed. Since the trustworthiness levels and costs of component services have discrete values and because of the non-linearity of those attributes, linear programming and other solutions that require continuous variables and/or linearity are not suitable. Additionally, the number of services to select from may be large making heuristic methods a better option to provide fast and adequate results. Genetic algorithms are well-suited to these kinds of problems. A custom GA is required to suit the characteristics of the problem of service composition.

5   Simulation and Experiments

5.1   Description of GA

A custom GA is developed in MATLAB in which the fitness function uses Equation (27) together with the aggregation techniques that depend on the structure of the service composition. As illustrated in Figure 3 the genome is represented by a binary matrix where each row represents an ordered set of (concrete) services belonging to a single service task. In each round, a selected service is represented by 1 and an unselected by 0. Therefore, each row must have only single 1 as only one service can be selected from each type to become a component of the composite service. Each task (row in the representation) is associated with a construct in the composite service and with a weighting value. Since the number of available services may be different for each service type, the number of columns in the matrix equals the size of the largest set of services belonging to one service type S where there are m service types.

$$\max_{i=1}^{m}(size(S_i))$$

Empty elements in smaller sets are filled with Not-a-Number (NaN).

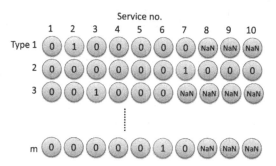

Fig. 3. GA Genome

A set of matrices (using MATLAB cell array) are created as an initial population. The custom crossover function takes the parents as cell arrays, and returns the children that result from a two-point crossover by exchanging randomly selected sections in the parents' matrices. The custom mutation function randomly selects two elements in a row of a parent and swaps their values. Since all elements except one are set to 0, the mutation may have an effect only if the value of one of the affected elements equals 1. The number of generations can be fixed to a constant number or set to be proportional to the number of service types and number of services. Figure 4 shows the improvement of the score of best composition over 50 generations for a simulation of services. Note that the problem is converted to a minimisation one. In the simulation there are 10 types of services (i.e. tasks) organised in constructs as illustrated in Figure 1 with each type having between 5 and 10 concrete services. The cost and trustworthiness of the services are randomly assigned.

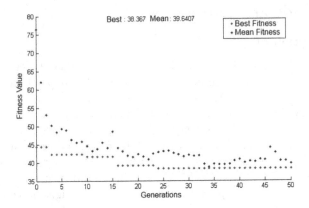

Fig. 4. Scores by Fitness Function

5.2   Comparison to Other Approaches

Figure 1 illustrates an example composite service used in the simulation that includes the composition constructs discussed earlier. Simulation services continue to receive new ratings over the duration of their runtime. The arrival time for service requests is based on Poisson distribution and the mean for the requests changes over time peaking towards the end. Ratings are created based on results of service executions and their values vary between services, the time of the rating and whether there is an increased demand. The high demand is set to cause consistent low performance (resulting in mainly low reputation) or fluctuations in performance (resulting mainly in low reputation confidence) in some of the services. A Gaussian random number generator is used to generate new ratings where the mean and the variance depend on the component service, its type (service task), and the time of rating (e.g. high demand).

During the simulations each of the services receives a rating after each request. The ratings trigger the update and checking of the trustworthiness of the composite service. Figure 5 shows an evaluation of the trustworthiness of the services using our approach compared to that using other approaches including:

- averaging of the reputation of components as proposed by Hwang et al. [18].
- taking the minimum reputation of the components as the reputation of the composite service based on the weakest link principle where the reputation of the composition is as good as that of its component with the lowest reputation.

In Figure 5 (A) only three out of ten component services significantly decrease in their trustworthiness during the peak time. Despite the low reputation of three component services, the reputation calculated using the averaging technique is still high. The weakest link technique only shows the lowest trustworthiness component but does not reflect information on other components with weak reputation while our approach maintains better view of the state of the composite service. In Figure 5 (B) all component services' trustworthiness levels

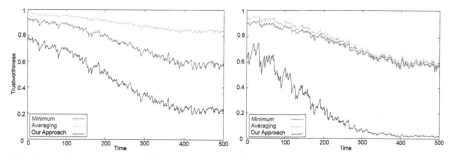

(A) Three Components with low reputation   (B) All Components with low reputation

Fig. 5. Comparison between Approaches to Trustworthiness Aggregation

decline significantly. The weakest link technique estimates trustworthiness of the composite service around the same value as in previous case despite the decline of trustworthiness of all component services. The averaging technique also does not reflect the low reputation of every component service. The trustworthiness based on our approach falls to a very low level indicating the low trustworthiness of the composition.

FIRE [2] is a widely cited trust management model and algorithm for the assessment of the trustworthiness of agents in open multiagent systems. FIRE extends REGRET system developed by Sabater [1]. Unlike our approach of using a moving average, FIRE algorithm recursively runs through all the ratings whenever a new rating is received. This results in an increasing delay in responding to requests for trustworthiness evaluation as ratings increase in quantity.

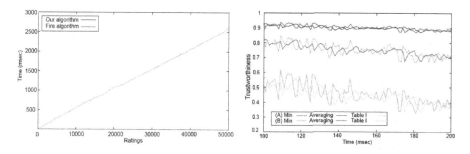

Fig. 6. Processing Time in msec for FIRE and Our Algorithm   **Fig. 7.** Effect of Processing Time on Trustworthiness Calculations

Figure 6 compares the processing times of new ratings required by the algorithm described in this chapter and that of FIRE. The figure clearly shows our algorithm is considerably more faster as the number of ratings available for assessment increases. Note that re-assessment of all ratings may be required in our approach after some configuration changes such as those that modify the weighting of reputation subcategories.

The delay in processing time has an effect on the trustworthiness evaluation because of the role of time in the computations. Figure 7 compares the trustworthiness evaluations when (A) our prediction algorithm is used and (B) with FIRE algorithm during the time interval between 100 and 200 msec. The trustworthiness levels differ because of the processing delay in case (B).

6 Summary

Composite service providers need to be able to select trustworthy components for new compositions and respond swiftly to changed trustworthiness requirements and behaviour of existing composite services through adaptation. With the availability of alternative components providing the same functionality as those already integrated in a composition, composite service providers can take advantage of this by replacing untrustworthy components.

This chapter presents the Aniketos approach to monitoring and predicting the trustworthiness of composite services. The dynamic plugin-based trustworthiness module continuously monitors the adherence the services to their contracts and receives metrics relating to the reputation, QoS, security and other events. Internal service ratings are generated using a rules engine and stored in the module's trustworthiness ratings' store. The computation of trustworthiness depends on the construction of the composite service and the relative importance of components.

The chapter discusses the aggregation of trustworthiness attributes to collectively evaluate services and their constructs. Component services in a composite service can be mandatory or optional components and may not all be equally important to the trustworthiness of the composite service. Additionally, component services are executed in business processes which consist of different types of workflow constructs. The aggregation is based on the common structures of BPMN business processes. A custom Genetic Algorithm is used to optimise the composition of services based on their trustworthiness and cost.

References

1. Sabater, J.: Trust and reputation for agent societies, PhD dissertation, Universitat Autònoma de Barcelona (2002)
2. Huynh, T.D.: Trust and Reputation in Open Multi-Agent Systems, PhD dissertation, University of Sourthampton (2006)
3. Noorian, Z., Ulieru, M.: The State of the Art in Trust and Reputation Systems A Framework for Comparison. J. Theoretical and Applied Electronic Commerce Research (2010)
4. Khalid, O., Khan, S.U., Madani, S.A., Hayat, K., Khan, M.I.: Comparative study of trust and reputation systems for wireless sensor networks. J. Security and Communication Networks 6(6), 669–688 (2013)
5. Hoffman, K., Zage, D., Nita-Rotaru, C.: A survey of attack and defense techniques for reputation systems. ACM Computing Surveys 42(1), 1–31 (2009)

6. WS-Trust specification document, http://docs.oasis-open.org/ws-sx/ws-trust/v1.4/ws-trust.html (February 2009)
7. Singhal, A., Winograd, T., Scarfone, K.: Guide to Secure Web Services, National Institute of Standards and Technology, Technical Report (August 2007)
8. Malik, Z., Bouguettaya, A.: Trust Management for Service Oriented Environments. Springer (2009)
9. Takabi, H., Joshi, J., Ahn, G.: Security and Privacy Challenges in Cloud Computing Environments. IEEE Security and Privacy 8(6), 24–31 (2010)
10. Paradesi, S., Doshi, P., Swaika, S.: Integrating Behavioral Trust in Web Service Compositions. In: 2009 IEEE Int. Conf. Web Services, pp. 453–460 (2009)
11. Hang, C.-W., Singh, M.P.: Trustworthy Service Selection and Composition. ACM Trans. Autonomous and Adaptive Systems 6(1), 1–18 (2011)
12. Lee, G.-G., Lin, H.-F.: Customer perceptions of e-service quality in online shopping. Int. J. Retail & Distribution Management 33(2), 161–176 (2005)
13. Li, H., Suomi, R.: A Proposed Scale for Measuring E-service Quality. Int. J. u-and e-Service 2(1), 1–10 (2009)
14. Parasuraman, A., Zeithaml, V., Berry, L.: SERVQUAL: A multiple-item scale for measuring consumer perceptions of service quality. J. Retailing 64(1), 12–40 (1988)
15. Udo, G.J., Bagchi, K.K., Kirs, P.J.: An assessment of customers' e-service quality perception, satisfaction and intention. Int. J. Information Management 30(6), 481–492 (2010)
16. Ciszkowski, T., Mazurczyk, W., Kotulski, Z., Hoßfeld, T., Fiedler, M., Collange, D.: Towards Quality of Experience-based reputation models for future web service provisioning. Telecommunication Systems 51(4), 283–295 (2012)
17. Moser, O., Rosenberg, F., Dustdar, S.: Non-Intrusive Monitoring and Service Adaptation for WS-BPEL. In: Proc. 17th Int. Conf. World Wide Web, pp. 815–824 (2008)
18. Hwang, S., Wang, H., Tang, J., Srivastava, J.: A probabilistic approach to modeling and estimating the QoS of web-services-based workflows. Information Science J. 177(23), 5484–5503 (2007)
19. Grassi, V., Patella, S.: Reliability prediction for service-oriented computing environments. Internet Computing 10(3), 43–49 (2006)
20. Elshaafi, H., Mcgibney, J., Botvich, D.: Trustworthiness Monitoring and Prediction of Composite Services. In: Proc. 17th IEEE Symposium on Computers and Communications, pp. 580–587 (July 2012)
21. Elshaafi, H., Botvich, D.: Aggregation of Trustworthiness Properties of BPMN-based Composite Services. In: Proc. 17th IEEE Int. Workshop on Computer-Aided Modeling Analysis and Design of Communication Links and Networks (September 2012)
22. Bianco, V., Lavazza, L., Morasca, S., Taibi, D.: A Survey on Open Source Software Trustworthiness. In: IEEE Software (2011)
23. Object Management Group, Business Process Model and Notation (BPMN) 2.0, http://www.omg.org/spec/BPMN/2.0
24. Weske, M.: Business Process Management. Concepts, Languages, Architectures, 2nd edn. Springer (2012)
25. Russell, N., ter Hofstede, A.H.M., van der Aalst, W.M.P., Mulyar, N.: Workflow Control-Flow Patterns: A Revised View, BPM Center Report BPM-06-22 (2006), http://bpmcenter.org
26. Workflow Patterns Initiative, http://www.workflowpatterns.com

27. Steel, C., Nagappan, R., Lai, R.: Core Security Patterns: Best Practices and Strategies for J2EE, Web Services and Identity Management, Pearson Education (2006)
28. Rehman, Z.U., Hussain, F.K., Hussain, O.K.: Towards Multi-criteria Cloud Service Selection. In: Proc. 5th Int. Conf. Innovative Mobile and Internet Services in Ubiquitous Computing, pp. 44–48 (June 2011)
29. OSGi Alliance Specifications, `http://www.osgi.org/Specifications`
30. Drools - The Business Logic integration Platform, `http://www.jboss.org/drools`

Monitoring Threats to Composite Services within the Aniketos Run-Time Framework

Brett Lempereur[1], Dhouha Ayed[2], Muhammad Asim[1], Madjid Merabti[1], and Qi Shi[1]

[1] School of Computing and Mathematical Sciences, Liverpool John Moores University, Byrom Street, Liverpool, L3 3AF
{b.lempereur,m.asim,m.merabti,q.shi}@ljmu.ac.uk
[2] Thales Services, Paris, France
dhouha.yahed@thalesgroup.com

Abstract. Creating complex systems by combining service components is becoming a fundamental way to create flexible IT solutions that can react to changing environment and comply with agile business. The dynamic nature of the Future Internet introduces new threats, and with wider deployment comes a greater need to identify and tackle these threats before they become attacks. For a composite service, this is even more challenging, since each individual service component will have a fluctuating threat picture and there is a broad combined attack surface when many service components are involved. In this chapter we present the design and implementation of the Aniketos Service Threat Monitoring Module. This approach applies runtime monitoring of a service that collects change events that occur and determines their impact on service compositions.

1 Introduction

The highly distributed and complex nature of composite services exposes a greater attack surface than traditional stand-alone systems. The nested usage of services and its dynamic behaviour exposes the composite service to various security threats [1]. A threat is defined as "a potential for violation of security, which exists when there is an entity, circumstance, capability, action, or event that could cause harm" [2]. According to NIST, a threat represents the potential for accidental triggering or intentional exploitation of a specific vulnerability [3]. The threat picture of a service will always be in constant evolution due to the fact that new methods for performing attacks emerge over time, the users find themselves in changing operating conditions, and the services themselves and their execution environment might be updated relatively frequently. For a composite service, this is even more challenging, since each individual service component will have a fluctuating threat picture and there is a broad combined attack surface when many service components are involved [4]. This chapter discusses a threat monitoring approach that applies runtime monitoring of a service for collecting change events that occur and correlating their impact on

A.D. Brucker et al. (Eds.): Secure Service Composition, LNCS 8900, pp. 173–191, 2014.
© Springer International Publishing Switzerland 2014

service compositions. In case the events describe the occurrence of a threat, a notification is sent to the affected composition.

We begin the chapter by discussing the requirements of a threat-monitoring solution within these service-oriented architectures and then introducing the high-level architecture of threat monitoring within the Aniketos platform. The chapter continues with the implementation of the threat-monitoring module, and we present an evaluation of the module in terms of its ability to represent complex threat types by composing primitive monitoring patterns, and its performance at detecting denial-of-service attacks. We conclude the chapter with a discussion of our experience while designing and implementing the threat-monitoring module, and future research directions for threat monitoring in composite service architectures.

2   Requirements for Threat Monitoring in Composite Service Architectures

A threat monitoring solution must predict the potential for security violations and detect malicious actions when it is possible. In a composite service architecture context such monitoring solution must capture the changing threat picture of a service composition, support all the threat categories that are specific to composite services such as incompatibilities or malicious activities, and have the capability to analyse the types of threats that are specific to service composition (see more details about the threat categories and types in Chapter 3).

Threats could appear after a composition of a set of atomic services that do not show any threat when they run independently of each other but the composition can cause vulnerability or make an existing vulnerability in an atomic service exploitable. A threat monitoring solution needs a capability to detect such threats in addition to the ability to collect and detect any type of change from the atomic services that can have an impact on the threat level of a composition. Such changes can have various types going from simple context change to service inherent or security properties.

Moreover, threat monitoring of service compositions has several requirements in common with monitoring systems for service compositions that we mention in the following:

- It needs to be platform agnostic in order to support monitoring of services and compositions using various technologies.
- It should be capable of integrating monitoring data from other subsystems in order to enable a holistic view of all monitoring data in a system.
- It needs to be unobtrusive so that no modifications to atomic services or compositions should be necessary to interact with the monitoring system.
- It should enable monitoring across multiple atomic and composite services, and must correlate monitoring data.

Moser et al. [5] demonstrated that a complex-event processing (CEP) approach guarantees a flexible monitoring solution that covers the previous requirements.

3   Architecture of the Service Threat Monitoring Module

The Aniketos Service Threat Monitoring Module (STMM), forms part of the Aniketos Complete Solution discussed in Chapter 2, and is built upon built upon a complex event-processing architecture. This event-driven approach allows the monitoring system to monitor changes to service as they occur, and lets the system respond in a much timelier manner to threats than a batch approach where the detection process executes intermittently.

Not all event-processing systems have the same structure, but they generally include the concepts of event producers and event consumers that are linked by an event distribution mechanism and intermediary event filtering and processing components. An event-processing network is "a collection of event processing agents, producers, consumers, and global state elements connected by a collection of channels" [5]. In this model, an event producer is an entity that generates a stream of events that is dispatched through the event-processing network, and an event consumer is an entity that is able to receive events and, if necessary, trigger actions in response. The intermediary event processing is generally specified as a sequence of subcomponents that are called event processing agents, these are typically divided into filter agents, pattern detection agents, and transformation agents, where

- Filter agents apply a test on incoming events to decide whether to discard it or to dispatch it for further processing;
- Pattern detection agents examine a stream of incoming events to discover the occurrence of specified or anomalous patterns; and,
- Transformation agents modify the content or structure of the received events.

Following this model, Figure 1 shows the platform independent architecture of the logical components within the module. The service threat-monitoring module contains a set of threat detectors, which represent a suite of core functionality, augmented by a collection of monitoring pattern definitions. To monitor events, services are bound to specific threats by the Service Runtime Environment, for which the STMM instantiates a threat detector as a threat binding. The service-monitoring module in particular, and any component in the Aniketos platform capable of sending alerts through the notification module, play the role of event producers by monitoring service compositions and their environments. The STMM automatically manages subscriptions for services and their dependencies with the notification module.

Logically, the service threat-monitoring module represents a network of processing agents, including a filtering component that discards irrelevant incoming events and dispatches the remaining sequence of events to all interested service monitors. In turn, the service monitors dispatch the event to all of their threat bindings, which apply their core functionality and pattern agents to determine changes in the level of a threat to a service.

The STMM is flexible enough to be applied to any service-oriented architecture that provides the necessary marketplace and messaging components. In the

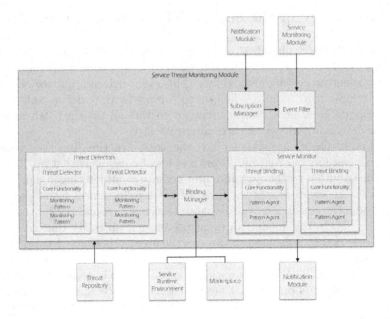

Fig. 1. Component diagram showing the structure of the implementation of the service threat-monitoring module

following section, we discuss the implementation of this platform-independent architecture within the context of the Aniketos platform.

4   Implementation

Like most of the Aniketos platform, we implemented the service threat-monitoring module as a web service using the OSGi framework. The implementation is separated into a collection of loosely coupled and cohesive components that are provided as bundles of functionality. For example, the data model shown in the next section is provided as one bundle, and a second bundle that depends on the model bundle provides the component that interacts with the Aniketos Marketplace to construct composite service dependency graphs. Our implementation accesses external components using their web service interfaces made available using the distributed DOSGi framework [8], with the exception of the Notification Module that we access by connecting directly to the AMQP broker [6]. Figure 2 shows the structure of the bundles in the implementation as a component diagram, where boxes represent components, circles represent interfaces, lines indicate that a component provides an interface, and lines ending in cups indicate that a component uses an interface. To simplify the diagram, we have hidden interfaces that are provided and consumed within the implementation and are not accessible to external components.

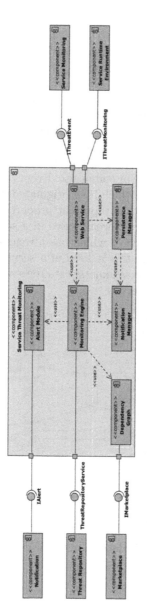

Fig. 2. Component diagram showing the structure of the implementation of the service threat-monitoring module

In the remainder of this section, we will present the design and implementation of the components of the service threat-monitoring module, beginning by presenting the common data model shared among all components of the module.

4.1   Data Model

The components in the service threat-monitoring module share a common understanding of the domain that is provided by the data model. Figure 3 shows a sketch of the classes that comprise the data model using UML class diagram notation, where each box represents a class, a filled-diamond denotes a composition relationship between classes, and an open-diamond represents an aggregation relationship between classes. Within this model, instances of the class service represent both atomic and composite services. The dependency class encodes a dependency relation between a parent service composition and a child service that can be either atomic or composite. Events describe the time at which they occurred, the service from which they originated, the composing service (if any), and a set of parameters that represent properties of the event. A threat represents a collection of potential weaknesses in a service or the environment in which a service executes, each of which has a weight that allows the service threat monitor to calculate the threat level of a service. Services are bound to threats for monitoring, with the weakness state representing the current state of a given weakness for a bound service.

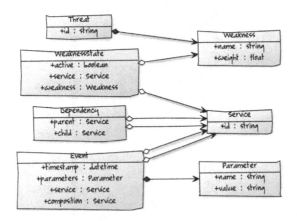

Fig. 3. Data model of the service threat-monitoring module

This model forms the basis of the implementation of the service threat-monitoring module. It allows us to apply complex event-processing techniques to streams of events that originate from environmental and service-level monitors, computing threat levels based on dynamically changing bindings between services on the Aniketos Runtime Environment and threats hosted by the Aniketos Threat Repository.

While the description of the architecture of the service threat-monitor explained the sources of the data in this model, we have not yet addressed where we derive service dependency information. In the next section, we will elaborate on this topic, and discuss how we construct a graph-based model of direct and transitive service dependencies.

4.2   Composite Service Dependency Graphs

To determine the presence of threats in composite service architectures, the service threat-monitoring module must not only consider threats to the service composition and its components, but also to any transitive service dependencies. Our solution to this problem is the concept of a composite service dependency graph, which models the relationship between a service composition and all of its known transitive dependencies. An example composite service dependency graph that consists of seven services and seven dependencies between those services is shown in Figure 4. We draw a distinction between services that we know are compositions, as their model is available in the Aniketos Marketplace, and services that we treat as atomic because their model is unavailable to the Aniketos platform, further discussion of this can be found in Chapter 2 and Chapter 3. In the case of Figure 4, we know that the root service, service a, service b, and service e are composite services, and we treat the remaining services as if they were atomic. From this model, we know that in order to correctly determine the actual threat level of the root service, we must also monitor events relating to the other services in the dependency graph.

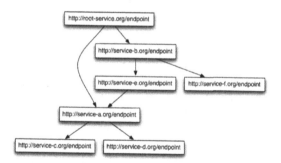

Fig. 4. Example composite service dependency graph consisting of seven services and seven dependencies

To construct and maintain the dependency graphs in the service threat-monitoring module, we use two iterative algorithms that interact with the Aniketos Marketplace to retrieve the composition plans for services in the dependency graph. The first algorithm, shown in Figure 5, accepts a root service as an argument, and constructs a dependency graph as a set of services and dependencies by iteratively traversing its set of unvisited child services, determining whether each child service is known to be a composite service, and if so adding its plan to a stack for processing. As explained earlier in this section, the resulting composite service dependency graph captures our best knowledge of the status of the composition and all of its dependencies.

Algorithm 4.1: CONSTRUCT DEPENDENCY GRAPH(c)

procedure CONSTRUCTDEPENDENCYGRAPH($root$)
  $services \leftarrow \{root\}$
  $dependencies \leftarrow \{\}$
  $stack \leftarrow \langle\text{GETPLAN}(root)\rangle$
  while NOTEMPTY($stack$)
  do $\begin{cases} plan \leftarrow \text{POP}(stack) \\ parent \leftarrow \text{GETSERVICE}(plan) \\ \textbf{for each } child \in \text{GETCHILDSERVICES}(plan) \\ \quad \textbf{do} \begin{cases} dependencies \leftarrow dependencies \cup \{(parent, child)\} \\ \textbf{if } child \notin services \\ \quad \textbf{then} \begin{cases} services \leftarrow services \cup \{child\} \\ \textbf{if } \text{HASPLAN}(child) \\ \quad \textbf{then } \text{PUSH}(stack, \text{GETPLAN}(child)) \end{cases} \end{cases} \end{cases}$
  return ($root, services, dependencies$)

The earlier chapters in this book have shown that composite services in the Aniketos platform are not static; they react to changes in the environment and user requirements by dynamically replacing services to ensure a high degree of availability, security, and trustworthiness. We should expect, then, that the dependency graphs we construct will not always be valid and our knowledge of a composition should be updated. While we could, in the event of a change, reconstruct the entire dependency graph, this will require a significant number of round-trips to the marketplace, and is unsuitable for volatile environments. Instead, the algorithm in Figure 6 allows us to reconstruct a dependency graph by only knowing the original state of the graph and the dependency graph of the replaced service. It accepts two dependency graphs, where , , and are the root service, services, and dependencies in the current graph, and , , and are the root service, services, and dependencies for the replacement subgraph. We traverse the original dependency graph, excluding all services that are only the direct or transitive dependencies of the replacement root , and return a new dependency graph as the union of the visited services, dependencies, and those in the replacement subgraph.

Algorithm 4.2: UPDATE DEPENDENCY GRAPH(c)

procedure UPDATEDEPENDENCYGRAPH$(r_p, s_p, d_p, r_q, s_q, d_q)$
$services \leftarrow \{\}$
$dependencies \leftarrow \{\}$
$stack \leftarrow \langle r_p \rangle$
while NOTEMPTY$(stack)$

$$
\mathbf{do}
\begin{cases}
parent \leftarrow \text{POP}(stack) \\
services \leftarrow services \cup \{parent\} \\
\mathbf{if}\ parent \neq r_q \\
\quad \mathbf{then}
\begin{cases}
\mathbf{for\ each}\ child \in \text{GETCHILDSERVICES}(parent) \\
\quad \mathbf{do}
\begin{cases}
dependencies \leftarrow dependences \cup \{(parent, child)\} \\
\mathbf{if}\ child \notin services \\
\quad \mathbf{then}\ \text{PUSH}(stack, child)
\end{cases}
\end{cases}
\end{cases}
$$

$services \leftarrow services \cup s_q$
$dependencies \leftarrow dependencies \cup d_q$
return $(r_p, services, dependencies)$

We use these two algorithms to create and update the dependency graphs for services for the duration that they are bound to threat monitoring. The information from the dependency graph is used by threat monitoring to determine which service monitors should receive incoming events, and within the service monitors to associate the state of a threat with each service participating in the composition. In the next section, we will present the design and implementation of the threat detectors and service monitors, explaining the complex event-processing engine in the Aniketos service threat-monitoring module.

4.3   Complex Event Processing Engine

The complex event-processing functionality in the service threat-monitoring module is built upon the Drools Fusion platform [7]. This platform, which is an extension of the Drools Expert knowledge-management software, allows us to implement the service threat-monitoring module in terms of temporal operations on streams and windows of events. Our implementation provides a mechanism for filtering, dispatching, and processing events using threat detectors and bindings constructed from a collection of primitive threat-monitoring patterns.

Figure 5 shows the event-processing pipeline, which we separate into stages involving management, event filtering and processing, and alert generation. Events are received from external components through the web service interface or from the notification module, filtered to check for relevance to monitored services, dispatched to relevant service monitors and threat bindings, and finally used to update the threat level of a service and raise an alert through the notification module if necessary. The four main entities in the service threat monitoring module that implement this event-processing pipeline are

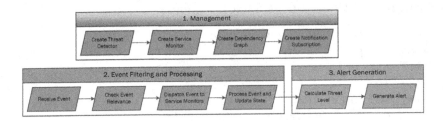

Fig. 5. Service threat-monitoring module event-processing pipeline

- Threat detectors that act as a repository of monitoring patterns instantiated from templates and spreadsheets.
- Threat bindings that are implemented as stateful and event-based Drools monitoring sessions.
- Service monitors that are a collection of threat bindings for each threat that a service has been bound to through the web service interface, they receive and process events, calculate the threat level for the bound service, and dispatch alerts when a service threat level changes.
- A monitoring engine that coordinates the creation of threat bindings, service monitors, subscriptions to the notification module, and the dispatch of events to the set of relevant service monitors.

We call the stream of events that arrive as the input to the event filtering and processing stage the list of participant events. Event filtering is one of the fundamental concepts of complex event processing, as it allows us to define facts on which it is possible to reason about the state of a system. The service threat-monitoring module is able to filter the list of participant events arriving from the Aniketos platform according to their associated service identifiers. As the module maintains a mapping that includes the identifiers of all bound services and their transitive dependencies to the relevant service monitor, we can achieve this filtering in constant time regardless of the number of services or bound threats, limited only by the available memory in the system hosting the module. Events from services that are not bound to a threat are considered irrelevant, however, they are always logged and can be used to detect threats to services at the point of their binding. This stage reduces the number of events that must be considered by the module, as we need not apply complex temporal reasoning to the subset of events that are irrelevant and will never trigger any changes in the threat level of bound services.

In the next section, we complete discussions of the implementation of the service threat-monitoring module by addressing the definition of threat-monitoring patterns, the specification of abstract monitoring templates, and the instantiation of concrete threat detectors through template parameter substitution.

4.4 Monitoring Patterns and Templates

The detection phase examines the stream of participant events and determines if they match the specific conditions of the threat that is being searched for.

In the previous sections, we have shown how the service threat-monitoring module provides an extensible platform for monitoring threats to composite service architectures that uses filters to allow for the expression of constraints on events. However, event filters only support the expression of individual constraints, which means that these constraints are applied on a particular event type. In order to be able to express complex constraints, for example a threat that is dependent upon several event types, we introduce the notion of threat monitoring patterns. Etzion et al. describe event patterns as

"An event pattern is a template specifying one or more combinations of events. Given any collection of events, we may be able to find one or more subsets of those events that match a particular pattern. We say that such a subset satisfies the pattern."

From this, we define a set of patterns for the detection of threats in composite service architectures to include

- The all pattern is a logical conjunction on the stream of events that is satisfied when the participant event list contains one instance of each event type that is specified in a relevant event types list;
- The any pattern is a logical disjunction on the stream of events that is satisfied when the participant event list contains at least one instance of any event type that is specified in a relevant event types list;
- The always pattern is a model pattern which is satisfied when all event instances in a participant list match a given assertion;
- The absence or non-event pattern detects the absence of specified events and is satisfied when the participant event list does not contain any instance of any event type that is specified in a relevant event types list;
- The threshold pattern involves an aggregation function that is applied to the set of participant events and the result of the aggregation function is then compared to a threshold value;
- The sequence pattern applies a temporal ordering to the participant event list and is satisfied if instances of events in the list occur in the same order as specified in a relevant event types list;
- The monotonicity pattern that is satisfied if the value of a given event attribute increases or decreases monotonically as we move forward through the participant event list; and,
- The functor pattern applies a derivation function to a specific event attribute over a set of event instances and then compares the result to a threshold, for example functions applied by this pattern can include min, max, average, concatenation, first, and last/

These patterns form the fundamental complex event-processing model of the service threat-monitoring module.

To allow for the specification of threat monitoring rules by users, we hide the complexity of the complex-event processing engine through the use of parameterized templates. These templates are constructed from the threat monitoring

Listing 1.1. Excerpt from the implementation of the any pattern as a threat-monitoring template

```
rule "Insecure Vulnerability {@name} Change"
    when
        $activator : ServiceEvent(type == "@{type}", parameters["@{key}"] != null, @{expression}, $service :
            service) from window RecentEvents
        not(ServiceEvent(type == "@{type}", parameters["@{key}"] != null, !(@{expression}), service ==
            $service, this after $activator) from window RecentEvents)
        $weakness : Weakness(name == "@{name}", weight == Float.valueOf("@{weight}"))
        $state : WeaknessState(service == $service, weakness == $weakness, !active)
    then
        logger.debug("Insecure vulnerability change for '@{name}' triggered");
        modify($state) { setActive(true) }
end

rule "Secure Vulnerability {@name} Change"
    when
        $activator : ServiceEvent(type == "@{type}", parameters["@{key}"] != null, !(@{expression}),
            $service : service) from window RecentEvents
        not(ServiceEvent(type == "@{type}", parameters["@{key}"] != null, @{expression}, service == $service
            , this after $activator) from window RecentEvents)
        $weakness : Weakness(name == "@{name}", weight == Float.valueOf("@{weight}"))
        $state : WeaknessState(service == $service, weakness == $weakness, active)
    then
        logger.debug("Secure vulnerability change for '@{name}' triggered");
        modify($state) { setActive(false) }
end
```

patterns as Drools rules with placeholders for variables that can be supplied through some external source, typically a spreadsheet, database, or XML document. As an example, consider the template excerpt specified in Figure 8. This template specifies a simple monitoring rule using the any pattern. It examines the stream of participant events for any event that contains an attribute matching the given value, and if it is detected it signifies this by activating the weakness state associate with the responsible service. This will, in turn, trigger a recalculation of the threat level for the service and if necessary the dispatch of an alert through the notification module. In the event that the constraint does not hold for any future event of the given type, the weakness state is deactivated, causing the threat level to return to its previous value and again triggering a threat level recalculation and resulting notifications if necessary.

The implementation of the service threat-monitoring module contains multiple templates that provide implementations of the any, threshold, and monotonicity patterns. To support additional threat monitoring patterns, further templates can be added to the implementation without requiring changes to the code.

To instantiate this template for their own needs, a user supplies the values for its parameters in a spreadsheet that is uploaded to the Aniketos Threat Repository as a monitoring control countermeasure. These spreadsheets contain multiple workbooks, with each row in a workbook providing the parameters to create an instance of the named threat-monitoring template. If we continue to consider the previous example, the following assignments of parameters will instantiate the any template to detect when the architecture providing a service moves into an untrusted legal jurisdiction:

- Name: Untrusted outsourcing or delegation;
- Weight: 1.0;
- Type: Context change;
- Key: Jurisdiction;
- Expression: parameters[jurisdiction] != Republic of Costaguana.

In this case, upon receiving an event of type context change, the service monitor will check whether the event has a key named jurisdiction. If so, it will check whether the given expression holds. If not, the weakness state associated with the service will be updated to active and an alert will be generated if this resulted in a change to the overall threat level of the service. If the expression does hold and the weakness state is active, the state will be deactivated, again triggering an alert if the overall threat level of the service changed.

This layered model, built on the concepts of threat monitoring patterns and templates, allows the service threat-monitoring module to provide a flexible solution for detecting changes and threats in complex service-oriented architectures. In the next section, we will present an evaluation of the implementation of the module, beginning by considering the effectiveness of the threshold-monitoring pattern.

5   Evaluation

In this section, we present a two-part evaluation of the service threat-monitoring module. In the first evaluation, we consider the functionality of the module within the context of the Aniketos platform, specifically testing our integration with the Aniketos Marketplace, Threat Repository, Notification Module, Service Runtime Environment, and the Service Monitoring Module. In the second part of the evaluation, we discuss the flexibility of the module, describing our implementation of a denial-of-service detector based on the threshold pattern discussed in the previous section.

5.1   Integration with the Aniketos Platform

For the purposes of this evaluation, we are hosting the Service Threat Monitoring Module within Apache Karaf [9] on an Amazon EC2 micro-tier instance. This cloud machine is running an up-to-date version of Karaf as a system level service, and the STMM and all of its dependencies are executing within this Karaf instance, as shown in Figure 6. Access to this cloud deployment of the STMM has been made public to allow other components within the Aniketos platform to test their integration with the module.

To conduct this evaluation, we used the SoapUI unit-testing suite. The tests are implemented as a SoapUI project, consisting of multiple unit tests that evaluate the functionality of individual methods offered by the STMM, and test cases that the behaviour of the STMM when sequences of methods reflecting expected real-world usage are invoked. The aim of the tests is to achieve coverage of all of the interfaces and methods provided by the STMM. To this end, the test suites implemented within the project include:

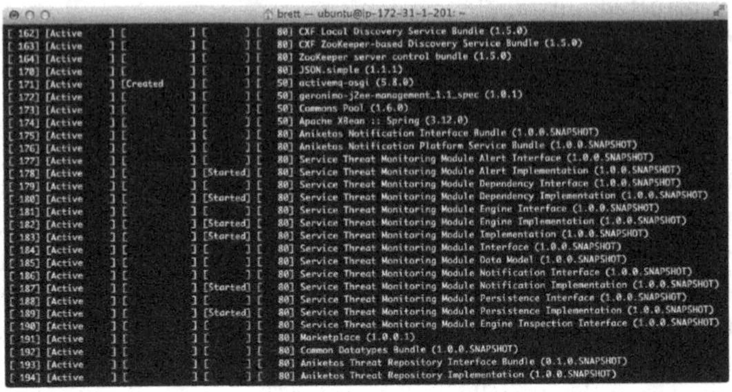

Fig. 6. Cloud deployment of the Service Threat Monitoring Module

- A set of six test cases that evaluate the STMM in isolation (i.e. with a dummy threat countermeasure implementation), these cover both successful operations and sequences of actions that are known to violate internal constraints maintained by the STMM, and
- A set of nine integration tests that evaluate both the functionality of the STMM and its integration with other Aniketos components.

The test case shown in Figure 10 first binds the service to the specified threat, it then sends a sequence of events with an increasing request count (and relatively close timestamps) that are designed to trigger the activation of the threat detector, and then sends an event with a lower request count that should deactivate the threat detector. Each of these actions sends a SOAP request to the relevant method of the STMM interface. We execute the test by selecting the play button in the top-left corner of the toolbar, and SoapUI handles dispatching the SOAP requests and testing the servers replies against expected responses.

As the design of the STMM interface does not send detailed reports back for each invocation, and we have not been able to integrate checking messages sent by the notification, the responses indicate only the success of the operation. That is, a successful test corresponds to a non-error reply from the web service. To evaluate whether the STMM actually performed the expected sequence of events, we must manually examine the logs produced by both the STMM itself, the threat detectors, and the notification module. In the next section, we detail the specific tests we conducted to validate the functionality of the STMM and the results of the evaluation.

We implemented two test suites for the Service Threat Monitoring Module. The first test suite, which evaluated the functionality of the module in isolation, tested its response to various valid and invalid inputs. The second test suite considered the functionality of the module as a part of the Aniketos platform, including testing whether three real monitoring controls function correctly when receiving streams of events. Table 1 shows an overview of the results of these test suites. For all test cases in both test suites the module performed

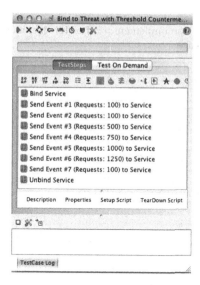

Fig. 7. Test case specification for an adaptive-threshold based denial-of-service threat detector

as expected, this includes our manual verification that the correct events were dispatched through the notification module. In the remainder of this section we will present detailed results for both of the test suites, providing descriptions of the operations invoked and their expected results.

Table 1. Overview of test-suite results for the Service Threat Monitoring Module

Name	Test Cases	Failures	Errors	Success Rate	Time (s)
Isolation	7	0	0	100%	20.2
Integration	9	0	0	100%	12.8

As part of these tests of the module in isolation and integrated into the rest of the platform, we used three separate threats from the threat repository to evaluate the functionality of the STMM in the specified test cases, which were

- A simple countermeasure that activates and deactivates its corresponding weakness state depending upon some test of the value of a parameter of a single event;
- A threshold countermeasure for the detection of denial-of-service attacks that uses an adaptive threshold algorithm, in this case based on the total number of requests a service receives within a specified time-window; and
- A monotonicity countermeasure that, in this case, checks whether a sequence number attached to events is strictly increasing.

Listing 1.2. Excerpt from the implementation of the threshold-monitoring pattern as a threat-monitoring template

```
rule "Threshold {@name} Calculate Moving Average"
    no-loop
    when
        $service : Service()
        $weakness : Weakness(name == "@{name}", weight == Float.valueOf("@{weight}"))
        $averageState : MovingAverageState(service == $service, weakness == $weakness)
        $events : ArrayList(size >= 2) from collect(
            ServiceEvent(type == "@{type}", parameters["@{key}"] != null, service == $service) from entry-
                point "Event Stream"
        )
    then
        // Calculate the updated moving average value.
        ServiceEvent initialEvent = (ServiceEvent)$events.get(0);
        float averageCoefficient = Float.valueOf("@{averageCoefficient}");
        float mu = Float.valueOf(initialEvent.getParameters().get("@{key}"));
        for (int i = 1; i < $events.size(); i++) {
            ServiceEvent event = (ServiceEvent)$events.get(i);
            float xi = Float.valueOf(event.getParameters().get("@{key}"));
            mu = (averageCoefficient * mu) + ((1 - averageCoefficient) * xi);
        }

        // Extract the latest observation value.
        ServiceEvent latestEvent = (ServiceEvent)$events.get($events.size() - 1);
        float xn = Float.valueOf(latestEvent.getParameters().get("@{key}"));

        // Update the moving average state.
        modify($averageState) { setAverage(mu), setObservation(xn) }

        // Allow inspection of rule progress through logs.
        logger.debug("Updated moving average state '{}'", $averageState);
end
```

These threats represent typical usage of the STMM in real-world scenarios; effectively we simulated inputs from the service runtime environment and the service-monitoring module to test the functionality of the STMM. In the next section, we present an evaluation of the flexibility of the module in terms of its ability to represent complex threats using the paradigms we have outlined in this chapter, and the performance of a denial-of-service threat detector.

5.2   Denial-of-Service Detection

Figure 11 shows an excerpt from the implementation of the threshold-monitoring pattern that uses the adaptive threshold algorithm to determine whether a monitored value exceeds normal behaviour. This algorithm collects a list of the participant events as those events relating to a monitored service that have been received from the Aniketos platform within the last ten minutes. It then calculates the exponentially-weighted moving average of some attribute of those events using the first event in the list as the initial value. If the latest observation is above a threshold computed using a given coefficient and the moving average, an alarm count is incremented. Another rule in the implementation that was omitted for brevity reacts to changes in the alarm count, determining whether the number of consecutive alarms is above a user-specified threshold, and if so activating the weakness and consequently triggering an alert to be generated.

This template accepts parameters that define the name of the weakness, its weight, the type of event containing relevant information, the name of the event attribute containing the value to use for calculation, the moving-average coefficient, the adaptive threshold coefficient, and a limit for the number of consecutive alarms. For the detection of denial-of-service events, we use the coefficient values demonstrated by Siris and Papagalou [10] to be effective at the detection of high-intensity denial-of-service attacks, constructing an instance of the template with the parameters:

- Name: Distributed denial-of-service;
- Weight: 1.0;
- Type: Context change;
- Key: Requests-per-minute;
- Moving average coefficient: 0.96;
- Threshold coefficient: 0.5;
- Alarm limit: 4.

To evaluate the performance of the threshold monitoring template, and the effectiveness of the service threat-monitoring module, we conducted an experiment that involved generating two different sequences of events.

Figure 8 and Figure 9 show the behaviour of the distributed denial-of-service threat detector in these two scenarios. In the first instance, we generated a sequence of requests per minute values that do not indicate a denial-of-service attack. While the number of requests per minute fluctuated between 45 and 60, the adaptive threshold remained relatively stable and was never breached. The second graph shows the behaviour of distributed denial-of-service threat detector when the requests per minute values indicate a denial-of-service attack, with

- The vertical magenta line indicating the point at which the number of consecutive alarms exceeded the alarm threshold, activating the vulnerability and generating a notification; and,
- The vertical cyan line indicating when the number of requests per minute fell below the adaptive threshold, causing the vulnerability to deactivate and a notification to be generated.

In this example, we have used distributed denial-of-service as an example threshold-monitoring pattern that uses fluctuations in the number of requests received by a service to determine whether it is under attack. The design of the threshold pattern, however, allows it to be used more generally for the monitoring of properties of events, and for their inclusion as part of any monitoring control specified in the Aniketos Threat Repository.

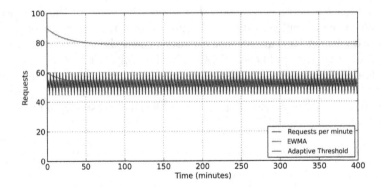

Fig. 8. Graph of the behaviour of the distributed denial-of-service threat detector when the sequence of participant events does not indicate an attack

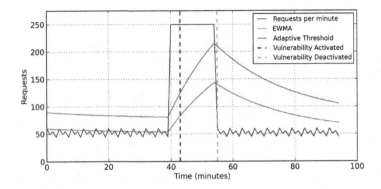

Fig. 9. Graph of the behaviour of the distributed denial-of-service threat detector when the sequence of participant events indicates an attack

6   Conclusions and Futher Work

The Future Internet will be populated not just by data and devices, but also by services. Creating complex systems by combining service components is becoming a fundamental way to create flexible IT solutions that can react to changing environment and comply with agile business. As a solution to this problem, in this chapter, we have presented the requirements, architecture, design, and implementation of the service threat-monitoring module that forms part of the Aniketos platform.

Within the scope of the current implementation, we intend to investigate methods for horizontally scaling the monitoring platform to improve its performance. This will involve distributing the monitoring components, either by having nodes be responsible for hosting a smaller number of threat detectors and a larger number of service monitors, or by ensuring each node holds a smaller number of service monitors and a larger number of threat detectors. The infrastructure to ensure the efficient distribution of messages can be built upon the existing Notification Module.

In addition, we believe that further work on the mechanisms for specifying monitoring policy will increase the usability of the service threat-monitoring module. That is, we aim to reduce the semantic distinction between the specification of the composition plan and its security requirements and the monitoring mechanisms that can detect the potential for threats to a service. While the existing monitoring template and spreadsheet-based instantiation process works effectively for experts, it requires expertise on behalf of users and the separation of monitoring specification between the Threat Repository and the Service Composition Framework. We believe that a more usable solution would be to encode and represent all information required to monitor a composite service as part of its plan.

References

1. Elshaafi, H., McGibney, J., Botvich, D.: Trustworthiness monitoring of dynamic service compositions. In: Proceedings of the 6th International Workshop on Enhanced Web Service Technologies, USA, pp. 25–29 (2011)
2. Shirey, R.: Internet Security Glossary, Version 2 (RFC4949) (2007)
3. Stoneburner, G., Goguen, A., Feringa, A.: Risk management guide for information technology systems recommendations of the national institute of standards and technology. NIST Special Publication 800(30), 55 (2002),
   http://csrc.nist.gov/publications/nistpubs/800-30/sp800-30.pdf
4. Meland, P.H., Guerenabarrena, J.B., Llewellyn-Jones, D.: The Challenges of Secure and Trustworthy Service Composition in the Future Internet. In: Proc. of the 2011 6th International Conference on System of Systems Engineering, Albuquerque, New Mexico, USA, June 27-30 (2011)
5. Moser, O., Rosenberg, F., Dustdar, S.: Event Driven Monitoring for Service Composition Infrastructures. In: Chen, L., Triantafillou, P., Suel, T. (eds.) WISE 2010. LNCS, vol. 6488, pp. 38–51. Springer, Heidelberg (2010)
6. Apache ActiveMQ, http://activemq.apache.org/
7. JBoss Drools, https://drools.jboss.org/
8. Apache CXF-Distributed OSGI,
   https://cxf.apache.org/distributed-osgi.html
9. Apache Karaf, https://karaf.apache.org/
10. Siris, V.A., Papagalou, F.: Application of anomaly detection algorithms for detecting SYN flooding attacks. Computer Communications 29(9), 1433–1442 (2006)

Security Policy Monitoring of Composite Services

Muhammad Asim[1], Artsiom Yautsiukhin[2], Achim D. Brucker[3],
Brett Lempereur[1], and Qi Shi[1]

[1] School of Computing and Mathematical Sciences, Liverpool John Moores University, UK
{m.asim,b.lempereur,q.shi}@ljmu.ac.uk
[2] Istituto di Informatica e Telematica, Consiglio Nazionale delle Ricerche, Italy
artsiom.yautsiukhin@iit.cnr.it
[3] SAP SE, Vincenz-Priessnitz-Str. 1, 76131 Karlsruhe, Germany
achim.brucker@sap.com

Abstract. One important challenge the Aniketos platform has to address is the effective monitoring of services at runtime to ensure that services behave as promised. A service developer plays the role that is responsible for constructing service compositions and the service provider is responsible for offering them to consumers of the Aniketos platform. Typically, service consumers will have different needs and requirements; they have varying business goals and different expectations from a service, for example in terms of functionality, quality of service and security needs. Given this, it is important to ensure that a service should deliver for which it has been selected and should match the consumer's expectations. If it fails, the system should take appropriate subsequent reactions, e.g., notifications to the service consumer or service designer.

In this chapter, we present the policy-driven monitoring framework which is developed as part of the Aniketos project. The monitoring framework allows different user-specified policies to be monitored simultaneously. The monitoring is performed at the business level, as well as at the implementation level, which allows for checking the policies of composite services as well as atomic ones. The framework sends an alarm in case of policy violation to notify the interested parties and triggers re-composition or re-configuration of the service.

Keywords: monitoring, secure service composition, security policy, complex event processing, SOA, BPMN.

1 Introduction

Applications based on a Service-Oriented Architecture (SOA) are highly dynamic and liable to change heavily at runtime. These applications are made out of services that are deployed and run independently, and may change unpredictably after deployment. Thus, changes may occur to services after deployment and at runtime, which may lead to a situation where services fail to deliver for which they have been selected and no longer satisfy user's expectations. Therefore, there is need to shift towards runtime monitoring of services [1].

One important feature of the Aniketos platform is the effective monitoring of services at runtime to ensure that services behave as promised. This paper presents a

A.D. Brucker et al. (Eds.): Secure Service Composition, LNCS 8900, pp. 192–202, 2014.
© Springer International Publishing Switzerland 2014

monitoring framework that is based on the runtime monitoring of a composite service to ensure that the service behaves in compliance with a pre-defined security policy. Alerts regarding policy violations are sent as notifications. BPMN [2] has been used for modelling and specifying composite services, and the Activiti engine [16] as a Business Process Management Platform. BPMN is widely used as a modelling notation for business processes as well as for executing them in a business process engine [3].

Current monitoring methods applied to service execution environments focus on generating alerts for a specific set of pre-built event-types. However, the dynamic nature of SOAs also extends to the end-user security requirements. An ideal system might allow different users to be given the opportunity to apply their own security policies enforced through a combination of design-time and run-time checks. This might be the case even where multiple users are accessing the same services simultaneously. Current monitoring techniques [4, 5, 6, 7] have not been set up with this flexibility in mind.

In this paper we aim to rectify the above weakness of the existing monitoring work by developing a novel policy-driven monitoring framework that allows different user-specified policies to be monitored simultaneously at run-time with the accuracy of a monitoring system that links directly into the service execution environment.

2   Service Composition: An Example

We will illustrate our approach by using a running example. In this example, we assume that we are a small company that designs, develops, and provides customized services to customers. Moreover, we assume that our customer wants to have an application that provides a location based information service, e.g., based on the current GPS coordinates of a mobile device or after entering an address. The application should display information such as the current weather or a map highlighting various points of interests.

As there are many services available that already provide information such as the current weather, it is quite a natural approach to build this new application based on already existing services, e.g.:

- a GeoCoding type service, which takes as input a street address and gets the associated geographical coordinates;
- a PointOfInterest type service that takes as input the geographical coordinates and returns the places that the end user can be interested in;
- an WeatherForecast type service that takes as input the geographical coordinates and returns the information about the weather observations at the station closest to the end user;
- a Map type service that takes as input the geographical coordinates and returns a map showing the position of the end user;
- a WebPageInfoCollector type service that takes as input a set of information related to a location and returns a web page that shows it.

The resulting composite service, named InfoService, takes as input a street address and returns the web page collecting all the information described above. For more details about this scenario and its implementation, we refer the reader elsewhere [17]. Fig. 1 presents an overview of the InfoService case study.

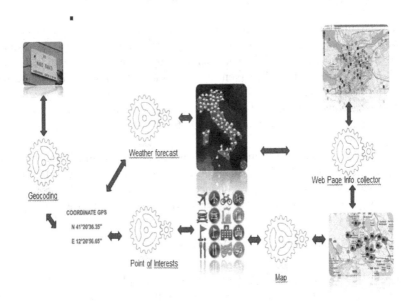

Fig. 1. Overview of InfoService Components

3   Policy Language

In the Aniketos project we were looking for a language which could: (i) express security properties and policies for hierarchical services; (ii) be expressive enough, clear and simple in processing at the same time; (iii) be generated by both humans and software.

We considered several candidates for such kind of language. XACML [9], Event Calculus [10], PROTUNE [11]. XACML is a general purpose language but hard to express policies and reason about them. Event Calculus has a complex syntax for expressing policies for composite services. PROTUNE [17] language has high expressivity and can be used to specify complex policies in a distributed environment. The main disadvantages of the method relates to its strength. Because of such enormous expressiveness the language is complex for policy writing and reasoning.

Based on the above analysis, we selected the ConSpec language [12] for our purposes. The ConSpec language was proposed by the University of Trento and Royal Institute of Technology in the scope of the S3MS project [15]. Briefly, we can see the language as follows (we refer a reader to Aktug and Naliuka [12] for the details):

```
RULE ID ruleId
SCOPE <Session | Multisession>
SECURITY STATE
<bool |int|string> VarName1 = <Value1>
<bool |int|string> VarName1 = <Value1>
<BEFORE | AFTER> event1 PERFORM
Gaurd11->Update11
......
Gaurd1N->Update1N
         ...
<BEFORE | AFTER> eventM PERFORM
GaurdM1->UpdateM1
...
GaurdML->UpdateML
```

Fig. 2. ConSpec Syntax

The tag RULEID simply defines the id of the policy. The tag SCOPE specifies whether the rule is applied to one specific execution or to all executions of the service. The tag SECURITY STATE defines the global variables and their initial values. Then several events are checked BEFORE or AFTER occurrence. If an event occurred we check guards one by one until find the one which is satisfied. In this case certain security updates are performed. If no guards are fired for the event, then the further execution is not permitted (and some further security actions, like notifying the customer, are triggered). In case no security updates are needed but the further execution is allowed, there is a special action SKIP which does not do anything but continues the execution. There is also a possibility for specifying an ELSE statement for the cases, when the further execution should be allowed even if no guards fired (we omitted this option here for simplicity).

There are a number of advantages of ConSpec. First, this language was developed for security purposes and allows guarding possible actions performed by a system (e.g., a service). It represents behaviour in terms of different events (originally, Java method calls) that allow policies to be checked at runtime. The policies written in ConSpec are easily understandable by humans (the language is similar to programming languages), has comparatively simple semantics, and is easy to learn. ConSpec is an automata-based language. Although this feature slightly reduces its expressiveness (in comparison with its predecessor PSLan [13], or other declarative languages as EventCalculus [10], XACML [9], PROTUNE [11], etc.), it allows automatic reasoning on it. For example, in the project we needed to check that requirements desired by a consumer could be fulfilled by a service provider. Furthermore, it is simple to define a policy decision point for monitoring purposes if automation is available. Finally, ConSpec defines different scopes of its application. Thus, we may define a policy for a single execution of a service or multiple executions.

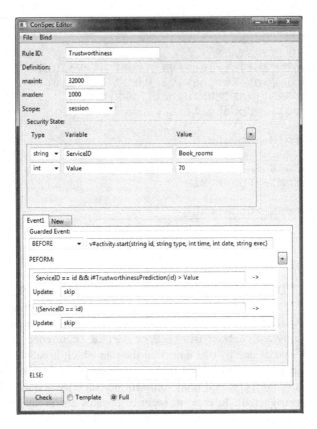

Fig. 3. ConSpec Editor

In the scope of the Aniketos project we have created a tool which provides a graphical user interface for making and changing ConSpec policies. The tool is called a ConSpec Editor and has been illustrated in Fig. 3. The tool also converts the policy in a specified XML format, which simplifies policy processing by the policy decision point (PDP) of the monitor. The tool checks the correctness of the written policy and notifies the writer about possible errors.

Moreover, the tool allows creating templates for policies, i.e., a predefined policy structure, which requires only initialization of input parameters. Thus, templates significantly simplify the work with ConSpec rules for inexperienced users, who now should simply insert context specific values in a selected policy template. Finally, the tool may be integrated with a service composition framework (e.g., the one shown in Chapters 4 and 9, and retrieve names of used constructs (e.g., IDs of services) or even policies themselves.

4   Event Model

The monitoring framework we propose is built around the concept of events. It is an event-driven approach that allows the monitoring system to analyse events and react to certain situations as they occur.

Figure 4 displays a simplified version of our proposed event model. This organises different event types allowing us to reason about and provide a generic way to deal with them.

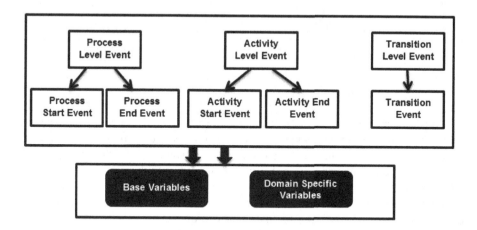

Fig. 4. Event Model

The Activiti engine provides an extension on top of the BPMN 2.0 specification allowing Execution Listeners to be defined. These listeners can be configured at the Process level, Activity level or Transition level in order to generate events. Our event model is based on two types of process variables: Base Variables and Domain Specific Variables. Both types of variable are available during the execution of a business process and could be used for monitoring. The listeners have access to these process variables and can create events populated using their associated values, sending for analysis. The Base Variables inherit common attributes from the process itself, e.g., the process ID, process name, activity ID, activity name, process start time. For example, to monitor the execution time of a particular service composition described as a BPMN process (possibly using an extension that supports the specification of security and trust properties [14]), both process start and end events could be used along with the common variables: event start time and event end time. However, the Domain Specific Variables are user-defined and may build upon the Base Variables. For example, to analyse the load on a particular service, we could accumulate all start process events for that service over the last hour. An alert message should be generated if the number of requests is more than a threshold value in the last hour. This threshold value is a user-defined attribute falling within the Domain Specific Variables.

In the following discussion, we try to determine the structure of events that should be received for analysis. In our proposed framework, an overall process could represent a composite service and an Activity could represent a service component. Fig. 5 shows an example of events for a BPMN process executed in a specific order.

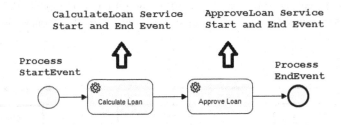

Fig. 5. Event Flow

In this example, a loan service is comprised of loan calculation and loan approval tasks. Therefore, it is not possible to define a single structure for monitoring the overall process. For example, to monitor an Activity, we cannot wait for the whole process to complete. The monitoring of an Activity may need only the process ID, Activity start and end events.

In our proposal, an event structure describes the data and structure associated with an event. It helps in organizing the data that is required for monitoring. Below we define the event structure for our proposed monitoring framework.

1) Process level event
   processName
   eventLevel (processLevelEvent)
   eventName (Start or End)
   eventTime (Timestamp)
   Variable 0...n –domain specific variables

2) Activity level event
   processName
   activityName (name of the Service or User Task)
   eventLevel (activityLevelEvent)
   eventType (Service Task or User Task)
   eventName (Start or End)
   processFlow (used to construct a composition work-flow)
   eventTime (Timestamp)
   Variable 0...n –domain specific variables
    eventDate (e.g. 2013/04/05)

5   The Monitoring Framework

The general architecture of the monitoring framework that we use to monitor the BPMN processes is shown in Fig. 6.

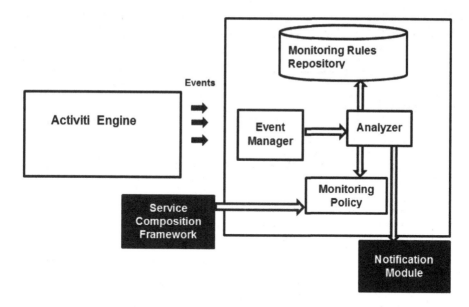

Fig. 6. Monitoring Framework

During execution, the Activiti engine generates events for the deployed BPMN process. The framework consists of an Analyzer that accepts a set of security requirements (monitoring policy) for a particular process to be monitored. The monitoring policy is defined by the service designer. The Analyzer then recovers the monitoring patterns that are related to the requirements from the monitoring pattern repository and checks whether the received events are consistent with the patterns and if it is not then it reports a violation. The monitoring policy is defined using the ConSpec language. The components of the monitoring framework are shown in Fig. 6. In the following, we describe the monitoring components:

Event Manager: This module is responsible for gathering events coming from the Activiti engine and forwards them to the Analyzer. The event manager is composed of an Event Filter that filters relevant events for compliance monitoring. The Event Filter relies on a filtering mechanism and acts as a first step to reduce the number of events that must be considered by the Analyzer.

Monitoring Policy: A set of requirements, specified in ConSpec, that describes what properties need to be monitored for a particular BPMN process. The monitoring policies are defined using the Aniketos Service Composition Framework (SCF), see Chapters 4 and 9.

Consider the following example where a service designer creates a travel booking composition that consists of several tasks, such as ordering, booking hotel, booking flight, payment and invoice, and each task is performed by a component service. The service designer might want that the payment service component should only be invoked when it has a trustworthiness value $\geq$ 90%. This requirement could easily be specified using the ConSpec language as shown in Fig. 7.

```
MAXINT 32000
MAXLEN 1000
SESSION session

SECURITY STATE
    int trust_threshold = 0.9;
    string ServiceID=PaymentService;


BEFORE v#activity.start(string id, string type,
    string time, string date, string exec)
ServiceID==id    &&    i#Trustworthiness(id)    >
    trust_threshold-> skip;
```

Fig. 7. ConSpec rule for Trustworthiness

Monitoring Rule Repository: It is a database of monitoring patterns used for monitoring services. The rules defined in the monitoring policy are translated into monitoring rules and are stored in the Monitoring Pattern repository. An example monitoring pattern might specify that the trustworthiness of a service should be continuously monitored so that a notification is generated as soon as the value falls below a given threshold.

Analyzer: It analyses the events coming from the Event Manager by using patterns stored in the repository. The Analyzer makes use of the monitoring policy to select the appropriate monitoring patterns for a particular process. Every policy is analysed according to the ConSpec specification, particular, if a policy has a Scope Session policy initialised when a service is invoked. The PDP helps in translating ConSpec policies into monitoring rules for decision making. Upon receiving events from the Analyzer, the PDP analyses them according to the order of the guard-update statements specified in the policy. The first guard returning "true" fires the corresponding update (i.e., actions, which have to be performed before continuing of the execution) and afterwards no more statements are checked. Thus, no conflicts are allowed to occur. Note that if no guards resulted to "true" (and updates for ELSE are not specified), this means violation of the policy. If no updates are necessary for some conditions, a special command skip is envisaged.

Notification Module: It is developed as a part of the Aniketos platform and is used by the monitoring framework to report any violations. The Notification Module is implemented as a cloud service and is based on a publish-subscribe paradigm that notifies the entities subscribed about contract violation.

6   Conclusion

The presented monitoring framework is tightly integrated into the Aniketos platform (See Chapter 4) which supports the design-time and runtime aspects of secure and trustworthy service compositions. The proposed monitoring framework provides a user friendly interface for service designers to specify their monitoring policies as ConSpec rules. A policy written in ConSpec is easily to understand and the simplicity of the language allows comparatively simple semantics. This enables the service designer to easily specify the monitoring requirements for their processes and monitor them using the framework. The monitoring framework is based on the way relevant information can be combined from multiple dynamic services in order to automate the monitoring of business processes and proactively report compliance violations. Alerts regarding policy violations are sent as notifications which other interested parties (generally the service composition providers) can subscribe to, allowing them to make verifications and take decisions and actions.

References

[1] Ghezzi, C., Guinea, S.: Run-time Monitoring in Service Oriented Architectures. In: Test and Analysis of Web Services. Springer, Heidelberg (2007)

[2] OMG, Business Process Model and Notation (BPMN) Version 2.0 (2011), http://www.omg.org/spec/BPMN/2.0/

[3] Rademakers, T.: Activiti in Action:Executable business processes in BPMN 2.0. Manning Publications (2012)

[4] Baresi, L., Guinea, S., Nano, O., Spanoudakis, G.: Comprehensive monitoring of BPEL processes. IEEE Internet Computing 14(3), 50–57 (2010)

[5] Haiteng, Z., Zhiqing, S., Hong, Z.: Runtime Monitoring Web Services Implemented in BPEL. In: International Conference on Uncertainty Reasoning and Knowledge Engineering (URKE), Bali, Indonesia, vol. 1, pp. 228–231 (2011)

[6] Wu, G., Wei, J., Huang, T.: Flexible Pattern Monitoring for WS-BPEL through Stateful Aspect Extension. In: Proc. of the IEEE Intl. Conf. on Web Services (ICWS 2008), Beijing, China, pp. 577–584 (2008)

[7] Baresi, L., Ghezzi, C., Guinea, S.: Smart Monitors for Composed Services. In: Proceedings of the 2nd International Conference on Service Oriented Computing (ICSOC 2004), New York, USA, pp. 193–202 (2004)

[8] Aniketos Consortium, Deliverable D9.2: Demonstration material and events from the complete project (2012)

[9] eXtensible Access Control Markup Language (XACML) Version 3.0, http://docs.oasis-open.org/xacml/3.0/xacml-3.0-core-spec-os-en.pdf

[10] Shanahan, M.: The Event Calculus Explained. In: Veloso, M.M., Wooldridge, M.J. (eds.) Artificial Intelligence Today. LNCS (LNAI), vol. 1600, pp. 409–430. Springer, Heidelberg (1999)

[11] Bonatti, P.A., De Coi, J.L., Olmedilla, D., Sauro, L.: PROTUNE: A Rule-based PROvisionalTrUst Negotia-tion Framework (2010)

[12] Aktug, I., Naliuka, K.: ConSpec: A Formal Language for Policy Specification. In: Proceedings of the First International Workshop on Run Time Enforcement for Mobile and Distributed Systems (2007)

[13] Erlingsson, U.: The inlined reference monitor approach to security policy enforcement. PhD thesis, Department of Computer Science, Cornell University (2004)

[14] Brucker, A.D.: Integrating Security Aspects into Business Process Models. IT - Information Technology 55(6), 239–246 (2013)

[15] S3MS project, http://researchprojects.kth.se/index.php/kb_1/io_9718/io.html

[16] Activiti engine, http://www.activiti.org/

[17] Aniketos Consortium, Deliverable D9.2: Demonstration material and events from the complete project (2012)

The Aniketos Design-Time Framework Applied –
A Case in Air Traffic Management

Stéphane Paul[1], Alessandra Tedeschi[2], Erlend Andreas Gjære[3], and Ivonne Herrera[3]

[1] Thales Research and Technology, Avenue Augustin Fresnel, 91767 Palaiseau, France
stephane.paul@thalesgroup.com
[2] Deep Blue, Piazza Buenos Aires, 20, 00198 Roma, Italy
alessandra.tedeschi@dblue.it
[3] SINTEF ICT, Strindveien 4, NO-7465 Trondheim, Norway
{erlendandreas.gjare,ivonne.a.herrera}@sintef.no

Abstract. In order to assess the industrial relevance of the Aniketos design-time framework, we report on its application to a typical use-case of the Air Traffic Management (ATM) System Wide Information Management (SWIM) system: a meteorological information request from a pilot in an aircraft involving air-ground data-link communications. The scope of the study runs from security requirements elicitation, to the deployment of dummy services implementing the meteorological request secured process and communication functions. The evaluation shows that a rich set of security requirements can be captured and managed throughout the design-time engineering process. The Aniketos design-time framework is assessed as a sound baseline. To allow for an industrial exploitation follow-up, some required improvements have been proposed.

Keywords: Evaluation, Design-Time, Security Engineering, Tools, Case-Study, Air Traffic Management, System Wide Information Management.

1 Introduction

The European airspace is fragmented and congested. Air Navigation Services and their supporting Air Traffic Management (ATM) systems are not fully integrated, and are based on technologies already running at their max. To cope with this congestion, early this century, the ATM community thought that a paradigm shift (i.e., a break-through) was required. This led to the creation of the Single European Sky ATM Research (SESAR) Programme. The SESAR Joint Undertaking (SJU) was created under European Community law to manage the SESAR Development Phase. During the recent years, a new operational concept (CONOPS) was developed for ATM. One of the main identified operational enablers is the System Wide Information Management (SWIM). SWIM is a distributed processing environment, which replaces data level interoperability and closely coupled interfaces with an open, flexible, modular and secure data architecture, totally transparent to users and their applications.

SWIM will be open to all traditional ATM stakeholders and systems. However, it is also planned to be open to non-traditional ATM stakeholders, thus giving birth to

A.D. Brucker et al. (Eds.): Secure Service Composition, LNCS 8900, pp. 203–218, 2014.
© Springer International Publishing Switzerland 2014

new and strong security needs in a domain that has always focused exclusively on safety. This makes SWIM a very relevant case for applying and assessing the new Aniketos security engineering design-time processes, methods and tools.

In order to assess the industrial relevance of the Aniketos design-time framework, we report on its application to a typical SWIM use-case: a meteorological information request from a pilot in an aircraft. Section §2 provides an overview of all the Aniketos design-time security engineering evaluation activities that were run. Another perspective is presented in Chapter 16: Supporting Security and Trust in Complex e-Government Services.

On our selected case-study (cf. section §3), we applied the overall Aniketos design-time process. The first step was the capture and documentation of the security requirements (cf. §4) using the Socio-Technical Security (STS) modelling method, language (cf. Chapter 5) and tool (cf. Chapter 7). This was compared to the existing list of security requirements, as extracted from the SESAR documentation [1-9].

Then, we realised a shift from the SWIM problem space to the SWIM solution space, by modelling the corresponding business processes (cf. §5), integrating the security measures along the path, and developing the corresponding web services for deployment. For this work, we used the Service Composition Framework (SCF) tool, which integrates interaction with several components and services developed in Aniketos (cf. Chapter 4, Chapter 6, and Chapters 8 to 11). This engineering work with Aniketos tools was briefly compared to the current industrial best practices.

2   Methodology

The evaluation activities and assessments presented in sections §4 and §5 are the result of many focused evaluation sessions carried out throughout the whole Aniketos project lifespan. These evaluation activities can be classified in three main categories:

- in-depth specific evaluation activities, to test and assess individual components, performed by the authors of this chapter, acting as Aniketos end-users (cf. §2.1);
- on-the-job evaluations, involving third-party operational and security experts, to collect detailed external feedback on methodologies and tools (cf. §2.2);
- presentations to ATM stakeholders and potential end-users, to collect high-level feedback and assess general applicability in an industrial context (cf. §2.3).

2.1   Single Components Evaluations

Single components evaluations were run as an iterative process. A first evaluation session was dedicated to the investigation of modelling practices of STS-tool users, in order to better understand the modelling flows, and develop the STS methodology. Then, a workshop was organised in order to test and assess the STS-tool in its early implementation stage and inform further developments. An interactive validation session was organised to evaluation the Module Transformation Module (MTM) in its final version. Finally, a long evaluation session was dedicated to SCF and its satellite tools.

The SWIM case also informed the evaluation and re-design of the existing supporting material, tutorial and guidelines for the Aniketos design-time tools. The availability of a challenging industrial scenario used as test-bed provided useful insights and feedback to the Aniketos tool developers. All comments were not taken into consideration due to project time and budget constraints.

2.2   On-the-Job Evaluation

The on-the-job evaluation was a one-shot experiment with three third-party SWIM operational and security experts. The main objective of this assessment was to provide detailed industrial feedback on the STS methods and tools. The method used for the assessment was simply to build and run a SWIM case study.

2.3   Presentations to ATM Stakeholders

In order to evaluate the impact of the design-time Aniketos solutions for the ATM domain, various activities were proposed for presenting Aniketos project results to ATM stakeholders:

- presentations to SESAR partners during security-related events and SESAR meetings were iteratively carried out, in order to gather feedback from relevant external stakeholders and refine the Aniketos results;
- the SWIM case study partners organised presentations and modelling sessions inside their own organisation with other departments working in the ATM domain;
- a final combined demonstration and evaluation workshop with ATM stakeholders (about 15 participants) was conducted in Rome on October 23rd, 2013.

The main aim of these activities was to present and evaluate the Aniketos design-time support tools for the ATM domain, with a focus on: (i) assessing the overall suitability of the Aniketos design-time solutions for the ATM domain and its compliance with existing methods, standards, procedures and work practices; (ii) evaluating the acceptability of the Aniketos design-time solutions for ATM practitioners, including how understandable, easy-to-use and effective they are in real operational and industrial contexts.

3   The System Wide Information Management Case

According to SESAR [4], the set of initial Air/Ground (A/G) SWIM applications includes: (i) the sharing of weather forecasts and aircraft weather observations for the reduction of impacts of hazardous weather; (ii) the sharing of traffic situation for reduction of impacts of traffic congestion; (iii) the sharing of temporary aeronautical data and collaborative diversion planning to improve the management of unexpected situations. The flight crew should be able access the data at any time (regardless of the flight phase, airspace or communication link used), instantly (seamless loading without a long wait before information gets displayed) and will be confident that the data originates from a safe source approved by Regulation Authorities. The A/G SWIM aims to be a fast and secure in-flight connection, which will enable the flight crew to share and download data in real time, in large volumes and only from authorized sources.

The baseline scenario retained for Aniketos is an aircraft requesting weather information via SWIM. Thus, the specific A/G SWIM service considered is Weather Avoidance. Through the Weather Avoidance service the A/G SWIM can provide: (i) weather and turbulence forecasts; (ii) current weather situation for areas beyond the range of aircraft sensors and on-board weather radar; data may include the graphical shape of a large hazardous area, or textual information on the weather situation at alternative diversion airports.

We consider an aircraft flying its en-route Business Trajectory [10]. Weather conditions are changing and the pilots make a data-link request for *Meteorological Information* (*MET Info*) provision via SWIM. The aircraft *Airborne Broker* calls an intermediary *Ground Broker*. The *Ground Broker* enriches the information and provides the most recent *MET Info* to the *Airborne Broker*. This *MET Info* is timely stored in the SWIM by a *MET Service Provider* to be exploited by all the *MET Service Subscribers*.

Table 1. Excerpt of Functional Security Requirements from the SESAR programme

Id	Functional Security Requirement	Rationale
AG-SR1	Only publishers authorized for given information category shall be able to publish information of this category.	Data must be provided by the authority responsible for producing it.
AG-SR2	Only consumers authorized for given information category shall be able to receive information of this category.	Data must be received by authorised customer for a specific category.
AG-SR3	Unauthorized information access shall be prevented.	Security requirement, derived by Risk Assessment.
AG-SR4	The air/ground information management shall be able to provide information integrity of 0,999999 (i.e. probability of undetected error 10-6).	Most stringent requirement from the AIS/MET SPR, EUROCAE ED-175 / RTCA DO-324. No safety conditions.
AG-SR5	The air/ground information management shall be able to protect authenticity of the transferred information.	Security requirement, derived by Risk Assessment
AG-SR6	The air/ground information management shall be able to provide confidentiality of the transferred information.	Security requirement, derived by Risk Assessment.
AG-SR7	The air/ground information management shall fulfil security requirements for segregation of services between the Aircraft Control Domain (ACD), the Aircraft Information System Domain (AISD) and the Passenger Information and Entertainment System Domain (PIESD) - see ARINC 664 Part 5.	Security requirement, derived by Risk Assessment.

In Table 1, we report some of the SESAR Functional Security Requirements that are relevant to our case-study. These requirements have been used as a reference through the whole Aniketos design-time security engineering process.

4   Eliciting the Security Requirements with STS

This section describes the activities performed using the Socio-Technical Security modelling language (cf. Chapter 5) and tool (cf. Chapter 7) to elicit and capture the security needs of our ATM SWIM case (cf. §3). The modelling work was done following the STS methodology [11]. This section also provides some initial assessment of the framework.

4.1   Study of the Context

The first step of the STS methodology is the "Study of the Context". The objective is to set the scene, from an organisational, technical and operational view point. This step aims for breadth, not depth. The result should be short and easy to grasp.

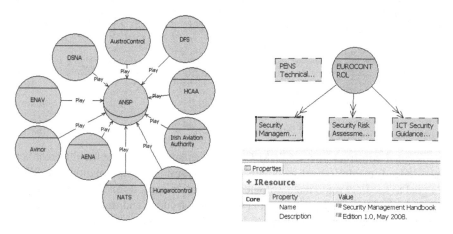

Fig. 1. Setting the scene: (a) roles and agents; (b) applicable standards and regulations

This step was particularly challenging in our ATM SWIM case-study. Indeed, many components of the considered ATM System of Systems (SoS) already exist, in terms of deployed and operated equipment, people and procedures. Building a relevant socio-technical abstraction adequate to reason about SWIM security requirements from the extremely complex SoS and very detailed legacy implementations described in hundreds of different documents, was very far from trivial.

Our first approach was to model common knowledge about the ATM context, including, for example, a fine-grained description of the actors at play (cf. Fig. 1a) and the way they could impact and / or influence the system-under-study through the modelling of the standards and / or regulation that they impose (cf. Fig. 1b). The STS tool proved quite efficient in capturing this common knowledge.

However, for such a complex SoS as the overall European Air Traffic Management system, this approach proved completely inappropriate. Too many details about common knowledge facts meant that the key elements of the study were lost. As a consequence, the ecosystem non-participant stakeholders were not modelled individually in the STS-tool. Instead, they were captured as a unique rag-bag actor called SWIM Context, with the exception of:

- the *Pilot* requesting meteorological information;
- the *Aircraft System* supporting the interaction between the Pilot and the SWIM;
- the *Meteorological Service Provider* providing the requested meteorological information to the *Pilot* via the *SWIM technical infrastructure* (TI).

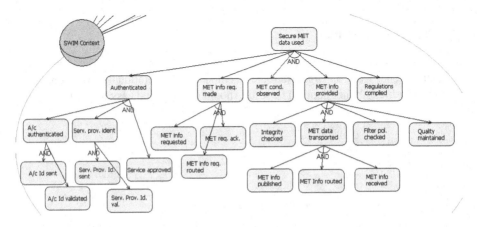

Fig. 2. Defining top-level goals

This original construct of the SWIM Context was key in defining the different actor goals. Indeed, a Pilot's goal to obtain fresh meteorological information, the SWIM TI's goal to securely route meteorological information requests and responses, and the Meteorological Service Provider's goal to provide accurate and timely meteorological information are all linked by some top-level soft-goals related, for example, to ensuring safe and efficient flights over Europe. Through the artificial SWIM Context construct, it was possible for us to define and decompose a top-level soft-goal related to the secure use of meteorological data (cf. Fig. 2) without too many discussions about who is at the origin of, or is responsible for, each sub-goal. This construct was also key in the following methodological steps, in particular when goal delegation was necessary (see below).

By contrast, the SWIM ecosystem participant stakeholders were modelled in more details, namely we chose to model individually: (i) a generic SWIM Access Point (SAP); (ii) the SWIM Transport Services, and (iii) the SWIM aircraft On-board Message Broker. The goals of these actors are defined later (cf. §4.3), through the delegation of goals defined in the SWIM Context.

4.2   Study of the Assets

The second step of the STS methodology is the "Study of the Assets". The objective of this step is to identify and describe all the assets relevant to the scope of the study, and capture their intrinsic[1] security needs.

This was done for all ecosystem participant actors. For example, for the *SWIM Access Point*, the following assets were identified: (i) in terms of information assets: *Meteorological Information Request, Meteorological Information, Aircraft Identification*, and *Meteorological Server Identification*; (ii) in terms of goal assets: *Meteorological Information Request Routed*, and *Meteorological Information Routed*; (iii) in terms of document assets: local copies of the *Meteorological Information Request*, local copies of the *Meteorological Information*, local copies of the *Aircraft Identification*, and local copies of the *Meteorological Server Identification*. Then, the assets were described in detail, and linked together (cf. Fig. 3).

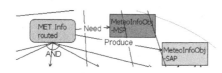

Fig. 3. Identifying assets and linking them together

The STS-tool allowed for the capture of quite a few intrinsic security requirements in a compact and formal way. For example, the model extract in Fig. 4 shows that the *SAP* is only allowed to access *Meteorological Information* in order to distribute it, as a sub-task of the *MET Info routed* goal. This implies that the *SAP* is never allowed to view, modify or produce *Meteorological Information*, and the *SAP* may not distribute *Meteorological Information* for other purposes than routing it to the specified addressee.

Fig. 4. Expressing a need-to-know and integrity requirement between the meteorological service provider and the system wide information management access point

Likewise, it was possible to capture some additional data availability and data transmission integrity requirements, but not all security needs could be easily expressed. To overcome these limitations, or to justify particular security requirements, the STS-tool allows for threats to be captured as threat events. Using the centralised Threat Repository Module (cf. Chapter 4 and Chapter 12), we searched for threats, by

---

[1] By intrinsic, we mean independent of the solution space, i.e. excluding any delegation / co-operation options; indeed, co-operation and delegation are the first steps in the solution space with respect to the problem space of top-level goal achievement by an actor.

keyword (e.g. *impersonation*) and by business domain (e.g. *ATM*). We selected a few relevant threats and created new ATM-specific threats, which were stored in the Threat Repository. Although not being a replacement for proper risk analysis, the inclusion of threats in STS allowed explicating and sharing awareness on situations that are not otherwise described in the desired system. The STS-tool capability of propagating threat impacts throughout the model (cf. Fig. 5) further increased this security issue awareness. Beyond this shared awareness, threat modelling did not help us improve the remainder of the STS model, as one could have expected. This is probably because in our case, threat modelling was performed quite late in the modelling process. It is reasonable to think that our STS model had already been designed with these threats in mind. Threat modelling only allowed for making these threats explicit to all.

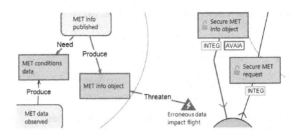

Fig. 5. Expressing threats with events, such as *Erroneous data impact flight*, allowing for the threat propagation analysis to be invoked (threatened paths and objects highlighted)

Although threat modelling was found to be quite appealing, we had to limit its usage because threats and their relations to actors and assets rapidly cluttered the diagram. A means to toggle threat visibility would have been of significant value.

Finally, let us recall that STS does not allow one to define scales for the security needs. This was found to be significantly detrimental in capturing security requirements.

4.3   Study of the Security Policies

The third step of the STS methodology is the "Study of the Security Policies". The objective of this step is to extend the analysis of the security needs by considering how collaborative goals are fulfilled. Collaborative goals imply security relevant features, namely, the delegation of all or part of the work, and sharing resources to support the fulfilment of those goals. Thus, the analysis performed in this step extends the scope of the capture of the security needs (cf. §4.2) to the delegation of rights over goals and to authorisations over data that are useful for the fulfilment of those collaborative goals.

In our case-study, we extensively used delegations between our *SWIM Context* and our three SWIM ecosystem participants (cf. §4.1). Delegation is one of the most powerful concepts of the STS modelling language (STS-ml). However, it is tricky to use and we found its semantics to be insufficiently defined. Typically, it remained unclear if goal delegation was a simple delegation of fulfilment of the goal, or a delegation of responsibility over the fulfilment of the goal, or a transfer of accountability. In our case-study, the actors interacting with the SWIM have no hierarchical relations[2] with the SWIM. Thus, neither of them can (legally) delegate a task to SWIM, and vice-versa. Typically, the Pilot and SWIM belong to independent organisations. When the Pilot uses SWIM to route a message to the Meteorological Service Provider, he does not (legally) delegate the routing, but he cooperates with a third-party, and he has to trust that third-party.

4.4   Conclusion

By contrast with traditional risk-based security requirement elicitation techniques (e.g., [12, 13, 14]), the Socio-Technical Security (STS) modelling approach of Aniketos is risk agnostic. Traditional risk-based security requirement elicitation techniques operate in the solution space, assessing the vulnerabilities of the designed solutions, in parallel to the assessment of the threats and impacts of the feared events. The STS modelling approach of Aniketos operates solely in the problem space, with a strong focus on business / operational goals. The intrinsic security needs can be elicited essentially based on the will to achieve those goals, whilst preserving the identified assets; the identification of feared events may help in this elicitation. As such the STS modelling approach of Aniketos is perfectly suited for a very early security engineering activity, during which business / operational staff can be easily involved, without introducing any complexity related to the solution space. For these reasons, the STS-ml and STS-tool were a perfect fit for the ATM SWIM case-study.

However, the current version of the STS-ml and STS-tool are not completely ready for industrial use. Based on our case-study, the main issues that would need to be solved beforehand include: (i) the impossibility of clearly defining the boundaries of the system-under-study; (ii) the impossibility of defining security need scales, in particular for the Confidentiality, Integrity and Availability (CIA) criteria; (iii) insufficiently formal semantics, in particular for organisation structures, goal delegation, asset ownership, and Role Based Access Control (RBAC).

5   Designing and Securing the SWIM Business Process with SCF

This section describes the activities performed using the Aniketos Service Composition Framework (SCF) to design and secure our ATM SWIM business process (cf. §3). This section also provides some initial assessment of the framework. For technical details relating to SCF and its satellite tools, please refer to Chapter 6 and Chapters 8 to 11.

5.1   Designing the (Unsecure) SWIM Business Process with SCF

The first step we carried out in running our ATM SWIM case-study was business process modelling without any consideration for security issues. We developed multiple BPMN diagrams, comprehending over thirty tasks. Some tasks were user tasks, e.g. *Login*, but most tasks were service tasks, e.g. *Authenticate*. SCF proved itself adequate for the job.

---

[2] This is a typical situation in the context of a System of Systems (SoS).

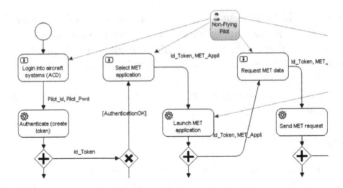

Fig. 6. Separating clearly user tasks from service tasks

Whilst the Business Process Modelling Notation (BPMN) specification allows for many types of tasks, including user tasks, the Aniketos service specifications consist of service tasks only. A service task is performed by a web service. A composite service process is hence an executable workflow that is realised by web services alone, and consumed as a web service itself. During the course of the case-study, this limitation proved to have significant but manageable impacts on our BPMN design. Some diagrams had to be redrawn to separate clearly user tasks from service tasks (cf. Fig. 6). For other processes with heavy human-machine interactions, this might however be a deterrent constraint.

5.2   Discovering Services: A Prerequisite to Security Specification

The next step in our engineering process should have been the securing of our business process. However, with the Aniketos engineering process, security specification on service compositions can only be done after atomic service discovery within the Service Composition Framework, in order to retrieve the atomic service signature. This approach is clearly disputable since, in a real industrial context, most of these services may not yet exist.

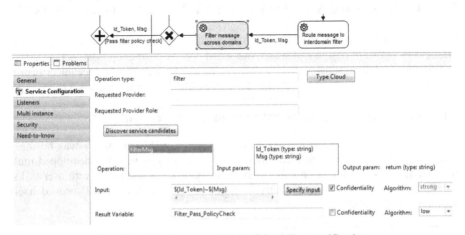

Fig. 7. Service discovery and confidentiality specification

To proceed with our case-study, we implemented, deployed and published 26 web services, using the Aniketos Marketplace. Most of these web services, e.g. *Log*, were dummy services doing nothing, but services that were key to observing the execution of the meteorological request-response scenario were effectively developed, together with their corresponding data flow interfaces and human-machine interfaces.

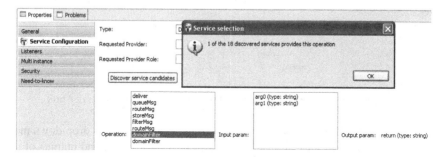

Fig. 8. Signature of composite service deployed and discovered with SCF

The first major issue we faced with service discovery in SCF was that the response to a discovery request was (only) a list of operations with their input and output parameters (cf. Fig. 7). This response is much shorter than the output that can be obtained from a search directly in the Aniketos Marketplace. Typically, the service names, the service descriptions, the service provider and the list of other tags were missing in SCF. An improvement of the Human-Machine Interface (HMI) is needed here, to avoid ambiguities in the identification of services.

The second major issue we faced with service discovery was related to method signatures. When a composite service is stored in and retrieved from the Aniketos repository, the 1st parameter of the associated method is an array of the names of all the parameters, whilst the 2nd parameter is an array of the corresponding values, cf. Fig. 8.

This implementation for composite services was found to be inadequate for service discovery, because it reduces the signature of the composite service to the sole name of the method. Moreover, it is different from the signature used for atomic services, cf. Fig. 7. An improvement of the implementation is needed here to support an effective discovery.

5.3   Securing the ATM SWIM Business Process

Having defined the business process (cf. §5.1) and performed service discovery for all atomic services (cf. §5.2), it was now possible to secure the business process. Each security property that was addressed in our test case is discussed below.

Separation and **binding of duty** (SoD/BoD) are the most straightforward security properties that can be modelled using SCF, integrated nicely in its GUI and tools palette. It is supported through the SecureBPMN extension (cf. Chapter 8) to BPMN and the Activiti tool. Although the SESAR SWIM project does not list any SoD/BoD requirement, this construct was extensively used during our case-study modelling, cf. Fig. 6. However, the concrete syntax makes it impossible to express SoD/BoD properties across diagrams. For example, it was impossible to capture a binding of duty between the logging services in all our BPMN diagrams. Another issue with the graphical notation was scalability, with quickly rising visual clutter in the diagrams.

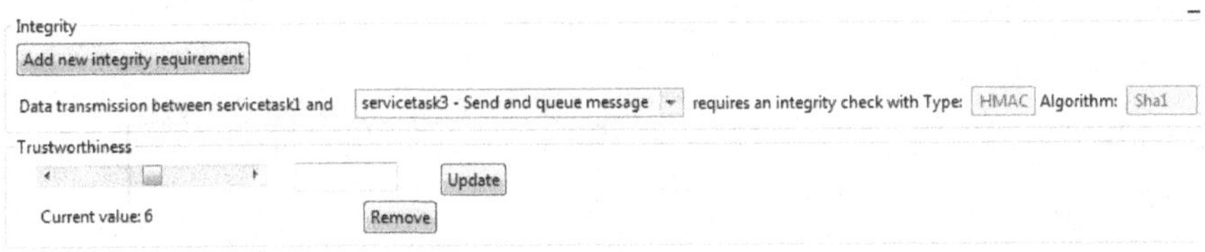

Fig. 9. Defining integrity and trustworthiness requirements for a service task

In SCF, **data confidentiality** is captured through a tick box and a drop-down menu for the selection of the confidentiality level (cf. Fig. 7), for inputs and outputs of service tasks. In our case-study, we first identified all confidential data (e.g., the pilot's identification token). Then, we expressed the data confidentiality property on each data flow comprehending at least one confidential datum. This modelling approach was found heavy and error-prone, because confidential data is involved in many flows. SCF should allow specifying data confidentiality on individual datum, rather than on data flows.

Data transmission integrity and **data authenticity** requirements were captured wherever needed with the choice of the *HMAC* construct and the *SHA1* algorithm. The notation was found to be very compact, as illustrated in Fig. 9, through the specification of the data flow source and target services, the type of integrity check to be implemented and the supporting algorithm. However, we deplored the lack of support for the choice of the construct and algorithm. Moreover, it was not possible to capture integrity requirements on control flows (by opposition to data flows).

In SCF, **Trustworthiness** is captured through an input field and an *Add* button (cf. Fig. 9). Lack of end-user documentation made the assessment of the capture of trustworthiness more complex than it should have been. We first thought that the initial trustworthiness values of atomic services were automatically assigned some neutral values. It turned out, that the initial trustworthiness values of atomic services needed to be initialised in the marketplace and that could only be done manually in an ad hoc fashion.

In SCF, **Role Based Access Control** (RBAC) allows for the specification of a Role's permission to perform an Action on the selected service; the possible actions are *Full Access, Claim, Assign* and *Complete*. The RBAC labels were found to be not self-explicit and the tool provided no definition for each of those actions.

In SCF, **Need-to-know (NtK)** allows for the specification of a Role's permission to perform an Action on a Process Variable of the selected service. The possible actions are *Read, Write* and *Read/Write*. In our case study, a number of NtK requirements were input. Coverage was good, but modelling work proved itself a long and tedious process. Indeed, input is done task per task, iterating on each applicable role.

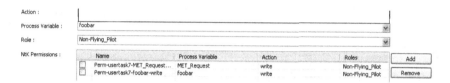

Fig. 10. Need-to-know specification

Delegation allows for the specification of delegation permissions on user tasks only, involving the definition of a Delegation Type, and when relevant, a Negotiable attribute and a Delegation Depth attribute. The possible delegation types are *None, Simple* and *Transfer*, whilst the Negotiable attribute can take its value in {*Yes, No, Dynamic*}: the labels were found to be not self-explicit and the tool provided no definition for each of those options.

In our SWIM scenario, we needed to model a **segregation** security requirement (cf. AG-SR7 in §3). This specification could not be achieved using SCF.

5.4   A Seamless Transition from Design-Time to Runtime

Our ATM SWIM case-study was planned as a design-time test case only. However, the Aniketos engineering process blurs the frontier between design-time and runtime (cf. §5.2). Thus, working on pure design-time engineering activities with the Aniketos tool suite proved impossible. We therefore briefly assessed a set of runtime tools that were required to perform design-time activities, i.e. tools supporting: (i) the compilation of security properties, (ii) the generation and validation of composition plans, and (iii) the deployment of a composite service. The corresponding feedback is provided below, but it does not go into as much details as for the aforementioned Aniketos design-time methods and tools.

The **compilation of security properties** is ensured by the Conspec editor. The Conspec Editor allows for the editing of the security properties specified in the Service Composition Framework. Encoding and saving is then done into an eXtensible Mark-up Language (XML) file, for reuse by other Aniketos modules. This additional and redundant format was found to be tedious and a potential source of inconsistencies and regression within the secure service engineering framework. Moreover, it is very complex to use, and the approach does not scale.

The SCF allows for **generating composition plans** for all possible compositions of service components. It is then possible to browse through the plans, as shown in Fig. 11. However, the number of plans rises dramatically fast, and the value of this browsing capability does not extend beyond toy examples, especially with respect to the human cognitive capability to select one composition plan amongst hundreds of options.

Generation and **verification of composition plans** allows for the short-listing and sorting of plans according to security properties: trustworthiness, credibility (based on how many security properties have been verified) and validity (based on when the verified security properties are to expire). This capability was not assessed.

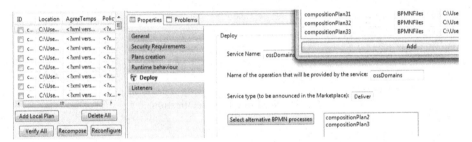

Fig. 11. Generating composition plans and selecting alternatives for deployment

Deploying composite services was however quite straightforward, using the built in function for connecting to a service runtime environment (SRE). We were able to use an already operational SRE infrastructure, with an execution engine for running the BPMN process provided by Activiti. The composite service process could be invoked as expected, as a web service.

5.5   Conclusion

The Service Composition Framework was found to be a reliable framework providing a rich set of security properties to work with. Even though the ATM SWIM test case provided us with a well-defined evaluation context, none of the security requirements that we worked on were ATM specific. Therefore SCF seems to be a sound and generic baseline for future industrial exploitation. However, the engineering process with SCF requires service discovery to support security requirements specification at design-time (cf. §5.2): this engineering process issue must absolutely be solved before considering industrial exploitation. Moreover, SCF suffers from a number of weaknesses that also need to be corrected before considering industrial exploitation, e.g. unclear semantics for some concepts (cf. §5.3), inconsistent integration of satellite tools, and unnecessary technical complexities (cf. §5.4).

6   Conclusion

The ATM SWIM case-study (cf. §23) was specified from the start as a design-time case. Naturally, it focused on the Aniketos Socio-Technical Security Requirements package and on the Aniketos Secure Service Specification and Deployment package (cf. Chapter 4).

The Socio-Technical Security modelling language, methodology and tool were extensively used. The overall assessment was definitely positive, even if some issues were raised with respect to rapid industrial use, but nothing unusual with respect to a research prototype (cf. §4). The main strength of the STS-tool is that it corresponds to a real Air Traffic Management (ATM) community need for a tool to support the elicitation of security requirements in the current phase of System Wide Information Management (SWIM) development.

The Aniketos Secure Service Specification and Deployment package prompts stronger reservations. This package was found to be a reliable framework providing a rich set of security properties to work with, and therefore seems to be a sound baseline for future industrial exploitation (cf. §5). However, SCF suffers from a number of weaknesses, e.g., unclear semantics for some concepts, fuzzy integration of satellite tools, and unnecessary technical complexities. Moreover, end-users (both Aniketos partners and external ATM and SESAR stakeholders) had difficulties in understanding and applying the overall design-time security engineering process. From our perspective, the Technology Readiness Level (TRL) of this package still requires to be raised before considering industrial application in the ATM domain.

More information on the Aniketos SWIM test case and its detailed evaluation can be found in [15, 16].

7   Disclaimer

© SESAR JOINT UNDERTAKING, 2014. The content of this section was provided under the responsibilities of the Aniketos Case Study B partners, including NATMIG for the SESAR JOINT UNDERTAKING within the frame of the SESAR programme co-financed by the EU and Eurocontrol. The opinions expressed herein reflect the authors' view only. The SESAR JOINT UNDERTAKING is not liable for the use of any information included herein. Reprint with approval of publisher and with reference to source code only.

References

1. Deliverables of SESAR Project 08.01.04 – Aeronautical information (AIS Airport Manning, Airport Network, Terrain and Obstacles)
2. Deliverables of SESAR Project 08.01.06 – Information Modelling Meteorological Domain
3. Deliverables of SESAR Project 08.03.03 – Identify and Develop Aeronautical Information ATM Services
4. Deliverables of SESAR Project 09.19 – SWIM Air-Ground Capability
5. Deliverables of SESAR Project 09.31 – Aeronautical databases
6. Deliverables of SESAR Project 09.48 – AIS/MET Serv. & Data Distr.
7. Deliverables of SESAR Project 13.2.2 – Aeronautical Information Management sub-system definition
8. Deliverables of SESAR Work Package 14 Projects – System Wide Information Management (SWIM)
9. Deliverables of SESAR Project 16.06.02 – Security support and coordination function
10. SESAR Joint Undertaking, SESAR Factsheet n°02/2010, Business Trajectory / '4D' Trajectory (2010),
    http://www.sesarju.eu/sites/default/files/documents/reports/
    SESAR_Factsheet_4DTrajectory__2_.pdf (accessed June 06, 2014)
11. Paja, E., et al.: Final version of the socio-technical security modelling language and tool. Deliverable D1.4, FP7 ICT Secure and Trustworthy Composite Services (ANIKETOS) project (Mai 2013)
12. French national agency for the security of IT systems (ANSSI). Expression of Needs and Identification of Security Objectives (EBIOS), Risk management method (2010)
13. CRAMM – the Total Information Security Toolkit, http://www.cramm.com/

14. Lund, M.S., Solhaug, B., Stølen, K.: Model-Driven Risk Analysis – The CORAS Approach. Springer (2011)
15. D'Errico, M., et al.: Final report on Aniketos applied to industrial case studies. Deliverable D6.4, FP7 ICT Secure and Trustworthy Composite Services (ANIKETOS) project (June 2014)
16. Beck, E., et al.: Results of the final validation and evaluation of the ANIKETOS platform. Deliverable D7.3, FP7 ICT Secure and Trustworthy Composite Services (ANIKETOS) project (June 2014)

Supporting Security and Trust
in Complex e-Government Services

Vasilis Tountopoulos[1,*], Ira Giannakoudaki[2], Konstantinos Giannakakis[1],
Lefteris Korres[2], and Leonidas Kallipolitis[1]

[1] Athens Technology Center S.A., Halandri, Athens, Greece
{v.tountopoulos,k.giannakakis,l.kallipolitis}@atc.gr
[2] DAEM, Athens, Greece
{i.giannakoudaki,l.korres}@daem.gr

Abstract. The next generation e-Government will be based on Future Internet applications, which can be dynamically composed of complex services, by utilising the mass data being made available in heterogeneous online archives and information sources. Such data can be synthesised as the outcome of a plethora of atomic services, which process and collaboratively handle digital information to facilitate the current business needs of the Public Administration. However, the providers of public services face the problem of maintaining security and preserving data privacy, when integrating this data into dynamically changing composite service environments. In that respect, this chapter presents the application of the design time and runtime capabilities of the Aniketos platform to support the whole data driven secure service development life cycle and ensure trust in service compositions, which can be consumed in value-added public service delivery processes.

Keywords: socio-technical security, trusted public services, secure service-based e-Government.

1   Introduction

The plethora of Web content offers the environment for leveraging innovation in ICT systems and building on new business paradigms to increase user satisfaction and bring benefits to society as a whole. Modern Governments try to follow the advances in the service and software engineering field to bring innovation in everyday life and offer a totally new experience of how public services are being provided to citizens, enterprises and other Governments as well, taking into account the need to address security and trust, when delivering such services.

Modern e-Government applications can integrate available common vocabularies, geospatial information, regulatory publications and citizens' deliberation data, which enhance the experience and the innovation of such applications. Towards this direction, the next generation of e-Government will involve a multi-provider environment

---

* Corresponding author.

A.D. Brucker et al. (Eds.): Secure Service Composition, LNCS 8900, pp. 219–233, 2014.

for delivering data intensive composite service processes, which expose a set of security and trustworthiness concerns.

During the composition of such service processes, the Aniketos platform (see Chapter 4 for details) can be adopted to fill in the current lack of existing secure solutions to effectively deliver data streams, being classified under various privacy and trustworthiness levels [1], according to stated legislation and public administration policies. These data may exhibit different security requirements on various dimensions, such as the value of the information that is delivered as a result of the service provisioning chain and the responsible organisation or the application role in providing the resulting information.

Subsequently, this chapter will elaborate on addressing the security and trust requirements attributed both to the data holders and the data content itself when designing, developing and implementing public services to deliver such type of data. The chapter is structured as follows. Section 2 identifies and elaborates on the problem for delivering secure public services. Section 3 describes the use of the Aniketos platform to support security requirements in the design and specification of secure composite service specifications, while section 4 presents the exploitation of the Aniketos platform offerings at runtime to consume the secure composite services in building business applications for the e-Government domain. Section 5 analyses our considerations and assessment from the application of the Aniketos platform in this specific domain and the chapter is concluded in section 6, briefly introducing the future directions for the further adoption of the Aniketos platform in the public service delivery process.

2   Problem Statement

In the context of online public services, security is considered as a major strategic and technological challenge that needs to be addressed in all e-Government service cases. Data exchanged among the involved parties in a public service paradigm should be safeguarded with respect to key security attributes, including data integrity and trustworthiness of the participating roles and systems.

The current European initiative for public services is headed towards a brand new approach, in which the technological advances in the ICT domain (including the Web2.0 paradigm and the SOA-based architectures) appear to be the solution for providing accurate, secure and trusted electronic public services to citizens, enterprises and public organisations.

2.1   An Introduction to Existing Solutions

Current e-Government systems focus on establishing the routes for making the public service delivery an online experience for all interacting stakeholders. Up to now, closed systems have been implemented, which may automate the processes, but they offer an isolating approach on the way data is exchanged between multiple providers and consumers. In alignment with the business needs in this domain and the pillars drawn in the Digital Agenda for Europe, e-Government applications move to the next step and aim to address the key objective of integrating service delivery at the most digital service level within the next few years. As a result, the achievement of interoperability between existing or developing IT systems arises as the major step to bridge the gap in existing complex e-Government applications.

However, the synthesis of heterogeneous data in composite public service chains raises major concerns about the security and trustworthiness maintenance, when offering such services. Thus, as the maturity level of the existing solutions on the field of electronic public services appears to be rather low, the majority of data exchange is currently handled manually, especially in cross public bodies transactions, which actually affects the performance and the quality of the service delivery process, especially whenever a critical decision has to be made on the process outcome.

Data involved in public service processes can be classified, according to their privacy level, as defined in local, national and international legislation, such as the Directive 95/46/EC [2], while the respective mechanisms for securing services may be controlled from the impact imposed by the loss of data integrity. The problem becomes more challenging as alternative end user devices (desktop PCs, mobiles, smart cards, etc.) and service channels, such as Central Governmental Portals, are to be supported in order to improve the citizens' experience on public service delivery and increase their satisfaction.

2.2   The Case Study

In order to define the problem we are trying to solve, we consider DAEM, the City of Athens IT Company, as the organisation dedicated in developing and providing e-Government related implementation services to local authorities and other public bodies and organisations. The following domain specific case study represents the implementation of the supporting service framework related to the scenario of when, where and what to acquire when searching for a piece of land (lot), so as to build a residence for individual or professional use.

Such a scenario involves many factors affecting decisions that should be made at various stages of the scenario implementation. Such factors involve among others the credibility of the lot owner to publish correct information about the lot, the trustworthiness of the solicitors that could be selected to assist in deciding which lot to acquire and the accuracy of the lot information, as it is delivered from the various roles involved in the scenario. In addition, for each decision point, a variety of security threats and vulnerabilities (i.e. denial of service, fake identity, inappropriate access control, breaches on sensitive data, etc.) are in place as a result of the nature of the e-Government scenario itself and the current regulatory framework. Therefore, in order to build the application that would facilitate the lot acquisition process, DAEM should meet the objective of enabling both citizens or the various service consumers and involved organisations to interact within a complex secure public service provisioning scenario.

Existing approaches limit the scope of this scenario by enabling partial electronic access to only a subset of available online information. On the contrary and in order to bypass the deficiencies of current systems in terms of trust and security, the complete service process for lot acquisition is split into manually and automatically accomplished steps. For example, as part of their commercial business, DAEM has developed two different systems, which are, currently, in operational mode to facilitate selected functionalities, while other steps can only be accomplished through individual and ad hoc access to external third party sources or public administrations.

This raises significant overhead, in both a time and cost manner, for those being interested in the lot acquisition service process.

Thus, the problem lies on how to use the Aniketos platform and develop a service-based application to effectively tackle the security and trustworthiness concerns that prevent the consumers of Governmental services from the use of electronic means to complete their interactions with the Public Administration.

2.3   Security and Trustworthiness Concerns

Focusing on the case of the lot acquisition service process, vast data is exchanged to accomplish the foreseen tasks for searching and managing a lot and issuing the relevant building permits as well. All this amount of information is generated by multiple providers, ranging from public organisations and the involved end users to other external stakeholders. Based on both the European and Greek e-government interoperability frameworks [3,4], which provide the specifications and guidelines on how such public services can be electronically assembled, the relevant infrastructure should implement many interaction points and interfaces, through the realisation of secure Web services.

Security at this point spans across many attributes due to the fact that the exchanged data can be classified according to their privacy level, as it was stated above. A general classification can, for instance, be the following:

- Information on the lot properties, such as the geographical coordinates, the building terms that apply to the specific area that the lot resides in and other lot information are considered as data publicly available, which can be subsequently accessed by all involved stakeholders without any need for authentication.
- Lot owner information, such as the VAT number and personal ID card number, which should be securely submitted to the relevant systems in DAEM in order for the house building permit to be issued.
- If the application process for issuing the house building permit is performed over a Governmental Service Portal (GSP) and not directly from DAEM systems, the necessary trustworthiness between both the end user and the GSP, and the GSP and the DAEM system as well, should be established.

In the above described examples, we can identify two different levels of data privacy. In the first case, we deal with public data, which can be accessed by anyone, thus the services exposing such data should bear trust properties only with respect to the data accuracy. However, if a security service violation occurs and the relevant trust level is not contained, then the impact of inaccurate data on the process may not be critical.

In the second case, the data exchanged refer to private data, which should be as accurate as possible in order for the permit to be issued and access is only granted to authorised roles. In consequence, the trustworthiness of services is extended to the authenticated and role-based service access.

In the third case, a different business model is adopted by introducing the concept of a service broker that can act on behalf of the end users. The problem of security and trustworthiness in service engineering (including service design, access, execution and consumption) is further extended here to the exchange of service trust levels among multiple stakeholders.

2.4   The Aniketos Platform Perspective

In order to address the challenges raised in the previous section, the Aniketos platform (see Chapter 4 for details) is used by DAEM to support the specification and development of secure composite public service processes, involving sensitive classified information. The platform offers design time and runtime support of security and trust in the development of the service processes that will be used in the Web application, which DAEM will offer to citizens, enterprises and any other interested party to facilitate the needs of the lot acquisition case study.

The Aniketos platform is exploited in the development process of the lot acquisition case study in two different phases, as explained here:

- At design time, the composition of the services processes involved in the execution of the application for the lot acquisition case study is specified, based on the security requirements of the business stakeholders and the required trust level of environment, in which these processes will be executed
- At runtime, the execution of the composite public service processes is monitored to ensure that the security and trust properties of the service-based environment are maintained, while appropriate service adaptation actions are enforced, as a response to changes in the security provisions of the service execution chain.

Through the Aniketos platform, this case study can be eventually evolved to a secure Web application, which fades the security concerns of the Internet-skilled users and boosts the economic impact from the adoption of secure ICT systems in the e-Government domain. At design-time, the platform offers the providers of public and private services the capability to identity the security breaches and the relevant threats, which are associated with the particular service processes that need to be implemented,   and control the runtime behaviour of such services to effectively respond to environment changes.

Furthermore, the use of the Aniketos platform in the development of this case study demonstrates how specific end user security and trust requirements are evolved to system level security mechanisms to offer complex interactive Web service based applications that require the integration of open, linked, personal and sensitive data.

The next section provides highlights on the use of the Aniketos platform software components and the technologies developed there, as they are analysed in Chapters 3, 4, 5 and 8, to support the full scale development cycle of this case study.

3   Developing Secure Public Services

3.1   Requirements-Based Service Specification

In order to define the abstract level security requirements for the lot acquisition case study, the relevant service designer, the public administration business executive and potentially a security expert can work together using the Socio-technical Security Requirements software package (see Chapters 4 and 7 for details). Through this package, all the necessary actions that should be taken in order to realize the case study, along with the involved stakeholders for the objective of identifying a suitable lot and building permit to be issued from the local authorities and handed to the interested party as well.

Each objective is presented in the form of goals that are decomposed and delegated among the scenario roles and agents based on specific security and trustworthiness requirements and the possible security threats involved in the scenarios. The steps that the service designer should follow to model the use case, with the support of the public administration executive and the security expert, are based on the STS-ml methodology (see Chapter 5 for details) and can be summarised in the following:

1. Identify and structure the ecosystem actors
2. Describe the ecosystem actors
3. Identify the assets of the ecosystem actors
4. Identify actor capabilities and potential co-operations
5. Describe the resources
6. Link the primary assets together
7. Delegate collaborative goals and describe security needs
8. Ensure validity of delegations
9. Identify possible threats
10. Define, review and approve the security requirements (Trustworthiness, Integrity, Availability and Confidentiality)

Through these steps, the service designer can have the complete overview of the definition and specification of the security requirements needed for each scenario of the land acquisition and building permit case study. An extract of the generated model is depicted in Fig. 1.

Here, we focus on the goal for getting a map view of the available lots when searching for the most suitable one in the area of interest. For this goal, we are interested in defining a minimum threshold for the trustworthiness of the services accomplished this goal. The extracted set of commitments [5, 6] that are generated from the above model into a machine readable (XML like) security requirements specification (SRS) document is shown in Fig. 2.

Using the Secure Service Specification and Deployment package (see Chapters 4 and 9 for details), the SRS commitments can be translated into a formal service specification language, which is a variant of the Business Process Modelling Notation (BPMN) [7], enhanced with security properties [8], for our case (see Chapter 8 for details). This specification is a process diagram that depicts the process flows of the described scenarios. The SRS commitments are inherited into the corresponding services tasks to exhibit the service level security requirements that should be fulfilled. Such requirements, include the trustworthiness of the providers, the integrity of the data involved, the confidentiality of the data-based service delivery, fundamental access control checks with respect to separation and binding of duty restrictions and the threats that can be associated with specific actions in this case study. The visual depiction of the package to perform these service level requirements is shown in Fig. 3.

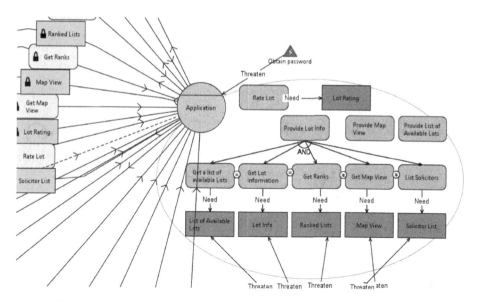

Fig. 1. The generated socio-technical security requirements specification model

```
- <commitment id="C5">
  - <debtor>
      <role id="1319459864828_0.740009334714889">IP</role>
    </debtor>
  - <creditor>
      <role id="1319459864828_0.740009334714889">IP</role>
    </creditor>
  - <precondition>
    - <trustworthiness minLevel="7">
      - <destination>
          <agent id="1342017247588_0.2748681103185343">Application</agent>
        </destination>
          <goal id="1381745334239_0.6995791735772233">Get Map View</goal>
      </trustworthiness>
    </precondition>
  - <postcondition>
    - <delegation>
      - <source>
          <role id="1319459864828_0.740009334714889">IP</role>
        </source>
      - <destination>
          <agent id="1342017247588_0.2748681103185343">Application</agent>
        </destination>
      - <goalSet>
          <goal id="1381745334239_0.6995791735772233">Get Map View</goal>
        </goalSet>
        <transferable>true</transferable>
      </delegation>
    </postcondition>
  </commitment>
```

Fig. 2. The security requirements specification document

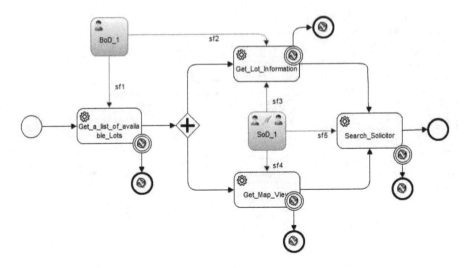

Fig. 3. The formal representation of the service process for Process for retrieving a lot

3.2   Analysis of Security Properties in Service Specifications

The defined values for the security requirements that should be addressed by the service specification can be modified or updated through the Secure Service Specification and Deployment package (see Chapters 4 and 9 for details). This package offers a service configuration tab, which hosts the security requirements that have been associated with a certain service process task. Additionally, the package provides the definition of requirements for the composite service process view. The whole set of security requirements, either referring to the composite process or the process tasks, is considered as the policy to which the actual service process execution should comply with. For example, as shown in Fig. 3, the task for getting a map view of the area of interest with the available lots should be provided by a separate service provider compared to the one delivering the lot information, since a separation of duty requirement is applied.

The service process view defines an abstract view of the functional and security characteristics that should be addressed by the actual implementation. In order to realise the composition and associate it with existing services, the package facilitates service discovery requests to identify the most suitable service components, which should be attached to the service process tasks, according to functional and security characteristics checks. An example of the service discovery process for the case of the available service implementations with respect to getting a list of lots is depicted in Fig. 4. In order to accomplish this step, the service designer has to define the type of the operation of the web service that must be bound to the selected service process task.

Following the service binding process, a number of available combinations for the composite service specification of retrieving a lot are created. The service developer is assisted in the selection of the most appropriate one by invoking the Security Service Validation and Verification package (see Chapters 4 and 10 for details), which performs security analysis checks, both for the composite service process and the atomic service components. The checks aim to identify which are the strongest combinations of existing service parts that can satisfy the range of the already defined security requirements and facilitate the secure and trusted execution of the composite service. The outcome of this process is the selection of the most suitable secure composite service specification.

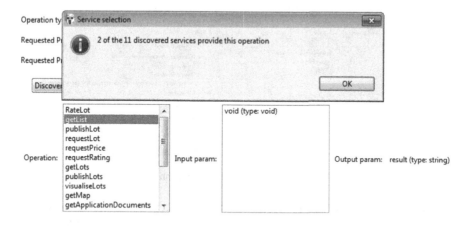

Fig. 4. Discovering existing service implementations

4 Using Secure Composite Services in Operational Environments

4.1 Monitoring Secure Service Compositions

Using the Aniketos platform, a service developer in DAEM can deploy the selected secure service composition and monitor the proper execution to ensure that the defined security properties are continuously monitored to verify the maintenance of certain trust and security values. DAEM needs this service to be consumed in the context of a business application that is implemented to facilitate the lot acquisition and issuing the building permit business case study. Given the operational environment of such an application, the identification of vulnerabilities and the exposure of threats are probable to the extent that the secure composite service execution might be at risk. As such, the deployment of the selected secure composite service specification needs to be enriched with the definition of rules, which should govern the runtime behaviour of the service execution for appropriate response.

Thus, upon the development of the composite secure service specification and prior to the actual deployment of the selected composition as a Web Service, the service provider needs to define rules for the runtime behaviour. This can be done through the Security Monitoring and Notification package of the Aniketos platform (see Chapters 4, 12 and 13 for details), which enables defining multiples rules that can be created for different security violation cases, such as threat level change, trust level change, security property change, etc. For that reason, a rule editor has been developed, as depicted in Fig. 5. This figure shows a rule about a trust level change event occurrence during the composite service execution, which is associated to the "Get map view" process of the secure service specification of Fig. 3. The rule scope is set 'Anywhere in the process" and the action defined is 'Try re-composition and re-configuration'.

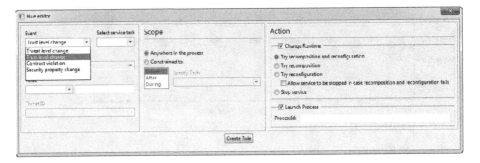

Fig. 5. Run Time Rule Definition

Furthermore, the Security Monitoring and Notification package (see Chapters 4, 12 and 13 for details) offers the ability for the composite service specification to subscribe to the Aniketos platform monitoring components for certain security violation cases. These subscriptions are used to track the normal operation of the composite service, within the context of the business application, and the generation of classified alerts, in case of an event exposure.

4.2   Dynamically Adapting Public Service Delivery Process

In order to trigger the Aniketos platform provisions to handle security violations and assess the effectiveness to dynamically support service adaptation, we have built the Lot Manager prototype implementation of the business case study for lot acquisition. Lot Manager is a Web application that consumes Aniketos compliant composite services, which are made available through the Aniketos Marketplace, and allows users perform lot management operations in a secure way. To this end, we have connected the Lot Manager application with the selected secure composite service deployment of the previous section so that it offers the end user functionalities with respect to publishing a lot that is for sale, searching for available lots near a specified address, getting a map view of the selected lots and selecting a solicitor to help the user across the lot acquisition process.

A normal service operation for this application is shown in Fig. 6. As it is seen there, the user can navigate to the Lot Search Tab in order to perform a search for available lots. This is done by defining values for lot type, registration date window and lot state. Also a desired address is given as well as the range from this address, in order to define the search area of interest. The output of this search is a list of available lots. Additional information for each of the lots of the list is provided, such as lot description, the seller contact information, etc. For this specific operation, the Lot

Manager application consumes the Aniketos compliant services that facilitate functionalities with respect to *getAlistofAvailableLots* and *getLotInformation* service process tasks of Fig. 3. These two processes are supported by the same (Lot Information)
service provider, implementing the binding of duty security requirement, which has
been specified for the respective service tasks on the process flow model.

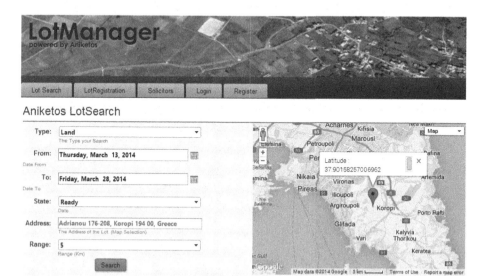

Fig. 6. The Lot Manager application – Facilitate maps through Provider A

By selecting a specific lot from the resulting list, the end user can navigate to the
list of available lots through a map view. At this specific step of the Lot Manager
execution, the getMapView service process is invoked, which consumes an external
Web service from a service provider A (see Fig. 6). During the service discovery
phase for the service process task, two candidate map service providers (A and B)
have been discovered, due to the fact that the trustworthiness requirement, which is
presented in Fig. 2, is being satisfied by both providers, and the selected secure service composition has been based on this service provider A.

The assessment of the service candidates is a dynamic process. If the bound actual
Web Service no longer fulfils the security requirements, then the Aniketos platform
should seamlessly react and determine the type of the service adaptation that should
be adopted. Thus, we assume that the trustworthiness value of the map service provider A deteriorates to be below the requirement of Fig. 2, which triggers specific
alerts and the service adaptation process of the Aniketos platform.

To this end, the runtime verification process of the Security Service Validation and
Verification package (see Chapters 4 and 10 for details) is invoked, which offers the
Aniketos platform a realisation on which is the most appropriate action to redress the
violation occurred. The decision is made as a combination of the outcome of the verification process and the expected behaviour of the composite service, as it has been
defined through the rules that were analysed in Section 4.1.

The result of the dynamic adaptation involves runtime recompositon, in which the map view process part of the composite service that is consumed in the Lot Manager business application changes to be provided by the map service provider B, as shown in Fig. 7. This result still addresses the security requirements, as they have been expressed in the design time.

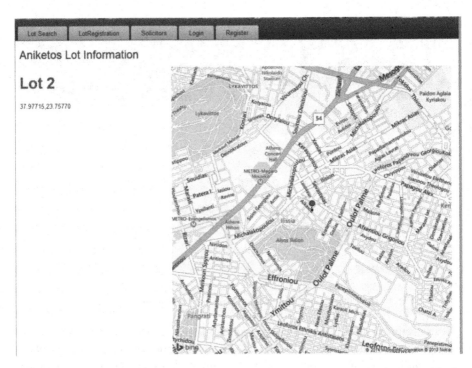

Fig. 7. The Lot Manager application – Adapt the provision of the map service from Provider B

5   Evaluation Considerations

Following the development of business case study using the capabilities of the Aniketos platform to support security and trust both at design time and runtime, we highlight that, in order to make use of the full range of the Aniketos functionalities, different levels of skills and expertise are required. Although this seems to be a considerable risk towards the adoption of the Aniketos platform in a business application, it is an actual benefit for the effective collaboration of various experts that should be inheritably involved to realise and build really trusted and secure services and applications.

At design time and based on the work that was described in section 3, the adoption of the Aniketos components enabled us to define security and trust requirements at two different levels. First, on a high, conceptual level, the use of the Socio-technical Security Requirements package helped us setting the problem, visually describing the security needs and for which goals and documents they should apply and assessing the risks arising from our perspective on how the scenarios should be executed business-wise. At this step, both business executives and security experts in the e-Government domain are required to assist service designers in effectively providing a representation of the high level requirements when designing secure public services.

As a second step, the use of the Secure Service Specification and Deployment package brought to us the depiction of the service developer perspective. However, even at this point, the contribution of the security experts and the business executives is necessary to calibrate the secure specification of the composite services and align it to the actual business needs and security restrictions that are applied in the public service delivery domain, as a result of both the legal framework and the public administration security policies.

At runtime and based on the work that was described in section 4, the Aniketos platform has been used to deploy and operate secure composite services, which have been consumed in order to build the application logic of the lot acquisition business case study. The enactment of rules to control the runtime behaviour of the services helped us building on test scenarios and assessing how we can bring the notion of business continuity to the e-Government sector, by attributing the monitoring of composite public services, with respect to their security robustness, to the Aniketos runtime components. Through the runtime service adaptation features, we evaluated the efficiency of the Aniketos platform to dynamically support the business continuity when operating open to the public services for citizens and enterprises with completely different computer skills.

At this point, we should also consider that the e-Government domain strongly involves the legal dimension in the provision of online secure applications. By bringing together multi-discipline experts in front of simple and usable ICT-based tools, they are capable of "communicating" their own knowledge in a transparent way, making the tools their semantic playground to mutually understand the objectives of the different worlds.

Using the Aniketos platform, it turns out that service composition can be enhanced, enabling the involved stakeholders establishing a sense of trust when using the respective software packages. In many business domains, like the e-Government one, service composition is subject to restrictions, concerns and, in general, considerations, which have to be effectively tackled if service and application providers want to offer real secure products to their customers.

In the e-Government domain, in which citizens and enterprises' trust on ICT systems, owned by the local authorities, increases with the credibility of the public bodies, a third party "certification" of best practice development is necessary. The methodology and tools that the Aniketos platform brings to the open source ICT market can facilitate this specific need. We highlight here the reference to the Aniketos open source solution, because the research trends in the e-Government field encourage the use of open source (and open standards) solutions, which may minimize the final costs for developing applications for secure public service delivery, both for the public authorities, which provide these applications, and the citizens and enterprises, which consume such applications.

6   Conclusions and Future Directions

The business case study that was presented in this chapter refers to a real life application example, targeting the e-Government domain. It involves multiple service providers and consumers, who interact with each other to enable accessing the most up-to-date procedures, information on relevant regulations and advice on associated costs, which affect decisions when acquiring a lot and issuing the respective building permit. Within the scope of this scenario, the chapter presented how the Aniketos platform facilitates the definition of security and trustworthiness requirements, which are identified in order to address the corresponding security problems being faced today, when dealing with traditional approaches in applications for public service delivery.

As the information, which is exchanged between the relevant stakeholders in such a business scenario, can be classified according to privacy and trustworthiness levels, the Aniketos platform has been used to support the secure specification of composite service processes and the appropriate monitoring of their runtime execution, when such specifications are deployed and integrated into modern service-based systems. The lack of the currently available solutions on providing the adequate level of trust and security in the execution of the involved service processes reinforces the adoption of the Aniketos platform provisions to fill in the gap between policy-driven public service delivery and trusted service consumption.

As a future step, the platform has to be adopted in a number of public service delivery case studies to broaden the scope of the security property based service specification and enhance or even extend the functionalities provided by the platform both at design time and runtime.

Through the use of the Aniketos platform to design, develop and implement the Lot Manager application that consumes secure composite services, we managed to showcase that secure service composition can be achieved for real life situations. The Aniketos platform functionalities, such as the service discovery and composition, based on security properties and trust, the notification of service consumers with respect to the secure execution of the service compositions, and the runtime service adaptation for policy driven service provisioning scenarios, can potentially address the user expectations from a multi-service provider environment and improve their online experience on modern and secure public service delivery paradigms.

References

1. Meland, P.H., Guerenabarrena, J.B., Llewellyn-Jones, D.: The challenges of secure and trustworthy service composition in the Future Internet. In: Proceeding of 2011 6th International Conference on System of Systems Engineering (SoSE). IEEE Computer Society (2011)
2. Directive 95/46/EC of the European Parliament and of the Council of 24 October 1995 on the protection of individuals with regard to the processing of personal data and on the free movement of such data. Official Journal L 281, 0031–0050 (November 23, 1995)
3. EIF - European Interoperability Framework for pan-European eGovernment services, http://ec.europa.eu/idabc

4. Greek e-Government Interoperability Framework, `http://www.e-gif.gov.gr/portal/page/portal/egif/`
5. Paja, E., Choprab, A.K., Giorgini, P.: Trust-based specification of sociotechnical systems. Data & Knowledge Engineering 87, 339–353 (2013), doi:10.1016/j.datak.2012.12.005
6. Paja, E., Dalpiaz, F., Giorgini, P.: Managing Security Requirements Conflicts in Socio-Technical Systems. In: Ng, W., Storey, V.C., Trujillo, J.C. (eds.) ER 2013. LNCS, vol. 8217, pp. 270–283. Springer, Heidelberg (2013), doi:10.1007/978-3-642-41924-9_23.
7. Business Process Modelling and Notation (BPMN), `http://www.bpmn.org`
8. Brucker, A.D., Malmignati, F., Merabti, M., Shi, Q., Zhou, B.: A Framework for Secure Service Composition. In: Procs. of the International Conference on Social Computing 2013 (SocialCom), pp. 647–652. IEEE (2013), doi:10.1109/SocialCom.2013.97

Characteristics and Addressed Challenges in Evaluating the Aniketos Project Outcome

Elke Beck, Sandra Trösterer, Alexander G. Mirnig, and Manfred Tscheligi

HCI & Usability Unit, ICT&S Center, University of Salzburg
Sigmund-Haffner-Gasse 18, 5020 Salzburg, Austria
{elke.beck,sandra.troesterer,alexander.mirnig,
manfred.tscheligi}@sbg.ac.at
www.icts.uni-salzburg.at

Abstract. Aside from technical R&D and outreach activities in the Aniketos project, one part of the project work comprised of validation and end user evaluation tasks. We describe the particular characteristics of the Aniketos project evaluation and the overall challenges we encountered during our evaluation tasks. These challenges are structured along four elements of evaluation work; viz., 1) *project-internal stakeholders* who were doing evaluation work or benefiting from the findings, 2) the developed *objects* that were evaluated, 3) the *development process* in which the evaluation process was embedded, and 4) the *beneficiaries of the project outcome* who participated in evaluation studies. We outline the multi-perspective evaluation approach pursued to address these challenges and to ultimately conduct evaluations of such a highly complex and multifaceted project. We conclude with examples and lessons learned from our evaluation work and provide recommendations for project evaluations under similar conditions.

Keywords: Evaluation, HCI, user-centred evaluation, project management.

1 Introduction

As presented in Chapter 4, the Aniketos project's R&D outcome is the Aniketos platform, i.e., scenarios, methods, tools, and security services. Next to these technical R&D activities in the Aniketos project, one part of project work comprised validation and end user evaluation tasks. The objectives of these tasks were to systematically validate the Aniketos results with regard to specific quality criteria (e.g., functionality, usability), as well as to perform end user focused evaluations of the Aniketos platform in the context of the projects' three industry case studies representing future European composite services (see Chapter 14 and 15). The Aniketos project was a relatively large undertaking, divided into twelve work packages, eight of which were dedicated for research and technological development. It took seventeen partners from across Europe (all of them large

A.D. Brucker et al. (Eds.): Secure Service Composition, LNCS 8900, pp. 234–246, 2014.

players in either industry or research) 46 months to go from an initial concept to a working platform. In order to comprehensively assess the effectiveness and impact of the project outcome over such an expansive time period and project structure, we strived for an evaluation process with specific characteristics.

First, we aimed at applying a combination of different validation and evaluation approaches, taking into account the plurality of scientific and professional backgrounds in the project. For instance, we combined test-driven development [4] with a user-centred evaluation approach [5], which ensured that the developed modules, tools, and the Aniketos platform will be secure, trustworthy, and easy to use by developers and the diverse stakeholders. Since the project results were practically applied in the industry case studies, we were also interested in case study specific validation methodologies, such as the European Operational Concept Validation Methodology (E-OCVM) [6] for the Air Traffic Management case study (see Chapter 14).

Second, in striving for a comprehensive evaluation within Aniketos, we aimed at considering a multitude of evaluation objectives, criteria, and methods for assessing the projects' outcome. The Aniketos platform modules were assessed from a technical perspective with regard to, e.g., functionality, performance, scalability, and integration. Some of the methods used were, e.g., JUnit tests (TimedTests and LoadTests). From a Human-Computer Interaction (HCI) and Usability viewpoint, we were also interested in understanding users and their interaction with the user interfaces in Aniketos and thus investigated, for instance, usability, user experience, technology acceptance, suitability, and compliance with standard work practices of users. We conducted interviews, surveys, usability tests and inspections, observations, group discussions, expert reviews, and walkthroughs to assess these quality criteria.

While working towards a comprehensive assessment of the project outcome, we encountered several challenges and difficulties with the evaluation work in the course of the project, which we present and discuss in this chapter. More specifically, we reflect on the user and technology-centred evaluation work in the Aniketos project. We offer our experiential knowledge gained in our work, i.e., a summary of challenges and characteristics of the evaluation work and lessons learned from doing evaluation work. We hope this chapter will be helpful for project participants in similar projects, who want to design and conduct multi-perspective evaluations (i.e., technology- and user-centred) within these projects. The presented challenges and related recommendations can serve as an information pool for other project participants who (plan to) conduct evaluation work in large-scale interdisciplinary R&D projects.

2   Identified Challenges

In the following section, we provide an overview about the identified challenges. For describing the challenges we encountered, we structure them along four distinguished elements of evaluation work:

Project-Internal Stakeholder Related Challenges. One element of the evaluation work is the project-internal stakeholders who are doing evaluation work or benefiting from the findings. It took an effort to establish collaboration for aligning evaluation activities and communicating evaluation findings among project stakeholders due to a plurality of scientific and professional backgrounds in the project.

Evaluation-Object Related Challenges. Another element is the developed objects that are evaluated. In Aniketos, evaluation had to handle a highly complex and pioneering object of evaluation (i.e., the Aniketos complete solution, see Chapter 4).

Development-Process Related Challenges. The evaluation process was embedded in the overall development process in Aniketos in order to enable iterative evaluation of the developed components in the course of the project. Therefore both processes had to be aligned in terms of matching the evaluation procedure with the status of the developed component. Still, evaluation had to face the challenge that single components of the platform were developed at different speeds. Thus, in addition to the individual component evaluations, only at the end of the project was a unified whole available for evaluation.

Evaluation-Participants Related Challenges. Finally, there are challenges related to the beneficiaries of the project outcome, such as the envisioned future users of the Aniketos platform, e.g., composite web service providers, service developers, and service users. In a user-centred approach to evaluation, actual users are often invited to participate in evaluation studies. In Aniketos, we also aimed at accessing user groups for user-centred evaluations, which however was challenging due to the geographically dispersed and partly unknown group of prospective Aniketos users.

In the following sections, we will individually address each of the four types of challenges. Each section is organized by listing our recommendations and lessons learned related to the challenges as subsections. In each subsection, we explain the sources and characteristics of the challenges and how we tried to solve or mitigate them. Moreover, we provide examples from our evaluation activities over the lifetime of the project to better illustrate our lessons learned.

3   Project-Internal Stakeholder Related Challenges: Establishing Collaboration in Evaluation

3.1   Definition of Evaluation Standards and Structures Early in the Project

The project's partners come from a wide range of facilities and institutions, each with a lot of experience in their fields and an according number of work practices they adhere to. This includes how they structure their evaluation activities and format their outcome reports. Having access to existing expertise is beneficial, since it means that the partners can start their share of the work immediately. It also means that the results of their work can vary greatly in structure and detail, depending on their background and the workflow(s) they are used to. Evaluation results and written reports need to be brought into one single format, so consistency needs to be established early on in a project. The challenging aspect of this is that one cannot arbitrarily impose a certain workflow on other partners and hope that they adjust immediately to it (if at all). Enthusiasm is high, especially at the beginning of a project, and partners are often willing to get to work immediately, leaving details and organizational issues to be resolved at a later date. While this might seem reasonable in general, pursuing the complete opposite has turned out to be an effective and simple way to combat inconsistency; by establishing mundane details, such as a concrete semantic structure for all deliverables, down to the chapter names, total number of subsections, and page estimates, everyone had a clear idea about not only what their output would look like, but also knew, in principle, what everyone else would eventually deliver. In Aniketos, in addition to the pre-emptive deliverable structuration, a test case template (specifying, for instance, tested modules, preconditions, steps taken, expected and actual results) was developed and supplied to all evaluation work partners, which served as an aid for their evaluation activities and helped keep results in a consistent and easily readable format. This way, less effort is spent on editing partner contributions and, unintuitive as it may sound, it is worth spending a considerable amount of effort in the beginning phases on simple formatting and structure issues, as this will have to be done sooner or later anyway and ensures consistent output among project partners at the earliest possible stage in the project.

3.2   Networking and Multiple Communication Channels

Another aspect related to the different scientific and professional backgrounds of the Aniketos partners, in addition to the wide variety of nationalities, was communication. This concerned both overall coordination, as well as communication of evaluation findings to the technical work packages. A lot of effort could have been spent on finding a common communication terminology and format, but a completely different and overall more efficient approach led to just as positive results: open access and redundancy. Project partners had open access to all relevant data in the Aniketos project through not only the deliverables, but also through a project-internal repository, which contained evaluation planning files, study materials, raw data collections from evaluation studies, as well as separate evaluation reports. In addition, no single communication channel was enforced and communication among partners happened via e-mail, VoIP, or the online repository's notification function. If a partner could make neither head nor tails of, e.g., a result they read in another deliverable, they could simply have a look at the corresponding study concept and raw data in the repository or contact the author directly via their communication means of preference. In a nutshell, everyone was given different possibilities and more information than necessary, which was available to them at all times. This open approach eventually led to natural networking among project participants and commonly preferred communication channels.

3.3 Making Sure That the Results Reach Their Target Audience: Active and Passive Methods

Having an entire work package dedicated to evaluation tasks has both its benefits as well as drawbacks. The main benefit is obvious: a centralized location for all evaluation results and documentation makes it relatively easy to assess the current status of the project and identify areas for improvement (e.g., tasks for the immediate future). The potential problem of such a dedicated work package, however, is that it can devolve into becoming its own isolated entity, detached from the components it is supposed to evaluate. This happens when the results of the evaluations are not communicated clearly and transparently enough to the technical personnel on the implementation side. The technical work packages have to deal with their own slew of problems and it cannot be expected that every developer is aware of every single evaluation activity at all times, considering that only a small part of all evaluations will touch on the component they are actively developing. A way to bridge this information gap is to make sure that the partners who would benefit from a particular evaluation activity are involved in said activity in one capacity or another. For Aniketos, this meant that evaluations would always be conducted as joint activities between technical and scientific evaluation partners, if at all possible. While having many partners involved might initially seem like an inefficient use of resources, it is arguably much less wasteful than an evaluation conducted only by a single work partner, which is never read or acted upon by anyone. Whenever such collaboration activities were not possible or feasible for whatever reason, the work package coordinator took particular care to foster transparency further and communicate with the developers directly and update them on any on-going evaluation activities or outcomes regarding their component(s).

4 Evaluation-Object Related Challenges: Evaluating a Highly Complex and Pioneering Project Outcome

4.1 Method Triangulation to Tackle a Complex Evaluation Object

In order to achieve a high validity of our evaluation results, we pursued a method triangulation approach (e.g., [2]), i.e., evaluation data is collected via different methods, measures, and approaches, and the analysis and interpretation of the collected data should lead to similar conclusions [3]. Relying on more than one data source for answering certain research questions also helps to get a deeper understanding of the collected examined phenomena. This is very helpful if the evaluation object is complex. For example, during an evaluation workshop on the Socio-Technical Security modelling language and its support tool (STS-ml and STS tool, see Chapter 5), we used questionnaires, cards, observation, structured interviews, and a group discussion in order to gain a comprehensive assessment of the usability of STS-ml and the STS tool. All of those methods were carefully chosen in order to answer our initial research questions concerning the usability and adequacy of the modelling language and tool. Using such an approach certainly requires effort and also one has to carefully consider the data analysis procedure. However, the great advantage is the high degree of comprehensiveness. In the mentioned evaluation, some problems were identified with all methods, but some could only be detected with a certain method or method combination. In Aniketos we also aimed for the adjustment and customisation of existing evaluation methods to the particularities of the Aniketos project. Existing (user-centred) evaluation methods range from expert-based evaluations (e.g., walkthroughs, heuristics for usability and trust) to end-user-based evaluations (e.g., investigating trust-related end-user behaviour via logging analysis, surveys, interviews, focus groups). As an example, one of our current long-term evaluation activities is the collection of (general) feedback about the various Aniketos tools via a short online feedback journal (see Figure 1). We developed this feedback journal to enable people to take notes about positive or negative usability issues with Aniketos tools and services at any time and any place. In contrast to a usability test, the journal collects the issues close to their actual occurrence in natural work environments and with greater user-centred focus than more traditional methods such as, e.g., bug trackers.

4.2 Differing Abstraction Levels for Evaluation Objectives

To make the evaluation of the project outcome manageable, we followed two strategies in defining our evaluation objects when creating our evaluation plan. First, we decomposed the envisioned platform along its building blocks, namely the tools, modules, and components that were defined in the platform design process. This was a viable solution for the technology-centred evaluation activities, which aimed at testing, e.g., the functionality of each platform part. However, for the user-centred evaluation approach, this decomposition of the whole Aniketos platform into single parts for evaluation was less suitable. This approach required user scenarios and user interfaces (in the form of conceptual designs, low- and high-fidelity prototypes) for evaluation, whose definitions were naturally still vague at the beginning of the project. As a second strategy, we therefore also defined more generic, high-level evaluation objectives in the Aniketos Evaluation Plan [1], such as "Aniketos results for architecting and design phases" and "Aniketos platform concepts and user interface". Consequently, the Aniketos targets of evaluation ranged from work package related tools, modules, and components of the Aniketos platform to trans-work-package evaluation targets, i.e., Aniketos results for specific development phases (architecting and design phases), as well as general concepts and user interfaces of tools, methods, and techniques developed within Aniketos. These evaluation targets were also further investigated within each case study.

4.3   Identify Your Internal Users

From our experiences, we conclude that it is very important in a project with
such a complex and new evaluation target, to identify the designated project-
internal users of the Aniketos outcome – the people from the three industry case
studies, using the diverse modules and interfaces developed within the project
– as soon as possible. For our evaluation activities, which focused on diverse
bits and pieces of the unified whole and required different people to participate
depending on the evaluation target, it was always a challenge to find the appropriate people. For this purpose, an online project collaboration platform served
as a helpful starting point, as it provided an overview of all project members and
their company and work package associations. Furthermore, we, e.g., used a short
online-questionnaire (asking about project activities per person) in order to find
out which project members are involved in modelling tasks. This later helped

Negative feedback (e.g. what you dislike about Aniketos services and tools, encountered problems, difficulties, recommenda

Positive feedback (e.g. what you like about Aniketos services and tools, what turned out to be very helpful or useful)

*Briefly describe the issue / what has happened:

*How severe do you think is the issue?
Choose one of the following answers

I don't agree that this is a problem at all

Cosmetic problem only – need not to be fixed unless extra time is available

Minor problem – fixing this should be given low priority

What kind of feedback do you want to give?	Negative feedback (e.g. what you dislike about Aniketos services and tools, encountered problems, difficulties, recommendations for improvements)
Briefly describe the issue / what has happened:	When clicking "Create Composition Plans" in the "Plan&Deploy" tab, I am asked to insert a desired "Agreement template" and a "Consumer policy". The final action button states "Create and send to SCPM". Where do I find or how do I create these? Are they mandatory? Can they just be empty XML-files if I don't bother at this point? What do they actually do..?
How severe do you think is the issue?	Major problem – important to fix, so should be given high priority

Fig. 1. Online feedback journal and output excerpts

us to decidedly choose participants for the different evaluations concerning the modelling language developed within Aniketos.

4.4   Finding the Right Amount of Training Needed for Evaluations

Due to the complexity of the evaluation object, most evaluation studies had to be combined with presentation sessions and/or training activities for the study participants. In many cases, there were not enough or no experienced users available. Thus, the evaluation study participants would not have been able to sufficiently understand the evaluated object (e.g., the Service Composition Modeller (Chapter 9) or the Model Transformation Module (Chapter 6)) and perform tasks with it, without any presentation or training lessons beforehand. Furthermore, the differing maturity levels of the respective components or tools had to be taken into consideration for the training, as well as the interdependency with other modules (if applicable), which had to be made clear to the participants. But here also lies the challenge: What is the right amount of training? On one hand, the evaluation participants need certain guidance in order to perform their tasks. On the other hand, if the training already provides solutions for each step too accurately, the participants may just follow this way and certain issues may remain completely unnoticed. Within our evaluation activities, we tried to find a compromise, which was tailored to the evaluation objectives. For instance, in the very first evaluation workshop of STS-ml and the STS tool that primarily focused on usability issues and appropriateness of the modelling language, the participants were given a presentation about the modelling language and the modelling tool on the first day, each lasting about 90 minutes. During the presentations participants were allowed to ask questions at any time. The part covering the modelling language was a presentation, while the participants had the opportunity to do some exercises with the modelling tool on a predefined scenario during the presentation of the modelling tool. Also, for the actual evaluation session (see Figure 2), participants were provided a scenario description where certain stakeholders were already identified (a task that normally would be done by the modeller him/herself when modelling a scenario on his/her own). However, in this case, it made sense to provide the information, as otherwise it would have been rather difficult to use the tool. In another evaluation that aimed at evaluating the Aniketos design-time support tools for the ATM domain, we also pursued a combined demo and evaluation approach. From our perspective, we believe that it is very important to find the right balance of training levels.

4.5   Close Cooperation with Technical Partners in Evaluation Studies Needed

A general challenge within the Aniketos project was that the evaluation researchers who focused on the human-centred perspective came from a different research area (HCI). However, experiences with and knowledge of the – sometimes less familiar – technical details of the object of evaluation was still an absolute necessity. Therefore, even for less technical (i.e., user-centred) evaluation activities, we experienced it as very important to closely cooperate with the technical partners in our evaluations. For example, we conducted a workshop with four technical partners who, apart from providing demos of Aniketos design-time support tools, were also available for the actual evaluation sessions in order to answer upcoming questions. We believe that this is very important, especially to avoid the identification of pseudo-problems – issues that only seem problematic due to missing knowledge about the tools. However, one also has to keep in mind that the presence of module developers might also lead to unnecessarily lengthy and/or digressive in-depth discussions. Therefore, it is important that the evaluator also takes care in terms of an adequate moderation. Furthermore, it is also important to define with the technical partners their degree of involvement in advance. That is, for some evaluations it can also make sense that technical people only react to severe issues because otherwise a certain task would become too easy if a developer answered any upcoming question. In conclusion, the close cooperation with the technical partners is important *in advance* – in order to define a tailored evaluation procedure –, *during* the evaluation activities – in case the evaluator does not have an in-depth understanding of the evaluation object –, and also *afterwards* – when it comes to the interpretation of evaluation results.

4.6   If Possible, Keep It Simple

Within our evaluation activities, we had to investigate whether users were able to use certain developed modules and interfaces without problems. That is, we took

Fig. 2. Workshop participants creating a STS model based on a scenario description

a closer look at issues regarding usability, suitability, or scalability. In order to do so, we used different scenarios or user interface prototypes within our evaluation activities. From our experiences, we conclude that in order to identify very basic issues (especially at the beginning), it is feasible to keep the complexity of the scenarios rather simple as long as it makes sense. For example, for identifying usability issues of STS-ml and the STS tool, we used a straightforward scenario that had to be modelled by the participants. Hence, we primarily focussed on the use of STS-ml and the STS tool rather than on issues that might relate to scalability issues, which may arise if the complexity of the scenario increases. However, in order to investigate the appropriateness of the modelling language and tool for more complex scenarios, further evaluations were conducted within the Air Traffic Management case study (see Chapter 14) to address the issue of scalability and suitability for the case study domain. Regarding user interface prototypes, low-fidelity prototypes have generally proven to be at least as important as functional prototypes and should not be seen as tools suitable merely for the preliminary phases of development. For example, for investigating a tool to generate training materials, we conducted a heuristic evaluation with a paper prototype in order to identify key problems. This strongly helped to guide the further development of the tool. In conclusion, we believe that it is important to always keep in mind which objective needs to be investigated and to choose the scenario accordingly. At the same time, one has to keep the big picture in mind, and should invest in an evaluation at least once that brings in a higher degree of complexity.

5   Development-Process Related Challenges: Aligning Evaluation with Development Processes

5.1   Early Conceptual Evaluation of the Aniketos Platform

The development process of the Aniketos platform is, like in most large-scale software development processes, characterized by parallel work on different components in order to achieve common project goals. As defined in the Aniketos architecture description, the platform consists of various parts, which are individually built and put together by the technical partners as the project progresses. However, components are developed at different speeds and only towards a later phase of a project are the components integrated into a unified whole. This poses a challenge for evaluation work, which also aims at doing "whole platform" evaluations. It's important to ensure an early start of such iterative evaluation activities and receive feedback for improvements early in the development process to save development time and costs, even when there is no coherent platform available. In the first half of the projects' timeline, comprehensive platform concepts and scenarios were therefore developed, which could then be evaluated in order to get an early assessment of the project's planned outcome.

5.2   Strong Focus on Formative, Chunk-Wise Evaluation

When planning the evaluation work at the beginning of the project, we aimed at balancing formative evaluation (evaluation that is carried out during the development process) and summative evaluation approaches (evaluations of the final system). Ideally, evaluation takes place continuously and iteratively during the course of the project. Once the evaluation of initial concepts (see section 5.1) was complete, we then moved on to test non-functional, as well as functional, user interface prototypes and finally investigated the quality and impact of different versions of the Aniketos platform modules. An example for such activities is the intense evaluation efforts spent for the STS-ml and its support tool (STS-ml and the STS tool), which were developed for Aniketos, allowing for continuous improvement of the language and tool. In summary, there have been three usability evaluations of STS-ml and STS tool and six end-user evaluations in the Air Traffic Management case study during the lifetime of the project. Performing summative evaluations of the final system turned out to be more critical and difficult to accomplish, mainly due to the aforementioned component-wise development process of the Aniketos platform. Consequently, in order to match our evaluation work with the development processes (see section 5.1), we had a strong focus on formative evaluation of single platform chunks. The vast majority of evaluation studies were performed during module development, accompanying the development process and offering findings for iterative improvement of the single modules and components.

6   Evaluation-Participants Related Challenges: Identifying and Accessing User Groups

6.1   Small-Cale User Studies

In a user-centred evaluation approach, a large amount of evaluation work is done with the participation of actual users of a developed system who provide the researchers with their points of view and experiences. For Aniketos, however, there was no existing pool of prospective Aniketos user from which individuals could be recruited for evaluations, mainly due to the pioneering research topic of the project. Thus, we had to face the challenge of doing user-centred evaluations of the Aniketos outcome with very small groups of potential (but not actual) users. We mainly conducted small-scale user studies (i.e., studies with a small number of people from the industrial case studies as study participants) while large-scale user studies were not feasible. For instance, in the first STS-ml and STS tool evaluation workshop, we had in total seven application domain experts who participated at the workshop and worked with the modelling language and tool. The third usability evaluation of the STS modelling language and tool was completed with people who were not associated with the Aniketos project, i.e., students who learned to use the modelling language and tool in a course conducted at the University of Trento. In total, 36 students participated in the evaluation. Aniketos-external experts from different fields (Institutions, Industry,

ASNPs, Research) are also hard to reach and motivate to take part in evaluation studies. For instance, for a one-day ATM case study evaluation workshop, we had ten selected ATM experts that took part in the validation and consolidation process of Aniketos results applied to the ATM domain. A larger number of participants would have been too difficult to get. Still, we can say that even such small sets of study participants helped us greatly to detect possible problems with the projects' outcome early.

6.2   Remote or Local Evaluation Study Set-Ups, but No Mixture of Both at the Same Time

For some user-centred evaluation methods, there is a need to (geographically or virtually) bring together people in one place to take advantage of group dynamics in group work. In Aniketos, this was relevant in most cases because of geographically dispersed user groups and project partners. We, therefore, tried different study set-ups in several evaluation workshops. We held evaluation workshops which required participants to be locally present, workshops which connected remotely located participants via Internet-based facilities, and workshops which had one part of the participants work together face-to-face, while the other part was virtually present. Based on our experience, we can conclude that a solely remote or local setup of a workshop worked well and arguably better than a combination of local and remote participants would have. In such a mixed study set-up, workshop participants unfortunately rarely discussed with each other.

7   Conclusion

In this Chapter, we have given an overview of the Aniketos evaluation approach, the overall challenges we encountered during evaluation, and practices employed to address these challenges. We structured the identified challenges with regard to which evaluation aspects they were related to. These aspects were 1) project-internal stakeholders, 2) evaluation objects, 3) development processes, and 4) evaluation participants. The applied practices comprise measures related to project-internal communication, evaluation planning and methods, and evaluation study designs. As our discussion of theses methods and practices showed, addressing the Aniketos challenges required not only evaluation best practices, but also project management and communication strategies. In fact, both aspects received an approximately equal degree of attention and consideration.

The Aniketos project was a difficult case for user-centred evaluations, due to its structure of multiple intertwined components with different development cycles, combined with a very wide potential user base. Careful planning and execution was necessary to ensure that user-centred evaluation activities covered all necessary aspects of the Aniketos framework, without exceeding the allotted resources. In today's age of ever-increasing demands and complexity in IT, highly complex and multi-faceted projects, like Aniketos, are not a rarity anymore. Thus, it will be increasingly important to gather and exchange knowledge of evaluation-related best practices, so that evaluation does not lag behind the bars set by technological progress in modern IT projects.

References

1. Aniketos D7.1 - Validation and evaluation plan, `http://www.aniketos.eu/content/deliverables`
2. Golafshani, N.: Understanding Reliability and Validity in Qualitative Research. The Qualitative Report 8(4), 597–606 (2003)
3. Wilson, C.E.: Triangulation: the explicit use of multiple methods, measures, and approaches for determining core issues in product development. Interactions 13(6), 46 (2006)
4. Janzen, D.S., Saiedian, H.: Test-driven development: Concepts, taxonomy, and future direction. Computer Science and Software Engineering 38(9), 43–50 (2005)
5. International Standard: ISO 9241-210:2010: Ergonomics of human-system interaction – Part 210: Human-centred design for interactive systems
6. EUROCONTROL. European Operational Concept Validation Methodology (E-OCVM),
`http://www.eurocontrol.int/eec/public/standard_page/validation_ocvm.html`

Author Index